Macroeconomic Methodology

Macroeconomic Methodology
A Post-Keynesian Perspective

Jesper Jespersen

Professor of Economics, Roskilde University, Denmark

Edward Elgar

Cheltenham, UK • Northampton, MA, USA

Published by
Edward Elgar Publishing Limited
The Lypiatts
15 Lansdown Road
Cheltenham
Glos GL50 2JA
UK

Edward Elgar Publishing, Inc.
William Pratt House
9 Dewey Court
Northampton
Massachusetts 01060
USA

Cased edition reprinted 2010
Paperback edition reprinted 2014

Originally published in Danish as *Makroøkonomisk Metodologi – i et samfundsvidenskabeligt perspektiv* (2007) by:

Jurist- og Økonomforbundets Forlag
Lyngbyvej 17
Postboks 2702
2100 København Ø
Denmark

A catalogue record for this book is available from the British Library

Library of Congress Control Number: 2009930427

ISBN   978 1 84542 736 8 (cased)
       978 0 85793 758 2 (paperback)

Printed on FSC approved paper

Printed and bound in Great Britain by Marston Book Services Ltd, Oxfordshire

Contents

Figures, tables and box

FIGURES

TABLES

BOX

Preface

This book has been a long time in the making. My interest in methodological questions arose already in the early stages of my studies. I was captivated by the question: why was there such a wide gap between the macroeconomic reality that unfolded before our eyes and the theories and models that were presented in our lecture halls? There must have been something wrong with the method that macroeconomists were using. To the surprise of many established economists, unemployment, contrary to the many fine theories, began to rise throughout the 1970s – all the while inflation and the current account deficit also grew. The current macroeconomic theories simply could not explain reality.

I wrote my Master's thesis on macroeconomic method in 1974 under the skilled supervision of Professor Poul Nørgaard Rasmussen and Professor Niels Thygesen at Copenhagen University, who both directed my focus on this disturbing macroeconomic problem: that mainstream economic theory could not explain the macroeconomic development of stagnation and financial instability. There seemed to be an increasingly yawning gap between theory and reality.

Concurrent with my studies, I was employed as an intern for Statistics Denmark, where I took part in creating and running simulations with the macro-econometric model ADAM, under the guidance of Professor Ellen Andersen. I later continued this empirically guided research as an assistant in the Economic Advisory Council with inspiration from Professor Anders Ølgaard and head of office Arne Mikkelsen.

Since the beginning of my university career, it has been the Keynesian macroeconomic tradition that has been at the core of my research in an attempt to build a bridge between theory and reality. I have taken up a number of current socio-economic questions including unemployment, monetary union in the EU, and sustainable development, and attempted to use these to develop the post-Keynesian theory so that it could give more relevant answers to these current issues. Time and time again I ran into the same problem: the lack of a methodological basis upon which a more realistic understanding of these issues could be achieved. Therefore, my work on the role of methodology in forming macroeconomic conclusions that could be drawn upon a scientific basis took centre stage. The research being conducted within the framework of the Critical Realist

Workshop at Cambridge University, led by Dr Tony Lawson, was of great importance for this later work. I was able to develop my contact with this group through a number of visiting fellowships at Churchill College, arranged by the Carlsberg Fund. Furthermore, since 1988 I have been a member of the Post-Keynesian Economics Study Group, with, among others, Professor Victoria Chick (University College London) as an inspiring organizer. These stints at Cambridge and London have given me invaluable inspiration for my research.

Finally, I would like to highlight my tenure at Roskilde University from 1991, first as a lecturer and then as a professor of economics. Here, I found an interdisciplinary and cordial environment that has contributed to broadening the scope of my research, both within macroeconomics and, of equal importance, within scientific theory.

The writing of this book took more than two years. Regardless of the fact that the process must have been a challenge for my family, not in the least my wife Annette, they supported me immensely. In the final phase of the project, Rosa Haslund has been very helpful in completing the Danish manuscript. I would like to offer a heartfelt thank you to my family, colleagues and the students whose contribution enabled the Danish edition of this work to be completed more or less according to plan.

The process of getting the manuscript translated into English was a rather long one. Fortunately, I had good support in the beginning from Ben Hope and later on from Diarmuid Kennan. They have made a great effort to convert my not so simple Danish into proper English. I am also grateful to Palgrave Macmillan on behalf of the Royal Economic Society for permission to quote extensively from *The General Theory of Employment, Interest and Money* and to my Danish publisher, Wilfried Roloff at Danmarks Jurist- og Økonomforbunds Forlag, who helped me with the Danish dissertation and later encouraged me to get it published internationally. Finally, I should mention that my mentor Victoria Chick has been so encouraging in her willingness to discuss a number of these theoretical and linguistic difficulties, and indispensable in her unlimited effort to complete the book. I am very grateful for this personal support which has made the completion of this English edition of my book possible.

Summary

Macroeconomic Methodology: A Post-Keynesian Perspective consists of nine chapters, all of which explore scientific theoretical content. The primary result of the book is a demonstration that macroeconomic theory and analysis are method-specific. Macroeconomic results, such as policy recommendations, cannot be assessed independently of the methodology employed. This conclusion is new insofar as there is very little overarching discussion of method to be found within the main-stream macroeconomic literature. Method is something to be used and rarely discussed. The absence of a discussion of method makes it difficult to interpret the analytical results for use in economic policy.

The book begins with an introduction wherein it is shown that if methodologically founded criteria for delimitation of macroeconomic theories are established, then it is possible to observe an overlying pattern within the existing macroeconomic literature. It can be substantiated that two entirely different methodological traditions within macroeconomic theory have developed. The first of these, a neoclassical-inspired line of theory, utilizes general equilibrium models as its analytical method, and the model of the ideal market equilibrium is central. This tradition includes both the new-classical and the new-Keynesian schools. Second, the post-Keynesian tradition employs path-dependent causal analyses, where uncertainty, incomplete information, societal power structures and institutional relationships are of greater interest. It is shown in Chapter 1 that this methodological border splits the Keynes-inspired macroeconomists into these two camps. The new-Keynesians utilize – contrary to their name – the same neoclassical equilibrium model to which Keynes was opposed in his major work, *The General Theory* (1936). It is therefore predominantly the post-Keynesians that carry on his methodological stance, the importance of which Keynes increasingly emphasized throughout the 1930s.

The methodological discussion is the heart of Chapter 2. With inspiration from Tony Lawson and Karl Popper among others, a scientific-theoretical template is developed, which then can be employed to identify the practical method. Within this template, a distinction is made between the real, the analytical and the strategic levels. It is shown that the general equilibrium theory predominantly, if not completely, operates on the analytical level. Opposite this stands the post-Keynesian methodology that enlists some critical realist arguments to explain why the preferred methodology should include all three levels. It is recommended, when conducting a post-Keynesian analysis, that one first make an ontological reflection, leading to a sketch of the contours of the macroeconomic landscape. The further investigation of this landscape must continue as a reciprocal action between the analytical and real levels *via* a retroductive process. This process leads toward a model for analysis, the results of which can be transferred to the operational level by modifying some of the delimiting assumptions in relation to the analytical results.

Chapter 3 explains how ontological reflections, in practice, can lead to the development of a macroeconomic landscape. This is meant to consist of macroeconomic actors, macro-markets, macro-institutions and political decision-makers. The individual components in the landscape are held together by causal relations that, *inter alia*, can be described as macroeconomic behaviour relations, institutionally defined market adjustments or political regulation.

Chapters 4 and 5 expound how the macroeconomic behavioural relations can be partially anchored by microeconomic theory and partially by the macroeconomic landscape. In the first case, this happens through a critical assessment of the neoclassical assumption that a 'representative agent' can give macroeconomic models a solid microeconomic foundation. In particular, the assumption that these representative agents maintain rational expectations, meaning that they have perfect information concerning the (modelled) future, is discussed at some length, with the aim to assess the realism of the model-related expectations. It is shown that a microeconomic foundation anchored in empirical evidence on the one side can maintain the assumption of rational individual behaviour, yet it must also formulate expectations that do not take full knowledge of the future as being given. The creation of expectations ought to reflect the notorious uncertainty to which each and every economic disposition is subject. The difference between risk and uncertainty is illuminated through a number of examples. Against this background, it can be concluded that individual behaviour will always be influenced by uncertainty. Conversely, macroeconomic behaviour can, under certain somewhat idealized assumptions with respect to the 'law of large numbers', take on a character similar to that of risk; it is an area where the empirical research unfortunately still lags behind.

Later, Chapter 5 highlights the analytical problems related to how the individual elements of the macroeconomic landscape can be bound together to form 'the economy as a whole'. Neoclassical theory (including new-Keynesian theory) often uses at the analytical level a laboratory analogy, assuming it to be possible to conduct controlled experiments where different mathematical solutions are compared. Such 'laboratory trials' are often illustrated in textbooks through a labour market analysis, where for example a fall in demand is analysed by describing how, through market forces, the actors in the labour market return to the general equilibrium, usually under the assumption that all other markets remain undisturbed. These thought experiments use general equilibrium as the analytical point of reference and are therefore a form of 'closed-system analysis'.

In post-Keynesian macro-theory, on the other hand, it is assumed that the macroeconomic landscape is under constant change and can be advantageously characterized as being open, in that considerable uncertainty exists in respect to future development. A common conclusion within post-Keynesian economics is that the sum of the parts will be different from the whole. There are several arguments which lead to this conclusion; one is that the interaction of the designed macro-markets must be explicitly drawn into the analytical model. Macro-markets cannot be analysed in isolation, which is illustrated by an example of a model-based linking of the goods and labour markets. This leads to more ambitious analytical results, in that the labour market even with full wage flexibility does not automatically return to equilibrium. Results become more ambiguous as the model is made more realistic.

In Chapter 6 the many different meanings of the analytical concept of equilibrium are presented and discussed. Equilibrium can be a solution to a mathematically formulated model. It can also be interpreted as a market-clearing condition, where planned supply and demand are of equal size. Finally, equilibrium – specifically where it is seen within the new-Keynesian or neo-Ricardian traditions – is given the form of a gravitational centre towards which the macroeconomic system is moving, but in a process characterized by various inertia caused by rational behaviour.

The post-Keynesian use of the term 'equilibrium' diverges from those just mentioned. With inspiration from *The General Theory*, a number of useful methods of analysis are described. Keynes also used the term 'equilibrium', but primarily meaning 'standstill' or 'repetition'. Here, he was inspired by the empirical state whereby unemployment in England, in the period between the two world wars, persisted at around 10 per cent. He spoke explicitly about the empirically observed unemployment equilibrium, which was in direct methodological opposition to the understanding of his neoclassical colleagues: they understood involuntary unemployment as an instance of *disequilibrium*, as it violated market clearing. Keynes, however, saw it as his task to explain this sustained high level of unemployment. Following Keynes's suggested method of analysis, this can be described as an attempt to demarcate a 'subsystem' (semi-closure) in the macroeconomic landscape and assign a temporarily closed character to it. The assumption for making such a semi-closure is that the development in that section of the landscape displays a significant pattern of regularity. A semi-closure can be established on the assumption, for example, of expectations of the future being temporarily locked in place. Jan Kregel (1976) was a pioneer in suggesting that in *The General Theory* Keynes initially locked all expectations of the future at their current level. He thereafter loosened them one by one and investigated how the macroeconomic model developed when an increasing number of changing expectation factors entered the arena. The model quite quickly became rather incalculable. Instead, it was suggested by other post-Keynesians to combine these closures with a path-dependent method whereby a selected few variables were followed on their course through the macroeconomic landscape. This led to the development by Mark Setterfield (2001) of the 'open-systems *ceteris paribus*' method (OSCP method), where a number of variables were fixed for shorter or longer periods, while the paths of selected endogenous variables were followed. This method can be traced back to Keynes, in that he used the expression *quaesitum* ('that which we seek') in referring to the outcome of the analysis of developmental trends in output and employment in *The General Theory*.

A notable consequence of going from a closed to an open analysis model is the opportunity to avoid 'false atomic conclusions' – the so-called 'fallacy of composition'. Chapter 7 deals with how to analyse the fallacy of composition within macroeconomic theories. False atomic conclusions are made when conclusions about the macroeconomic reality are drawn from an incorrect analogy to the individual level. In a general equilibrium model it might hold true, for example, that the macroeconomic result can be derived from the sum of the microeconomic actions. But such an equilibrium approach may lead to a false conclusion with regard to reality. A classic example to illustrate the fallacy of composition is the 'savings paradox', where an increased individual propensity to save makes the total amount of savings fall. In this case, the generalization of microeconomic behaviour would lead to the wrong conclusion that at the macro-level the sum of savings would increase when all individuals intend to save more. Another example is that a reduction in individual wage claims would increase the number of employed people at the macro-level. Also here, a generalization from the individual level to the macro-level can lead to a fallacy of composition.

In Chapter 8 it is demonstrated how Keynes's principle of effective demand, using the OSCP method, can give a far more nuanced interpretation than that which is commonly presented by neoclassical theorists (*inter alia*, new-Keynesians). It is shown that the theory of effective demand consists of both supply and demand arguments, in that it is based on the cost structure of firms as well as expected sales. Assuming that firms have given expectations of sales, then the cost structure and the competitive pressure on the goods and labour market would be the decisive factors in determining how much is produced, and consequently the macro-demand for labour. Should the supply factors change in the event of increased productivity or changes in the competitive environment (due, say, to increased globalization), then firms will likely adjust their planned productions and hence employment to match the new situation. It can thus be concluded that the principle of effective demand should be interpreted to include supply as well as demand factors in the production sector. By using a causal analysis, a number of variables that include production, profit and competitiveness are integrated in the term 'effective demand'. Hence, the myth that the Keynes model does not cover the supply side of the economic system is repudiated.

Finally, in Chapter 9, the threads are woven together. First, it is concluded that if the aim of an analysis is to understand the important trends in macroeconomic reality, then one must strive for a meaningful congruence between the real and analytical levels. As the number of unrealistic assumptions underlying the model increases, one compromises the relevancy of the results, making it more difficult to operationalize them when planning economic policy. A number of examples are given to show that unrealistic assumptions lead to a narrower range of validity, which in a number of relationships will limit the operational relevance of the results. It is concluded that the macroeconomic ontology should be decisive in the selection of the method of analysis, whereby it can ensure that the analytical results that underlie economic advice have a solid theoretical foundation.

The chapter, as well as the entire book, ends with a schematic overview of the results reached in relation to the three dominant schools: new-classical, new-Keynesian and post-Keynesian macroeconomics. It is concluded that there are significant methodological and theoretical characteristics that differentiate these schools and consequently their ability to analyse a macroeconomic reality characterized by uncertainty and continuous change.

Introduction

INTRODUCTION: DIFFERENT POINTS OF VIEW

John Maynard Keynes's macroeconomic theory was developed in the interwar period as a reaction to great imbalances in economic development, nationally and internationally. Up to and following the First World War, there were significant variations in respect to inflation, unemployment and the national budgets.

The macroeconomic imbalances of this time were to a certain degree self-amplifying in that they contributed to creating an atmosphere of uncertainty on all societal levels, particularly concerning what the future would bring, economically and politically. Lacking a macroeconomic-theoretical basis, politicians were advised to re-establish the economic world order that had dominated in pre-war times in the major economies of the UK, the USA, France and Germany.[1] The aim was for the international economic system to function the way it did before 'the world got off track'. Unfortunately, it became clear during this interwar period that the macroeconomic system lacked stability: high inflation was followed by a sharp drop in prices; unemployment was rampant and there were recurrent currency crises.

The macroeconomic thinking at that time did not really differentiate between theories for personal households, the state budget and the national economy; rather, they were lumped together. As Adam Smith, back in 1776, had stated: 'What is prudence in the conduct of every private family, can scarce be folly in that of a great kingdom' (Smith, 1776 [1976]: 457). On this point, Smith was not correct, as seen in Keynes's groundbreaking discoveries in macroeconomic method in the 1930s: drawing a parallel between micro- and macro-levels brings with it the risk of committing the so-called fallacy of composition (atomistic fallacy) (see Chapter 7). Macroeconomic developments, an example being unemployment, cannot be fully explained via a theory concerning optimal microeconomic behaviour. This leads us to the need for a distinct macroeconomic theory, furthermore demanding an explicit methodological basis, allowing for a holistic explanation rather than a summation of individual activities.

In the first decade after the First World War, politicians, following the advice of economic experts, tried to create economic stability through the use of 'classic' economic arguments and institutions: balancing the public budgets, re-establishing the gold standard, and exercising tight controls over the money supply through discount rate adjustments. Balance, or better still, surplus on the state budget (so that national debts accrued during the war could be repaid), was not up for discussion.[2] It was seen as an intrinsic welfare gain to make the state debt-free. To reach external stability, the international gold standard was seen as the anchor that could re-establish equilibrium on the balance of payments. And finally, through controlling the money supply, the aim was to create a national financial anchor to slow inflationary forces. In such case, when the national budget, current account deficit and inflation were under control, persisting high unemployment (which was the situation in Europe in the 1920s) could only be attributed to wage-earners refusing to accept the necessary reductions in money wage levels. Unemployment was not seen to be a macroeconomic problem; rather it was seen as a microeconomic problem stemming from a lack of adequate competition and flexibility in the labour market (see *inter alia* Pigou, 1933).

A balanced state budget, combined with a stable price level and the currency rate bound to the gold standard, were together expected to create a stable environment around the socio-economy. Unemployment could only, as mentioned, be attributed to labour being too expensive. If wages were stuck at too high a level, then it would not pay for firms to employ the entire labour force. Therefore, a reduction of unemployment demanded a lower wage level. Such was the economic advice of the time. It meant a lower real wage, which the employed wage-earners at the time understandably opposed; yet the state refused to budge. When the reduction of unemployment came to be seen as a microeconomic question, it was then up to the partners in the labour market to find a solution. Or rather, the solution was seen as the responsibility of the 'working class', which opposed a reduction in real wages, making unions stand out as being (morally) responsible for unemployment.

The economic thought of the time was dominated by the neoclassical equilibrium model,[3] which until the early 1930s was not really theoretically challenged in the English-speaking world. The empirically inspired challenge caused the paths of development within macroeconomics to split into the two separate schools of methodology: respectively, the neoclassical equilibrium school and the 'uncertainty' school, the latter mainly with inspiration from Keynes's writings of the 1930s and carried on by the post-Keynesian school.

NEOCLASSICAL MACROECONOMIC METHODOLOGY: KEY TERMS

Partial Equilibrium

The dominating (macro)economic reasoning in the interwar period was derived from the neoclassical market economic theory, which did not differentiate specifically between the micro- and macro-level. Macroeconomics was understood as a summation of individuals' (households' and firms') dispositions coordinated via a well-functioning market system. Within each well-functioning market, a well-defined equilibrium was found, where the supply and demand curves met. This was called partial (market) equilibrium. If no hindrances counteract the adjustments of market prices, wages and interest rates, then it was demonstrated that each and every market will reach such a partial equilibrium. When all markets are in equilibrium, then the entire macroeconomy is defined to be in equilibrium – the so-called 'general equilibrium'.

Partial equilibrium and analyses were the core of Alfred Marshall's *The Principles of Economics*, first published in 1890, which was the backbone of neoclassical theory that dominated the economic teachings in England until the 1930s. True macroeconomic theory was unknown, with the exception of the 'Quantity Theory', which postulated a narrower causal relationship from changes in the money supply to the development of the aggregate price level (see Estrup et al., 2004). The macroeconomic reasoning at that time was based upon a generalization of partial market equilibrium models.

Quantity Theory

The 'Quantity Theory of Money and Prices' had already been developed by the classical economists near the end of the 1700s. It linked the quantity of money (from where it gets its name) to the absolute price level. At this time, the logic was that the amount of (monetary) gold determined the absolute purchasing power of the society. The amount of goods available – predominantly then agricultural production – was (largely) constant. Should the quantity of gold be increased – as was the case after the discovery of South America – then prices must rise accordingly; otherwise the market system would never again reach a new and balanced equilibrium. In the interwar period, the argument was refined to include the balance of payments. The increased purchasing power would either force prices to rise or increase imports from abroad. It would create a deficit on the balance of payments, which would then slowly drain the country of its gold until purchasing power was once again equal to equilibrium on the balance of payments.

The quantity theory was the 'missing link' that could explain how the national market economic system could establish both internal and external equilibrium through the adjustment of price levels and via changes in the money supply (determined by the gold supply).

This total market economic system is a beautiful construction: if only there was perfect competition on all markets, then general equilibrium would exist, ensuring harmony, balance and full utilization of society's scarce resources. The inspiration from Newton's astronomical model is undeniable.[4]

The General Equilibrium Model

This market economic system was set into mathematical formulae by Frenchman Léon Walras (1874 [1954]). He linked the individual markets together by making explicit the inter-relationship between demand in one . market and supply in at least one other market. The typical example is that the household which demands some goods simultaneously must supply labour to be able to finance the purchases. If there is an excess demand within one market, then according to Walras's logic there has to be a similar excess supply in another market. If we now use the aforementioned example of the agricultural society, the excess demand for corn will make the price of corn rise, reducing the purchasing power of the money supply and thus reducing the excess supply of (real) money. In the industrialized society, a rise in consumer prices will erode the purchasing power of money wages. This adjustment of purchasing power via the change in the real value of money and of the real wages of labour will re-establish equilibrium in both the goods and labour markets; for if there were only two markets, then equilibrium in the one (net excess demand = zero) means equilibrium in the other (net excess supply = zero). Walras generalized this logical implication to include all (*n*) markets. Regardless of the fact that a surplus of demand could be spread over numerous markets, it would still hold true that there must be an aggregated surplus of supply of exactly the same magnitude in the other markets considered as a whole, as the market actors surely must finance their planned purchases. For Walras, the significant result was that, by adding some further assumptions about the mathematical formulation of the equations, he could demonstrate that a price vector existed (meaning, could be calculated), including the prices on all markets. This price vector contained the solution to the mathematically formulated system. The solution ensured that excess demand and supply could be nullified on every market. This mathematical solution is characterized as a general equilibrium, in that there are no private economic incentives to change the behaviour of firms and households, while at the same time it ensures an overarching macroeconomic balance: equilibrium of the public budgets, the balance of payments, full employment and no inflation.

The Existence of General Equilibrium

The importance of this proof of the existence of general equilibrium in a well-organized market system can hardly be overestimated in the history of economic theory. It constitutes the axiomatic framework within which neoclassical macroeconomic theory has since been developed. There is a straight theoretical-historical line from Walras's original equations to the more refined, Arrow–Debreu model from the 1950s, which could be used specifically for uncovering the conditions for the existence of an even more general equilibrium, which was broadened to include the formation of prices of future economic transactions, in correspondence with actors' expanded planning horizons and expectations with regard to demand and supply.

Parallel to the mathematical analysis of this idealized market system contained in the Arrow–Debreu model, the neoclassical school developed more pragmatic macroeconomic models for use in policy analysis. All share in common a belief that the market economic system has a general equilibrium solution that market forces by themselves (via perfect competition) are able to establish. Neoclassical (macroeconomic) theory of the post-war period has as a shared feature that a general equilibrium exists, which is characterized by full resource utilization and macroeconomic balance, and is a relevant tool for understanding how a modern market-based economic system functions. This assumption, as will be thoroughly discussed in the following chapters, has dictated the neoclassical school's macroeconomic conclusions and thereby its policy recommendations.

Can a General Equilibrium be Realized?

To what degree does a price vector that can ensure one unequivocal solution to a market-economic system even exist? This is an interesting system-theoretic question (Arrow and Hahn, 1971). But it would be of more practical relevance to investigate if the market-economic system, starting out of equilibrium, would be able to adjust itself in the right direction and (re)establish a general equilibrium. In other words, which adjustment mechanisms can be assumed to work outside prior equilibrium?

One example is the Walrasian *tâtonnement* process, where through a trial and error process excess supply and demand functions in the different markets are reduced and in the end become zero. If all actors had the same information, which is the case when perfect competition is prevailing, then this *tâtonnement* process is assumed to converge to a general equilibrium. The crucial assumption is that when agents know the n-1 (correct) equilibrium prices, and if the excess demand functions are 'well behaved', then the *tâtonnement* process (under ideal conditions, including the absence of transaction costs, and so on) will establish equilibrium in the nth market, whereby general equilibrium is ensured. Furthermore, this general equilibrium was assumed to correspond to the solution of the mathematical system of market equations, where the sum of net excess demand functions adds to zero. This market system condition was at a later stage given the name of 'Walras's Law' expressing that whenever n-1 markets were in equilibrium, then the nth market would also, by definition, be in equilibrium (Hansen, 1970).

The natural starting point for a more realistic market analysis is, though, as mentioned, a situation where imbalances persist in multiple markets. The price information acquired by actors is essentially plagued by imbalances and has a much more random nature, as there is no established theory for the creation of prices on markets which are out of balance. This means that the equilibrium prices, which the 'existence vector' uses as information conditions, are unknown until equilibrium has been realized. Sonnenschein (1972) has shown that given the lack of perfect information concerning correct prices out of general equilibrium, one cannot conclude that a smooth-working *tâtonnement* process based on excess demand and supply functions exists outside of equilibrium. The prices – namely those concerned with future transactions – which actors perceive as a basis for their economic behaviour will not be uniform; rather, they are dependent on the price signals sent by the market participants at large, and the individual formation of expectations. Without general equilibrium, the market participants are groping in the dark; they have no commonly known general equilibrium price vector to which they can adjust their supply and demand. This means that if the economic system is not resting at general equilibrium, then it is theoretically undetermined whether they ever will reach it; in fact, it would be a mere coincidence if the market economy subsequently moved in the direction of general equilibrium. It cannot therefore in any case be taken for granted that within a Walrasian model an automatic adjustment to general equilibrium – which for the actors is unknown – will ever occur.[5]

In an attempt to overcome this lack of information, a group of neoclassical economists, led by Robert Lucas, posed the question in the beginning of the 1970s that can be restated as follows: 'What would happen if actors knew the equilibrium vector prices? Or if actors were assumed to have so-called "rational expectations"?' In such a case, market participants with sure knowledge of the future could 'hit the mark', meaning that they could re-establish the general equilibrium. This is still the founding assumption in the new-classical school of theory.

Hahn and Solow (1996) showed, though, that the condition of rational expectations was not enough to ensure the establishment of a unequivocally defined general equilibrium, which is an important condition for the assumption that equilibrium can be known in advance. The lack of clarity is substantiated by, *inter alia*, the possibility that the system has multiple solutions that cannot *a priori* be discriminated between.

This result implies that any equilibrium will be specific and cannot be analysed independently of the traverse. Thus equilibrium will be determined not only by the specific institutions of the market system, but also by the initial conditions, by both supply and demand factors, and by economic policy (Østrup, 2000).

Regardless of the fact that disagreement exists between neoclassical economists as to the character and clarity of the general equilibrium solution, it is a methodological requirement that each and every market economic model, where perfect competition is assumed to exist, should be 'well behaved', meaning that the system must converge towards a general equilibrium with full resource utilization.

This neoclassical precondition that a macroeconomic model of analysis should be formulated as a general equilibrium model – which economic development of itself must converge upon – is not theoretically supported (Andersen, 2000). These model properties are postulated as a part of an axiomatic basis that is rarely subject to an empirical test.

The question of convergence to a general equilibrium discussed above is therefore of major system-theoretical interest when an analysis of the postulated market system's dynamic and statistical equilibrium properties is conducted. The analytical results are dependent on the characteristics of the model employed, and are primarily relevant to the system world from which they have been derived. The results of the analysis will conversely only be relevant to macroeconomic reality to the degree that the model and the conditions are realistic. Fulfilling this request is a challenging problem in itself, as will be thoroughly demonstrated in the following chapters.

The important issue is not whether or not one can theoretically find an existence vector, but rather whether this vector is relevant for a realistic macroeconomic analysis.

Solow's Growth Model

The Walras model was constructed so that its components formed an analytical model that should ensure a general equilibrium in a single period – a so-called flow equilibrium. An important test criterion for equilibrium is that there should be full employment (no involuntary unemployment). The fulfilment of this demand therefore stood central to the discussion that arose after the publication of *The General Theory* and which subsequently divided 'the Keynesians' into separate camps; this is the subject of the following chapter.

Concurrent with the 'Keynesian' debate about the character of and reason for unemployment, the desire to develop a model of analysis to understand economic growth rose in the theoretical agenda. Not least, seen in the light of the post-war period's high growth rates, economists began to question how positive real investments and technology influence productivity. Here the Cobb–Douglas production function was instrumental, in that within the framework of equilibrium models, it linked the capital apparatus and future production together. It was assumed that an increased number of production factors automatically created growth, as they would always be fully utilized in a permanent flow equilibrium. Saving is automatically converted in the Walras model to real investments, just as labour is always fully utilized. The growth tempo in the model is assumed for technical reasons to be moderated in step with expansion of the capital apparatus. The growth model rests at so-called stock equilibrium, when the capital apparatus stops growing, measured in relation to the number of employed wage-earners. This equilibrium is characterized by all production being consumed – except for needed reinvestment. An eventual continuation of growth must be attributed to either technological innovation or growth in the population.

This expansion of the Walras equilibrium to include a stock equilibrium with constant capital equipment was presented by Robert Solow (1956). Here, it is the full-employment model (flow equilibrium) that is assumed to converge towards stock equilibrium (stationary state equilibrium).[6]

Neoclassical theory in this way leaves us with a 'broadened' general equilibrium term, which *inter alia* constitutes the model-based framework for empirical models, such as the Danish Rational Economic Agent Model (DREAM) which applies to the Danish economy. These models are constructed so that the analysed macroeconomy is assumed to be in permanent Walras equilibrium (with full employment), which slowly – over more than 100 years – converges towards the stock equilibrium, characterized as the point where growth in physical capital per employed wage-earner ceases. This general equilibrium growth model builds in such a way on its terminal position of fulfilling no less than three equilibrium criteria:

1. Walras equilibrium or flow equilibrium.
2. Continuous Walras equilibrium while converging to a stock equilibrium.
3. Stock equilibrium.

The question that therefore ought to be raised in relation to the formulation and use of a general equilibrium growth model is: 'To what extent is the object's empirical nature (the ontology) congruent with the model of analysis and the method?'

POST-KEYNESIAN MACROECONOMIC METHODOLOGY: IMPORTANT TERMINOLOGY

On the one side are those who believe that the existing economic system is, in the long run, a self-adjusting system, though with creaks and groans and jerks and interrupted by time lags, outside interference and mistakes. ...

On the other side of the gulf are those that reject the idea that the existing economic system is, in any significant sense, self-adjusting. ...

The gulf between these two schools of thought is deeper, I believe, than most of those on either side of it are aware of. On which side does the essential truth lie? That is the vital question for us to solve. ...

The strength of the self-adjusting school depends on its having behind it almost the whole body of organised economic thinking and doctrine of the last hundred years. ... There is, I am convinced, a fatal flaw in that part of orthodox reasoning which deals with the theory of what determines the level of effective demand and the volume of aggregate employment ... (*CWK*, XIII: 486–9)[7,8]

I shall argue that the postulates of classical theory are only applicable to a special case only and not to the general case, the situation which it assumes being a limiting point of the possible positions of equilibrium. Moreover, the characteristics of the special case assumed by the classical theory happen not to be those of the economic society in which we *actually live*, with the result that its teaching is misleading and disastrous if we attempt to apply it to *the facts of experience*. (Keynes, 1936: 3, emphasis added)

Economics is a science of thinking in terms of models joined to the art of choosing models which are relevant to the contemporary world. It is compelled to be this, because, unlike the typical natural science, the material to which it is applied is, in too many respects, not homogeneous through time. (*CWK*, XIV: 296)

Macroeconomic Method and Reality

The message contained in the first quote above, taken from the so-called 1934 paper by Keynes could also have been formulated the following way: What do we really know about how the overall macroeconomic system functions? Is it reasonable to assume that the system is self-regulating? Does the system, left to its own devices, have intrinsic adjustment mechanisms, which like a heat-seeking missile aim the individual markets towards full utilization of resources?

In 1936, Keynes took an important step forward in his critique of the neoclassical macroeconomic theory. He presented in the introduction to *The General Theory* the distinction between the economic society in which we actually live and the facts of experience on the one hand, and on the other the model through which we choose to see the world. For Keynes, economic theory also became a reflection upon the method-related choice of model, and not just the analytical use of a model, something which must constantly be adapted to society's changes. The central issues for Keynes, during his macroeconomic exploring that took place in the first half of the 1930s, were the criteria for selecting a relevant model of analysis, and thereafter, the use of the model. To understand this, a number of scientific-theoretical questions are raised and answers sought in the following chapters.[9]

The Consequences of Uncertainty

Keynes's and perhaps also the post-Keynesians' ontological starting point is the need to include uncertainty in macroeconomic analysis. This line of theory can hereby, without exaggeration, be summarized in the title 'the economics of uncertainty'.[10] Uncertain knowledge is present at all levels of human behaviour: the individual's understanding of his or her own choices and situation, the social consequences of our activities, external events and the overarching (macro)economic development. Post-Keynesian literature is influenced by the aspiration to understand the importance of uncertainty in an epistemological perspective. For this reason, among others, Keynes's writings have inspired post-Keynesian economists to ask a number of methodological questions: What do we really know about macroeconomic convergence and equilibrium? Is the selected model relevant for obtaining answers to these questions? For if it is not, then the analytical results will be irrelevant. If the hypothesis that the real macroeconomy is convergent cannot be substantiated through empirical studies, then it will remain an empirically unfounded restriction – a hypothesis which is *a priori* attributed to the analytical model.

A parallel problem is connected with the more specific use of a formalized model of analysis. Within the neoclassical tradition there are no limitations on the use of formal mathematical analysis. In the words of Varian (1999):

> An analytical approach to economics is one that uses rigorous, logical reasoning. This does not necessarily imply the use of advanced mathematical methods. The language of mathematics certainly helps to ensure a rigorous analysis, and using it is undoubtedly the best way to proceed when possible. ... [C]alculus is

not just a footnote to the argument of the text, but is instead a deeper way to examine the same issues that one can explore verbally and graphically. (Varian, 1999: xix–xx)

The point of the above methodological suggestion is that economic analysis, if one has the required mathematical insight, ought to be used, as it gives a deeper insight than can be acquired through verbal and graphical presentations. Only the mathematical method can ensure the highest degree of logical consistency, and thus precision, in the results. Hence, it is the method that defines the deepest way of doing economic analyses.

Even if this limitation of analytical economics is accepted it still does not free the researcher from having to justify further how the mathematically formulated model can give a relevant analysis. Relevance – meaning, here, to ensure that there is correspondence between the object's ontology and the method deployed – is a completely basic scientific criterion; this will be put into perspective in the following chapters by, among other things, reviewing scientific theory, particularly that inspired by 'critical realism'.

Can Trend and Cycle be Separated?

Ontological and analytical uncertainty means that general equilibrium and automatic convergence cannot be *a priori* assumed to be relevant model-related properties – unless we are speaking of a 'perfect' market economy without uncertainty and with well behaved mathematic functions. In that case the analytical focal point is the (very) long-term perspective, where the market economic system is designed to convergence to the predetermined general equilibrium. Here, we know by assumption (not by experience) that the closed system will end up in a 'Walras equilibrium', determined by the predesigned structural conditions. The model may be less clear-cut about the traverse towards general equilibrium. There may even be formulated alternative traverses leading towards the equilibrium; but the equilibrium itself is independent of the traverse. Hence, the shorter-run adjustment process causing 'conjectural waves' (business cycles) are of less interest, as they have no long run. In most general equilibrium models the growth trend is determined by structural conditions leaving business cycles without any impact on the macroeconomic performance.

The opposite condition would be true if the existence of uncertainty were introduced. In such cases growth trends and business cycles cannot be analysed separately and an eventual long-term equilibrium would not be unique (Hahn and Solow, 1996). In that case the long-term goal would be of less analytical interest and the traverse would gain attention. When uncertainty is recognized the macroeconomic analysis becomes open-ended. The further into the future we try to see, both as economic actors and as analytical economists, the more uncertainty will dominate and the more open-ended will be the analysis.[11]

Uncertainty about the future and expectations are narrowly connected. Keynes introduced short-term and long-term expectations as significant determinants of macroeconomic development. The weights attributed to expectations in the decision-making process change with the planning horizon and with the state of confidence (a term that covers variations in the level of uncertainty). In an uncertain world, the analysis with the shortest time horizon is in most cases the least uncertain, for instance daily consumption, while investment decisions are made in the light of longer-term, and therefore more uncertain, expectations.

In general equilibrium theory, the conditions are opposite: in the short term, actors can be surprised by unexpected events, but in the longer term, depending on the model's specifications, the model will adjust towards the general equilibrium. The certain point is therefore the long-term equilibrium.

The two macroeconomic schools therefore reach different results concerning the question of whether the growth rate and business cycles can be analysed independently of one another. To the degree that the average growth rate (the trend) is affected by the short-term conjuncture-determined development (the cycle), these two terms cannot be analytically separated. This means that macroeconomic development will always be decided by a mix of demand, supply and price-affecting institutions. Here, the 'traverse'[12] takes centre stage for the macroeconomic analysis, both in the short and long run, where irreversible factors such as 'path-dependency, hysteresis, cumulative causality and lock-in' are also of great importance (Kriesler, 2003).

Can the Microeconomic Foundation be Unequivocal?

To start, I would like to pose the question: Why is an explicit micro-economic foundation at all relevant for a macroeconomic analysis? The macro-model should draw broad lines in economic development and leave the details to microeconomic analyses. The analogy of making a map comes to mind. For the map to be useable the scale must be reduced, leaving out much detail.

Neoclassical theory works with an analytical concept called a 'representative agent', to which is attributed traits as though this were an acting individual, but how, in the model, can one agent represent a whole category of individuals, for example, all consumers wrapped into one? In this way, we are speaking about a stylized average of an entire category, which is then given individualistic behaviour such as utility maximization, most often under the assumption of full knowledge. Should these microeconomic conditions be carried over to the macro-level, then the representative agent is assumed, on behalf of the entire group, to know the general equilibrium, which is the macroeconomic equivalent to having perfect knowledge of the future. This was, as mentioned above, the model-related reason for formulating the hypothesis of rational expectations in new-classical macro-theory. But if the behaviour of the representative agent is not a representative for the whole group (perhaps because the group members act interdependently) or if the condition of full knowledge of the model's general equilibrium is not in agreement with macroeconomic reality, then this microeconomic foundation becomes less relevant for macroeconomic analysis. This rather trivial conclusion, however, has not hindered neoclassical macro-theorists from making the requirement that an analytical macro-model has to be based on an explicit microeconomic foundation, starting with individual optimizing agents with exogenous preferences.

The Fallacy of Composition

One of the great controversial questions in macroeconomics is to what degree is it possible to conclude from the particular to the general. Adam Smith wrote, as already mentioned: 'What is prudence in the conduct of every private family, can scarce be folly in that of a great kingdom' (Smith, 1776 [1976]: 457). He equates individual sense and societal sense – not a bad starting point *per se*, particularly not in a poor agricultural society with few supply factors and governed by a small upper class with autocratic tendencies.

As mentioned in the introduction to this chapter, macroeconomic theory has had to reflect on the question of the relevance of equating household economics and societal economics. General equilibrium theory is an attempt to generalize microeconomic behaviour to hold true on the macro-level. As an alternative to this stands the Keynes-inspired tradition, which concerns itself with the fact that uncertainty drives an epistemological wedge between individual behaviour and macroeconomic outcomes, because not even a super-rational actor can be all-knowing and act independently of the context. In the situations where uncertainty plays a significant role in economic decision-making, a macroeconomic generalization, based on a method-individualistic microeconomic theory, will carry the risk of committing the so-called 'fallacy of composition' (atomistic fallacy), which is caused by the fact that: '[i]ndividual actions, if common to a large number of individuals, will generate an outcome different from what was intended by each' (Dow, 1996: 85).

Smith's morally-founded statement should instead be formulated as follows: That which is right for one person is not necessarily correct for the entire society, when the action is conducted by a large number of people at the same time.[13] In other areas, Smith was well aware of the divide between morally-founded behaviour on the one side and the macroeconomic result on the other. He shocked the people of his time when concluding that following one's own interest in economic questions concerning production and employment could also be in the interest of society. He saw the selfish quest for greater income, which resulted in specialization and division of labour, as important sources of 'the wealth of nations'. Increases in economies of scale and productivity could stimulate the individual profit motive, which might make not only the producer but also the entire society richer.

The risk of committing a fallacy of composition lies in the case where the macro-conclusion is based on an unrealistic generalization of microeconomic behaviour. The significance of the fallacy of composition lies primarily in the warning against uncritically equating the individual and collective levels.

CONCLUSION: METHODOLOGY AS A MAJOR DIVIDING LINE WITHIN MACROECONOMICS

Within macroeconomic reasoning, two completely separate methodologies have been developed: one for neoclassical theory based on equilibrium models, and another for post-Keynesian theory based upon causal relationships and path-dependent analysis, where uncertainty, a lack of information, institution and supply and demand factors under constant change create a sustained and (partially) unpredictable dynamic structure.

Neoclassical macro-theory focuses on the analytical model built up around the criteria for a well-functioning and equilibrium-creating macroeconomic system. Here, the focus is on the idealized basic model built on the assumption of rational expectations. It is through this set of lenses that macroeconomic problems are viewed. It is a standard model that serves as the basis for all neoclassical-inspired macroeconomic theory. As is shown in Figure 0.1, within this line of neoclassic theory, there are a number of sub-schools and divisions which, to a varying degree, have dominated the post-war period. Of great importance for this discussion is the fact that, in the actual macroeconomic discussion, neoclassical macro-theory is represented by the new-classical and new-Keynesian lines, each of which has their specific characteristics, but both of which use the general equilibrium method and assume that representative microeconomic agents have rational expectations. It is, to put it mildly, terminologically confusing that one of the dominant schools within neoclassical theory uses the name 'new-Keynesian'. This apparent paradox will be discussed in the following chapter, which goes into more detail as to how Keynes's book from 1936 was later interpreted within the neoclassical tradition.

As shown in Figure 0.1, there is nothing less than a methodological abyss that divides the neoclassical macro-theory from Keynes's own contribution and its subsequent theoretical and methodological developments, called the post-Keynesian macro-theory. The domain here is the macroeconomic reality characterized by uncertainty. In the early post-war period all the post-Keynesians consisted of a relatively mixed bag of macroeconomists (see King, 2002). The school had its origins in the circle around Keynes in Cambridge. It took part in the discussions behind the creation of *The General Theory* and was, like Keynes, influenced by the big problem of the times: high unemployment. The post-Keynesian line of theory has continued to have the desire to understand reality as a central point in its research and theory development. The gravitational point since has shifted from the more specific theory development to a greater degree of methodological and method-related reflections, with significant inspiration from the scientific-theoretical direction called critical realism. This work was carried out, in part as an acknowledgement of the fact that many of the great macroeconomic challenges were still theoretically unanswered,[14] and partially in light of the renewed reading of Keynes, on the release of *The Collected Writings of John Maynard Keynes*, with greater emphasis on his methodological reflections and less on the more concrete theories and policy recommendations.

The argument of this introductory chapter could be summarized as follows: the selection of a method of analysis is a particularly important, yet often underestimated consideration that ought to be connected to each and every scientific work. On professional grounds, the choice between various macroeconomic theories ought to be justified. This is no easy task, as economic theory is, like all other social sciences, burdened by political interests that see science as a source of leverage for more specific concerns. As mentioned, I will attempt to filter out some of the more ideologically conditional overtones from the scientific discussion. For me, it is the primary aim of macroeconomic science to illuminate macroeconomic reality, independently of particular interests. This means creating the best possible accord between theory and reality, thereby providing the best basis for decision-making, from which one can subsequently make political decisions. This is an important project because macroeconomic theory

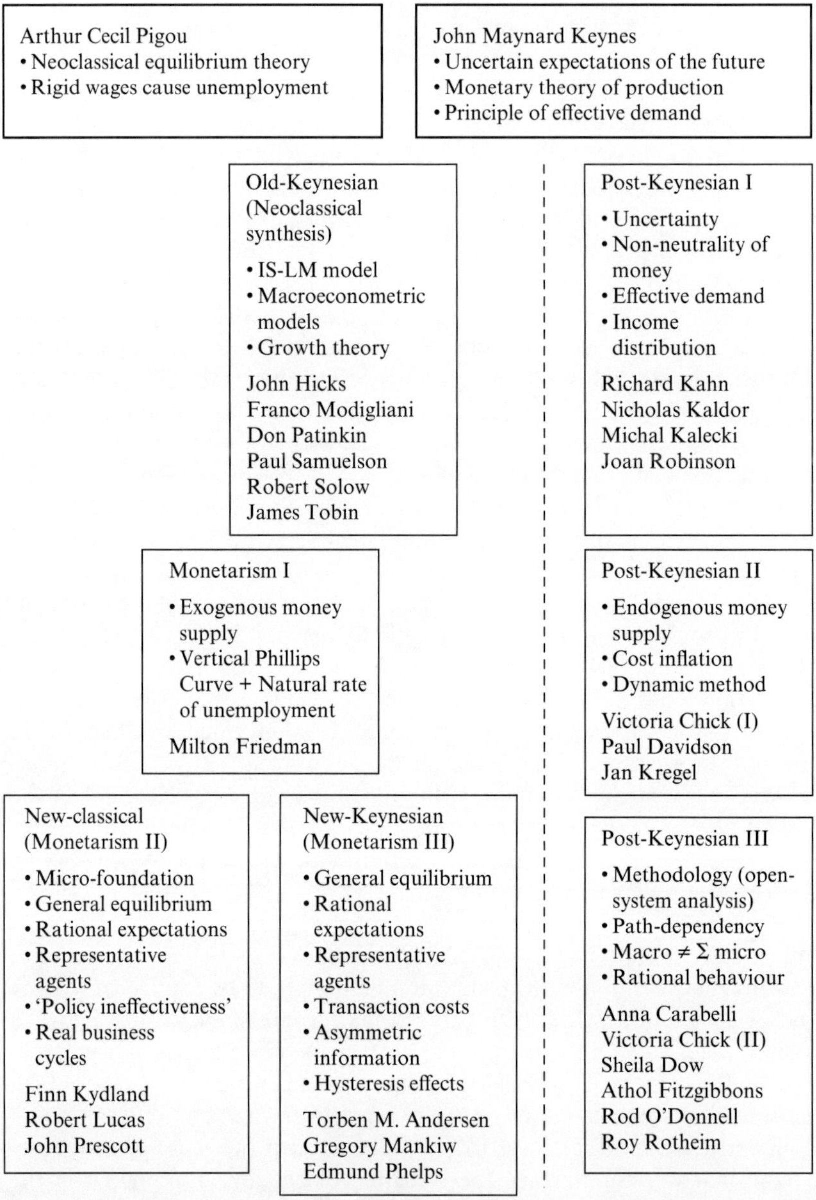

Arthur Cecil Pigou
• Neoclassical equilibrium theory
• Rigid wages cause unemployment

John Maynard Keynes
• Uncertain expectations of the future
• Monetary theory of production
• Principle of effective demand

Old-Keynesian
(Neoclassical
synthesis)

• IS-LM model
• Macroeconometric
  models
• Growth theory

John Hicks
Franco Modigliani
Don Patinkin
Paul Samuelson
Robert Solow
James Tobin

Post-Keynesian I

• Uncertainty
• Non-neutrality of
  money
• Effective demand
• Income
  distribution

Richard Kahn
Nicholas Kaldor
Michal Kalecki
Joan Robinson

Monetarism I

• Exogenous money
  supply
• Vertical Phillips
  Curve + Natural rate
  of unemployment

Milton Friedman

Post-Keynesian II

• Endogenous money
  supply
• Cost inflation
• Dynamic method

Victoria Chick (I)
Paul Davidson
Jan Kregel

New-classical
(Monetarism II)

• Micro-foundation
• General equilibrium
• Rational expectations
• Representative
  agents
• 'Policy ineffectiveness'
• Real business
  cycles

Finn Kydland
Robert Lucas
John Prescott

New-Keynesian
(Monetarism III)

• General equilibrium
• Rational
  expectations
• Representative
  agents
• Transaction costs
• Asymmetric
  information
• Hysteresis effects

Torben M. Andersen
Gregory Mankiw
Edmund Phelps

Post-Keynesian III

• Methodology (open-
  system analysis)
• Path-dependency
• Macro ≠ Σ micro
• Rational behaviour

Anna Carabelli
Victoria Chick (II)
Sheila Dow
Athol Fitzgibbons
Rod O'Donnell
Roy Rotheim

*Figure 0.1   Overview of the most significant macroeconomic schools from
a methodological point of view*

lies behind a number of policy recommendations, which then affect the daily economy of common citizens: employment, the welfare state, sustainable development, the national accounts and inflation.

For this reason it is important to develop professional argumentation for how one can differentiate between more and less adequate macroeconomic methodologies to enlighten others on a given macroeconomic problem. This means developing criteria for choosing a macroeconomic theory and the method of analysis.

This is the theme of the present book.

NOTES

1. After the revolution of 1917, Russia had embarked on a radically different economic path, based on collective ownership and central planning.
2. See Birk (1925).
3. The term 'equilibrium' has multifarious meanings, which will be analysed more thoroughly in Chapter 6.
4. Adam Smith's first book was published in 1750: *The Theory of Astronomy*, Kurrild-Klitgaard (2004).
5. This paragraph is inspired by my reading of Joan Robinson's 'Oxford lecture' reprinted as Chapter 13 in Robinson (1978).
6. The Solow model has since been expanded with both inexhaustible resources and endogenous growth factors, though still held within the confines of a general equilibrium model; see Sørensen and Whitta-Jakobsen (2005).
7. There will be many references to Keynes's works. They have been collected and published under the title of *The Collected Writings of John Maynard Keynes*, in 30 volumes. To make the references more simple, I use the acronym *CWK*, followed by a roman numeral to mark the volume. I make an exception in the case of *The General Theory*, citing it as Keynes (1936).
8. This, in my view programmatic, paper was originally delivered as a radio talk and later printed in *The Listener*, 21 November 1934 under the title 'Poverty in plenty: is the economic system self-adjusting?' (*CWK*, XIII: 485–92). In the text I refer to this paper as the 1934 paper.
9. I here have chosen Keynes as an exponent for the so-called heterodox economic tradition. It is a natural choice because macroeconomic theory and method is at the heart of this book. As put forward by *inter alia* Lawson (2003), within many other economic subdisciplines there are writers who have connected their economic theory to their method-related reflections, such as Karl Marx, Torstein Veblen, Friedrich Hayek and Milton Friedman.
10. The historian Eric Hobsbawm describes the twentieth century as the 'century of extremes', which naturally brings the reader to the idea that this century, to a much greater degree than its predecessors, has been influenced by uncertainty. This is an important factor for the shift in the scientific-theoretical foundation for macro-theory. However, macroeconomic uncertainty is not merely a consequence of political upheavals, but just as much a result of an increased division of labour – nationally and internationally.
11. An example: I feel confident that there will be sufficient supplies of energy for the next 20 years, even though political upheavals can hinder sections of the global energy supply. But were I responsible for the energy supply in a 50-year perspective, I would be rather uncertain, and even after being presented with the very best analyses, I still

would start a massive investment in renewable energy and energy saving, just to reduce uncertainty.

12. 'The traverse defines the movement of the economy outside equilibrium ...

The traverse is of relevance both to economists who deny that the economy is attracted to any equilibrium, as well as to those who accept that the economy will tend towards equilibrium, but argue that the final equilibrium position is path-determined' (Kriesler, 2003: 355–6).

13. The problem can also be found outside of economics. The paradox of the voter is well known: one voice for or against plays no role in an election, but if a large number of individuals act in a similar manner, then the result of the election can be affected. The Millennium footbridge over the Thames needed to be rebuilt when it was proved to be unstable in the event that a large number of pedestrians suddenly made the same movement, for example when they were hit by a strong gust of wind, or saw the Royal Family.

If one has paid for a seat at a football game, there is nothing so frustrating as when the spectator in front stands up. Then the spectator behind must also stand, which inevitably forces the person behind him to stand. Very soon, everyone is standing, and no one – except perhaps the first – can see any better.

14. Joan Robinson (1977), rather disillusioned, posed the question of how it could be, that 30 years after publishing *The General Theory*, a period when the Western world had experienced a previously unseen level of high economic growth, that the five significant macroeconomic imbalances listed below could still exist without a satisfactory theoretical solution:

1. Consumption of resources, including air to breathe, has evidently impoverished (parts of) the world.
2. The long struggle over relative income shares has implanted a chronic tendency to and fear of inflation in industrialized countries.
3. The international financial system has weakened the structure of the world economy.
4. Growth in wealth has not removed poverty at home, and development aid (and more international trade) has not reduced poverty in developing countries.
5. Registered unemployment has re-emerged. In the EU it was around 5 per cent in 1977; 30 years later unemployment was in a number of countries fluctuating around 10 per cent.

1. Keynes-inspired macroeconomic theory in a methodological perspective

INTRODUCTION

This chapter will explain why the group of 'Keynesian' economists cannot be perceived as belonging to one homogeneous school of thought. As already indicated in Figure 0.1 which illustrates 'the macroeconomic family tree', there are a number of theoretical schools that employ the description 'Keynesian', regardless of the fact that they are located at opposite sides of the methodological chasm. This is confusing, to put it mildly, and this chapter will attempt to redress the issue. The reasons for this convergence of designation can be found in the sphere of political aspiration, since a common result from old-Keynesians, new-Keynesians and post-Keynesians is that macroeconomic policy can exert significant influence on economic development. That is something that the three schools of theory have in common with Keynes. In the 1930s, he developed his macroeconomic theory as a reaction to the prevailing (macro) economic orthodoxy that recommended a laissez-faire policy combined with a strengthening of market forces as means of curing unemployment. Keynes's *General Theory* contained some theoretical arguments as to why even within a well-functioning and competitive market economy full employment is a special case, so that economic policy can contribute to keeping macroeconomic development on the track of full employment.

Post-Keynesian theory is a direct continuation of Keynes's macroeconomic tradition, understood as theory and method, which was initiated in 1936. It maintains the requirement for an active economic policy derived from analyses within the framework of an open macroeconomic landscape.

We will return to these methodological issues in the following two chapters. Old- and new-Keynesians have in common that both schools, although with about 40 years' time difference, try to incorporate elements from Keynes's theory in the neoclassical general equilibrium model, which is referred to as the 'neoclassical synthesis'. To the extent that the project succeeded, it opened up the possibility, even within the framework of the neoclassical model, to explain the need to carry out macroeconomic policies. However, this was perceived as needed only in the short run in an attempt to smooth the economic cycles, because in the long run it is still assumed that the neoclassical theory of general equilibrium is valid.

The increasing criticism in the 1960s and 1970s from monetarists (especially Milton Friedman)[1] and later new-classical economists (like Lucas and Sargent)[2] against so-called 'Keynesian' economic theory and policies was aimed primarily at this neoclassical synthesis, which incidentally Friedman himself had been a part of (cf. the claim 'We are all Keynesians now' quoted in Skidelsky, 1996).

The new-Keynesian school (including Edmund Phelps, Gregory Mankiw and Torben M. Andersen) took a number of the neoclassical economists' criticisms seriously, in particular concerning the lack of microeconomic foundation and the so-called *ad hoc* nature of expectation-formation in the original neoclassical synthesis formulated by old-Keynesians. Despite the fact that the methodological basis for new-Keynesian theory therefore has much in common with the neoclassical critics of old-Keynesians, they have managed to develop a distinct new-Keynesian model that can establish a case for short-term demand management with the use of fiscal and monetary policies. The name 'new-Keynesian' should be seen as an acknowledgement of a certain kinship with old-Keynesians, but new-Keynesian theory rests on a different methodological basis, not least when it comes to the requirement of microeconomic foundations. Furthermore, it is a characteristic that new-Keynesians define themselves firmly within the neoclassical tradition, somewhat in methodological opposition to the old-Keynesians, by taking over the method of the new-classical school – methodological individualism, microeconomic foundations, including rational expectations and general equilibrium – but distinguish themselves by analysing different forms of market imperfections and short-term policy issues. It is characteristic that new-Keynesians, such as Lindbeck (1998) and Andersen (2000), present the new-Keynesian research programme without giving any recognition of post-Keynesian theory, much less method.[3]

FROM GENERALIZED MICRO-THEORY TO ACTUAL MACRO-THEORY

Generalised Micro-Theory

A stable macroeconomic development is widely accepted as a necessary assumption for ensuring continued prosperity and welfare in a democratic society based on a market economy, private property rights and a large number of wage-earners. On this basis alone, it is important to understand the social processes that determine the development of employment, inflation, unemployment, balance of payments and public sector budgets.

As already mentioned, macroeconomic theory was first established as a proper, independent, specialist research discipline in the interwar period. This was in direct response to the significant amount of macroeconomic instability that characterized this period. Macroeconomic models that had the primary goal of analysing the development particularly of unemployment became an increasing popular theme for the macroeconomic research of the period.

The starting point for this macroeconomic research was the existing neoclassical foundation, with its emphasis on market clearing, within separate markets where employment and relative prices were determined. Here, supply, demand and market prices on the separate markets were at the centre of neoclassical theory and were only organized into a macroeconomic unit via the 'quantity equation of money and prices'. In the Anglo-Saxon tradition[4] this specific equation had been founded more than 100 years earlier by Smith and Ricardo and carried on by Marshall and Pigou (in Cambridge); market (microeconomic) analysis remained the basis of the macroeconomic theory that was used as the basis for economic policy advice concerning, among other things, the relief of unemployment.

Until *The General Theory of Employment, Interest and Money* was published in 1936, macroeconomic theory of the interwar years consisted, therefore, of a number of mainly microeconomic (and therefore partial) analyses of the factors that influenced the development of the aggregated microeconomic variables. Each aggregated micro-market – that is, labour, capital, goods and currency – was analysed without explicit regard for their mutual interaction. This approach was legitimized, methodologically, through an assumption that 'everything else remained the same', the often-heard *ceteris paribus* assumption. In this way, macroeconomic theory came, in practice, to consist of partial (that is, independent) analyses of single markets, including the labour, goods and credit markets. Similarly, the absolute price level was determined in isolation from the real economic development, since the quantity theory of money and prices was assumed to be exhaustive in its description of the causal connection between the money supply and the price level, on condition of full utilization of productive resources; in other words, a given and constant output. As mentioned, this 'quantity theory' had already been formulated by the classical economists: that there can be established an unambiguous causal relationship between changes in the money supply and the development in the general price level (inflation).

Through the 1920s, Keynes had worked together with Dennis Robertson, Ralph Hawtrey and others in an attempt to explain the empirical fact of unemployment as a cyclical (that is, temporary) phenomenon caused by credit-cycle instability. According to the neoclassical argument, these credit cycles were a consequence of the financial sector having a partly independent capacity of expanding money and credit. But these cycles would only have a short-term, real economic effect. This was also one of the hypotheses of Keynes's *A Treatise on Money* (1930), which methodologically was confined within the overall framework of neoclassical macro-theory.

This was, in short, the macroeconomic frame of analysis that was available when the storm broke after the crash on Wall Street in October 1929. This framework is described in Pigou's book, *The Theory of Unemployment* (1933), which Keynes heavily criticized in his 1936 book with a frontal assault on all existing neoclassical macroeconomic theory. As a consequence of the partial, microeconomic market analysis, Pigou had necessarily to reach the conclusion that the persistently high unemployment was a result of the defective adjustment of the 'price variable' in the labour market (real wages). When the imbalance in the labour market could remain large and unchanged over such a long period, it had to be caused by an inflexible real wage, which was easily demonstrated in a neoclassical labour market model. Here it was not lack of demand for British products but too-high wage costs that was the cause of insufficient demand for labour. This conclusion was based on a partial microeconomic labour market analysis (without empirical testing); see Figure 1.1.

Actual Macro-Theory and Method

It is here that the publication of John Maynard Keynes's main work, *The General Theory of Employment, Interest and Money* makes quite a difference. This book presented for the first time an actual macroeconomic method that became the start of a fundamentally new understanding of macroeconomics as a research object. Methodologically, Keynes set a number of requirements that should be fulfilled before an analysis could be characterized as macroeconomics.

Firstly, the analysis should cover 'the economy as a whole', that is, the individual markets cannot be analysed independently of each other, because the assumption that 'all other things are equal' does not apply on the macro-level. As something new, Keynes succeeded in integrating the real and the financial sectors, which he emphasized in the title of one of the articles that pointed the way towards *The General Theory*: 'A *monetary* theory of production' (emphasis added) (1933, *CWK*, XIII: 408–11).

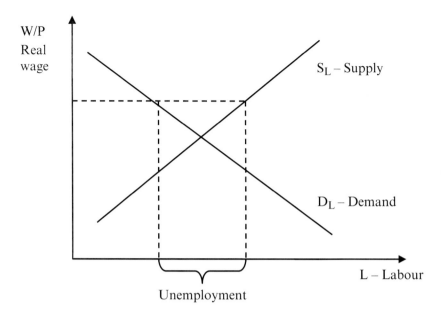

Figure 1.1   The neoclassical standard labour market model

Secondly, the macroeconomic theory should reflect the fact that the formation of expectations, according to the nature of macroeconomics, must be characterized by uncertainty with regard to what the future will bring. Keynes's often-quoted view of our possible knowledge about the distant future was: 'we simply do not know' (*CWK*, XIV: 142). This empirical statement rules out that the traditional microeconomic theory, with its assumption of full information, can be reflected within the macroeconomic landscape. The macroeconomic behaviour relationships must be formulated with respect for uncertainty and for the institutional circumstances that are established partly as a consequence of the fact that the future is uncertain.

Although the macroeconomic 'raw material' may consist of a number of perfectly competitive markets within the basic model, these markets cannot be analysed independently of each other, because the expected prices will change as a consequence of the interaction.

Hence, as a consequence of the second point in particular, it cannot be assumed *a priori* that the axiomatic assumption of (long-run) general equilibrium is relevant for macroeconomic analysis. If this statement is accepted, the discussion of whether the economic system as a whole is self-regulating becomes meaningless, because in that case there is no pre-defined fixed point that the macroeconomic system is moving towards. Without a general equilibrium, long-term expectations have no anchor and will continually be revised as a consequence of past events and present experiences. In Keynes's opinion, there was nothing (judged on the empirical data that existed in the interwar period) that supported the assumption that a well-behaved market economic system should be self-adjusting and generate a general equilibrium. In addition, the existing knowledge of the macroeconomic dynamics, particularly in relation to employment (and unemployment) was also unable to justify the assumption of a self-adjusting mechanism that pointed towards full employment and macroeconomic stability; see the quotation from Keynes's 1934 paper on p. 9 (*CWK*, XIII: 486–9).

Macroeconomic theory demanded a new methodological foundation if these theoretical questions concerning the more long-term dynamics were to be clarified. At the same time methodological 'space' was to be created to include the new analytical concept of 'fundamental uncertainty' that cannot be given a formalized representation. Fundamental uncertainty becomes a relevant concept in a macroeconomic context where reality cannot *a priori* be assumed to converge towards a general equilibrium, not even under the assumption of perfect markets. This new acknowledgement rules out that rational agents can have correct information about the future. Or in other words: theories of the economic behaviour at the micro- and macro-levels must reflect this systemically contingent ignorance.

Already here we are presented with one of the crucial contradictions within macroeconomic science, the issue of whether macroeconomic analysis should be based on idealism (how the economy could function in an ideal, but artificial, case) or on realism (how the economy actually does function). The idealists have an axiomatic point of departure: individual rationality, full predictability and general equilibrium. The realists, however, take their point of departure from the existing social ontology (reality, about which there is limited knowledge), where individuals act partly in communities, where knowledge of the future is limited and macroeconomic development moves towards unknown horizons:

> It may well be that the classical theory represents the way in which we should like our economy to behave. But to assume that it actually does so is to assume our difficulties away. (Keynes, 1936: 34)

Instead, Keynes wanted to construct a realistic macroeconomic theory. He achieved this partly in confrontation with the dominant idealistic theoretical construction, represented by Pigou (1933). The completely different perception (compared to the existing macroeconomic theory) of the ontological point of departure also had decisive importance for the analytical method that should be used to understand the factual macroeconomic relationships.

Of course, it is not only Keynes who can provide inspiration for the construction of a realistic methodological basis for macroeconomic theory in the twenty-first century. The problem of how to ensure correspondence between reality and theory is a fundamental issue for any theory of how to undertake social science. This discussion is not only relevant within economic theory. However, I will stick to my own field, where the list of 'realist economists' is quite long. It includes: Smith, Malthus, Marx, Veblen, Keynes, Schumpeter, Myrdal, Polanyi, Hayek and Galbraith. All of them have to varying degrees been hesitant in relation to the relevance of the neoclassical assumptions about methodological individualism, individual optimization under the assumption of full information and systemic equilibrium. This list of characteristic 'methodologically aware economists' could without difficulty be expanded into the twenty-first century with, for example, a number of post-Keynesian economists who have in common that they have made macroeconomic methodology an important and integrated part of their research.

However, Keynes stands out because he was educated by Marshall in the neoclassical tradition. Right up until the end of the 1920s, he attempted to create a synthesis of realistic macroeconomics and neoclassical reasoning, which failed.[5] That made him go through 'a long struggle of escape from habitual modes of thought and expression', which he asks the readers to be willing to undertake, if 'the author's assault upon them is to be successful' (Keynes, 1936, viii). In that perspective Keynes became an exponent of the requirement of a more elaborate correspondence between theory and reality within macroeconomics – the quest for methodological realism.

A reading of Keynes's contribution to the macroeconomic literature can therefore even today provide inspiration for maintaining the quest for such an explicit correspondence between theory and reality in the twenty-first century. Both his intellectual struggle to free himself from the equilibrium methodology of his day and his subsequent constructive contribution to developing a realistic macroeconomic theory and its methodological foundation are probably just as stimulating and challenging today as they were 70 years ago, but, unfortunately, also just as difficult to make operational.

KEYNESIANS AFTER KEYNES

Keynesians as Different from Monetarists and New-Classical Economists

As already mentioned in the introduction to this chapter, it is absolutely vital to differentiate between the various 'Keynesian' schools of theory. 'Keynesians' are not just 'Keynesians', as they are often presented in neoclassical textbooks, for example Romer (1996) and Sørensen and Whitta-Jakobsen (2005). But before we begin to straighten out the Keynesian confusion, it may be useful to clarify the popular contradiction between monetarism, and the Keynesian macroeconomic theory, particularly in relation to policy.

Outside of a comparatively narrow circle of macroeconomists, 'Keynesian' is usually used as a populist contrast to economic policies inspired by monetarists (or new-classical economists). A monetarist economic policy[6] is perceived to include a strict control of the money supply, balancing of a small public budget and *laissez-faire* in relation to the market economy – a conservative economic policy. Keynesian economic policy, however, is often identified with 'demand management' that may result in a budget deficit, a comprehensive welfare state and some regulations of the market economy, or in popular terms, an (old) social democratic policy. This simplified presentation is almost a caricature of the policy recommendations of both schools of thought; see for instance Estrup *et al.* (2004).

Since my aim is to discuss and develop the Keynes-inspired macroeconomic methodology, in this chapter I will try to clarify the use of the term 'Keynesians', since the methodologically relevant division is not whether parallels can be found between the economic policies but, on the contrary, in spite of the shared view of economic policy it is the task of discussing the fundamentally different macroeconomic methods used by old- and new-Keynesianism on the one hand and post-Keynesianism on the other hand. Arising from these two schools are two very distinct theory-of-science positions: idealism and realism, respectively. It should be noted, however, that new-Keynesianism fully acknowledges its relationship with the 'ideal' methodological camp:

> ... Another recurring principle is the wish to create general equilibrium models. This is a consistency requirement.
>
> In a part of the newer macroeconomic theory, not least in the classical inspired theory, there is a tendency that 'the method is the message'. This is deceptive. The choice of method imposes discipline and consistency on the analysis and so a 'laboratory' is defined for the analysis. ... This is for example reflected in the fact that new-Keynesian macro-theory, despite a methodological kinship with classically oriented macro-theory, has significantly different views of the economy's mode of functioning and the need and effects of economic policy...
>
> It is interesting that proponents for various economic schools [new-classical, real business cycle models and new-Keynesians] all use the methodological point of departure described above. (Andersen, 2000: 21–3, my translation)[7]

The following part of this chapter will be used to illustrate the different paths that the two Keynesian camps have followed in their development of theories and models in the post-war period. Old- and new-Keynesians have primarily focused on whether the theory of aggregate[8] demand, which they regard as an important inheritance from Keynes, can be incorporated into a general equilibrium model; see the quotation above. Post-Keynesians, on the other hand, have been engaged in developing a theoretical and methodological foundation that can assimilate the phenomenon of fundamental uncertainty in the formation of expectations and in developing the macroeconomic analysis method.[9]

The Neoclassical Synthesis: Old-Keynesians

As already mentioned, Keynes's work from 1936 started an avalanche within the macroeconomic discussion. It was particularly 'the monetary production theory' with its message that money was not neutral in relation to the real economy, and the arguments for an unemployment equilibrium (understood as the absence of the self-regulating forces), that captured the interest of the younger economists.

Hicks's IS–LM diagram, which was presented in the autumn of 1936 (Hicks, 1937), quickly came to represent the model that the Keynesians, in sharp contrast to the mainstream economists of the day, could agree contained the main message of Keynes's new macro-theory. It is understandable that the IS–LM model was given this position, because the model gave Keynes's new analytical concept 'aggregate demand' a prominent position. Here it is the aggregate demand for goods and services that determines the size of production and therefore also the volume of employment. In the IS–LM model, unemployment can remain in a permanent position since there are no automatic mechanisms that create full employment. It should also be mentioned that Keynes did not reject Hicks's representation, which he perhaps should have done, since Hicks claimed that his model could accommodate both Mr Keynes and the 'Classics', see Hicks (1937). The difference between Mr Keynes and the Classics could, according to Hicks, be limited to the question of which explanatory variables should and could in a consistent way be accepted in the macroeconomic behavioural relations. Hereby, the first step was taken towards the neoclassical synthesis, or more accurately, towards the dominance of the neoclassical methodology, which came to set the macroeconomic agenda throughout the first three decades of the post-war period.

Modigliani (1944) took the next step by reintroducing the neoclassical labour market and Pigou's argument that only rigidity in real wages could explain persistent unemployment.[10] But, just like Pigou, Modigliani had the problem that aggregate demand had become an integrated part of mainstream macroeconomic theory and the conventional neoclassical model lacked a connection from changes in the wage level to aggregate demand. In a model without foreign trade, a flexible real wage cannot by itself explain how the aggregate demand on the goods market changes. This missing adjustment mechanism only fell into place with the addition of the real balance effect, or the so-called Pigou effect, in the consumption function by Patinkin (1956 [1966]).

The neoclassical synthesis had thus brought Keynes's macro-theory back to the 'equilibrium fold', where the macroeconomic system is self-regulating, where uncertainty is disregarded and where analysis of 'the economy as a whole' as different from the analysis of individual markets is only relevant in the short run, that is, until the entire economy has managed to adjust itself to the general equilibrium. However, on one issue the old-Keynesians[11] did remain faithful to their intellectual roots: that economic policy, particularly fiscal policy, can exert an influence on the speed with which the macroeconomic system adjusts.

The Keynesian Macro-Econometric Models and the Lucas Critique

It was also the neoclassical synthesis that formed the theoretical basis for the so-called macro-econometric models that were produced in the 1960s and particularly in the 1970s, at the same time as the calculating capacity of computers increased dramatically. It was particularly names like Modigliani and Klein who were the driving forces behind the statistically anchored development of the large macro-econometric simulation models.[12] This development ran contrary to the scepticism of the use of econometric methods in macroeconomics that Keynes had expressed as early as 1939 when Tinbergen, on a much smaller scale, presented his first econometric works for Keynes (see Sutton, 2002).

These Keynesian (in the 'neoclassical synthesis' sense) macro-econometric models were subjected at the end of the 1970s to significant criticism from a circle of strongly market- and individual-orientated economists. These so-called new-classical economists including Finn Kydland, Robert Lucas and John Prescott were looking for an explicit microeconomic foundation for macroeconomic theory. These economists claimed that the statistically estimated macro-behavioural relations could not remain stable over a longer period of time, since they were not consistently derived from rational individual economic behaviour (for example, Lucas and Sargent, 1978). According to that criticism the estimated macro-behaviour relations were lacking a theoretical basis anchored in individual (rational) behaviour, not least concerning the formation of expectations. Hence, Lucas and Sargent claimed that these relations had an *ad hoc* character and could not be expected to remain stable if there was a change in expectations concerning economic policy for instance. Such stability of parameters would require that the behaviour relations were formulated in accordance with microeconomic behaviour, since the individual preference functions were assumed to be exogenous and therefore independent of a change in policy regime. The behaviour relations should be specified on the basis of the so-called deep, individual behavioural parameters. This was the beginning of the 'rational expectations' revolution within the neoclassical camp. From then on, it became an established requirement of neoclassical macroeconomic models that an explicit, microeconomic foundation should be specified so that macroeconomic theory could be acknowledged as being anchored in rational economic behaviour.

Expectation formation, within monetarism and the neoclassical synthesis, was therefore subjected to criticism from the new-classical economists. They argued that the only expectation formation that would be in accordance with the hypothesis of rational economic behaviour, where systematic errors are avoided, must be the assumption of correct expectations based on full information, which led to the concept of 'rational expectations'. Economic agents are assumed to optimize on the basis of full information about the model's equilibrium solution. Any other expectation formation is described by the new-classical economists as *ad hoc*, since the agents will continue to make expectation errors unless a correct learning process is included. The monetarist assumption of adaptive expectation formation will thus reflect a behaviour that will not conform with the axiom about rational agents, since it would be defective.

The new-classical economists' criticism was so effective that the monetarist and 'Keynesian' ('neoclassical synthesis') models were either given up or respecified so that macro-behavioural relations were formed on the basis of the theory of representative micro-agents and the hypothesis of rational expectations. The 'deep' parameters in the behavioural relations were calibrated, that is, given empirically plausible values, without necessarily being anchored by formal statistical tests. It is considered more important that parameter values respect the theoretical requirements of a well-behaved general equilibrium model.

This changed model practice entailed that an assumption of full predictability was introduced, which ensured formal consistency within the model between expectation formation and the model's equilibrium solution, given the axiom of general equilibrium. The empirical macro-models were thus, under the label 'applied general equilibrium models', returned to their pre-Keynesian starting point as a consequence of the 'triumph of the rational expectation hypothesis'. At the end of the 1980s, Lucas formulated it as follows:

> The most interesting recent developments in macroeconomic theory seem to me describable as the reincorporation of aggregative problems such as inflation and the business cycle within the general framework of 'microeconomic' theory. If these developments succeed, the term 'macroeconomics' will simply disappear from use and the modifier 'micro' will become superfluous. We will simply speak, as did Smith, Ricardo, Marshall and Walras, of *economic* theory. (Lucas, 1987: 107–8)

As a consequence of this development all subsequent neoclassical macro-theory became subordinated to this analytical evolution of rational expectations. The empirical determination of parameters was also subordinated to the macro-model's analytical and theoretical structures. Theoretical considerations were given priority to empirical verification.

New-Keynesians to be called New-Pigovians?

The new-classical economists had set an expanded agenda with the demand for a microeconomic foundation for macroeconomic theory. Important representatives of the 'neoclassical synthesis' held a kind of crisis conference in a remote convent in northern Spain. Their deliberations were collected in Harcourt (1977): *The Microeconomic Foundations of Macroeconomics*.

Two questions in particular were discussed. Firstly, the proposed microeconomic foundation is only fully consistent in general equilibrium due to coordination failures outside equilibrium. Hence, the question is whether it is possible, within a framework of long-term general equilibrium, to introduce 'rational' market failures into the adjustment process (towards general equilibrium). Market failures could then take the form of rational 'misperceptions' of information without breaking the assumption of neoclassical microeconomics and rational expectations. Could it be rational to hesitate in a case where the general equilibrium solution is only known with some 'creaks, groans, jerks and interrupted by time lags, outside interference and mistakes' (*CWK*, XII: 486–7)? In such cases individual optimization might deviate from social optimization even if the hypothesis of rational expectation formation is accepted in the sense that the long-term state of equilibrium is known. Here, asymmetrically distributed information, market coordination failures, transaction and menu costs, credit rationing and market power were named as possible short-term inertia factors in the price–wage adjustment to the known general equilibrium within the model.

Secondly, how should the microeconomic foundation for economic behaviour be incorporated into the macroeconomic models in a methodologically consistent way? How, in a consistent manner, can an aggregation be performed of the behaviour of innumerable microeconomic individuals into a meaningful macroeconomic behavioural relation that is compatible with the microeconomic foundation of optimizing individuals, but not necessarily in a persistent and unequivocal general equilibrium?

The recommendations from the participants of the conference in the form of answers to these questions about market failures and aggregate relations were not clear; but they pointed in the direction of an altered methodological strategy in the new-Keynesian camp, away from the previous *ad hoc* macro-behavioural relations and to a clearer specification of general equilibrium as the overall model framework. An adoption of the assumption of rational expectations should ensure that the established micro-theory, based on the description of 'rational economic man', could be used in the form of 'representative agents', since all agents in that case are assumed to have the same expectation. In this way, the macroeconomic models could be reduced to a modest number of equations based on a few, precisely described, rational representative agents that should guarantee that the macro-model was anchored in a consistent, microeconomic foundation. The methodological focus changed the new-Keynesian research programme so that the emphasis was on the short-term deviations from general equilibrium due to market failures and 'rational' inertia in the adjustment to general equilibrium:

> The assumption of model-consistent (rational) expectations is often made. The motivation for this is not that it necessarily is a descriptively very precise model for expectation formation. On the contrary, the reason is that the assumption serves a useful theoretical purpose ...
> The purpose of theoretical analysis is to create a laboratory for testing the consistency of various hypotheses. (Andersen, 2000: 22, my translation)

New-Keynesians' research strategy consists therefore of developing a model, that is, a 'laboratory' that contains a framework, where temporary but rational deviations from perfect equilibrium are incorporated. These deviations are thus explained by rational, individual behaviour without systematic expectation errors. As noted by Andersen:

> The methodological aspects listed here all serve the purpose of imposing consistency and discipline on the analysis in the sense that we wish to discover whether a given problem can be explained as an outcome of economic behaviour. This is especially important in relation to the evaluation of economic policy ... (Andersen, 2000: 22, my translation)

New-Keynesians wish to discover the causes of 'rational' inertia in the adjustment to general equilibrium. Some issues related to the labour market

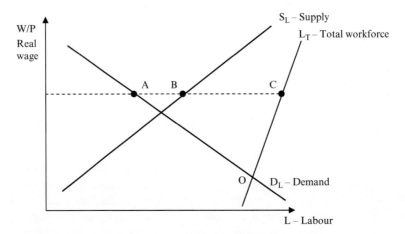

Figure 1.2   New-Keynesian labour market model

can be illustrated in the well-known form of Figure 1.2. Methodological individualism and rational expectations are assumed. Why is the socially optimal equilibrium point 'O' not realized? Two straightforward arguments can be put forward: (1) market failure (AB) and (2) policy failure (BC) causing voluntary unemployment.

Market failure is caused by a dominant group of agents having a shared interest in keeping the real wage above the market-clearing level: for example trade unions. The market power of this group might be eroded through time, reducing the involuntary unemployment. The theoretical point is that the trade union optimizes on the basis of knowledge of the general equilibrium. If the demand elasticity for labour is numerically less than one, it is rational to 'stick together', and the trade union can organize a redistribution mechanism that ensures all members (also the unemployed) a larger income than in the case of perfect competition. In addition to this there is, from the point of view of the trade union, an additional income from unemployment benefit paid by society, that is, employed wage-earners and owners of capital (Sørensen and Whitta-Jakobsen, 2005).

Voluntary unemployment is within the new-Keynesian tradition caused by welfare programmes changing incentives to supply labour. In fact, there are two negative effects. Unemployment benefit makes it tempting to withdraw from the active (wage-competing) part of the labour force. In addition, the wage taxes which are needed to finance the social benefit will reduce the supply of labour even further. This is the well-known trade-off in neoclassical literature between distribution and efficiency.

Firstly, it should be noted that, in this new-Keynesian labour market model, adjustment in real wages and employment is analysed in isolation, independently of repercussions from other macro-markets.

Next, it should be noted that the involuntary unemployment AB is explained by the inertia in adjustment of the real wage, for example caused by trade unions.

Voluntary unemployment, also referred to as natural unemployment, is indicated by the line BC and is determined by the rational representative supplier of labour balancing real wages (after tax) against income-replacing welfare benefits plus leisure time.

An increase in employment can, according to new-Keynesian theory, be deduced within Figure 1.2. One possibility is to make the real wage more flexible by weakening the trade unions' market power. The other possibility is to reduce the size of the income-replacing benefits and wage taxes. According to this analysis, if trade unions and the welfare state were dismantled, the Pareto-optimal point 'O' would be the outcome. This conclusion coincided with the results from monetarist analysis, which led DeLong (2000) to declare that: 'Now, we are all Monetarists'.

Not all new-Keynesians would unconditionally endorse this statement, since they also take note of the inertia in the adjustment to a new market equilibrium (under full or imperfect competition) that can cause cyclical movements in the wake of a demand or supply shock. Furthermore, some new-Keynesians have identified in their 'laboratory' a number of mechanisms based on rational microeconomic behaviour that could prolong the adjustment to the new equilibrium and create hysteresis effects. In that case, an active economic policy, especially for demand shocks, can contribute to reducing the cyclical fluctuations. Policy failures, on the other hand, should be alleviated through distributional changes that do not clash with individual preferences and incentive structures, including lump-sum taxes and subsidies. These conclusions advocating a somewhat active and countercyclical policy have lured some members of this school in opposition to new-classical economics to suggest the name 'new-Keynesian economists', because they saw that this active policy recommendation was in accordance with Keynes and his more realistic approach to macroeconomics. However, this is a misleading label, since the new-Keynesians' analytical point of departure, as described above, is an experimental laboratory also characterized by general equilibrium and rational expectations, which in fact is not realistic in any significant sense.

Arestis *et al.* (2001) have shown that it is possible to identify a so-called 'new consensus' macroeconomic theory that is primarily characterized by the methodological principles which focus on the ideal market model described in the previous chapter. The new-Keynesian models, despite the postulated inertia, lead in the long-term perspective to the same neoclassical policy conclusions as, for example, those undertaken by the European Central Bank (inflation targeting) recommending structural reforms in the labour market (greater flexibility and less welfare provision). For all practical purposes, it is impossible here to differentiate between recommendations from monetarists and new-Keynesians.[13] Hence, DeLong was in a methodological sense right because the general equilibrium framework seems to encompass monetarists and new-Keynesian theory equally well.

A Historical Comparison

It can be seen that new-Keynesians have renounced at least two of Keynes's methodological innovations: (1) that the long-period equilibrium is not well defined and cannot be known because of uncertainty and possibly does not even exist; and (2) that the market system cannot *a priori* be assumed to be self-regulating (with or without inertia). It can be concluded that the new-Keynesians' methodological approach is closer to traditional neoclassical theory than to Keynes's original macroeconomic contribution. Seen in this perspective, there is a striking similarity between Pigou's policy recommendations from 1933, where he recommended a lowering of real wages to increase employment. If this reduction was not possible for political reasons, then a temporary increase in 'the real demand for labour', that is, a displacement of the demand curve in Figure 1.2, was recommendable as a short-term relief, Pigou said. But here Keynes caught him making a theoretical error, since the demand curve of profit-maximizing firms is determined by the production function and is fixed by the technical conditions, that is, the marginal productivity of labour (Keynes, 1936: 278–9). The demand curve will only shift within the model when the shape or position of the production function changes, for instance due to improved productivity; so the demand schedule for labour in conventional neoclassical theory is independent of demand for goods and services. Hence, Pigou was not making a fully consistent argument, when he maintained within the equilibrium model that private sector employment could be increased by fluctuations in the real demand for labour caused by demand management policies, for example public investment. In Pigou's model, when Say's Law is accepted, these fluctuations are along the demand schedule and could only take place if either real wages or the supply schedule of labour changes. Later on, the old-Keynesians claimed, as mentioned above, that they had solved this problem of inconsistency by introducing the 'real balance effect' or the 'Pigou effect'. That is a kind of money illusion, where a lower nominal level of wages and prices – leaving the real wage unchanged – would generate higher private demand because it increased the purchasing power of money. But this argument was also fallacious because it overlooked the theoretical fact that the real wage together with productivity determine maximum profit; if neither real wage nor productivity change then the private sector is supply-constrained (see Keynes, 1936: appendix to Chapter 19 – discussed in Appendix 8.1 to Chapter 8 in this volume).

The new-Keynesians work in principle within the same labour market model as Pigou did. For instance, new-Keynesians have therefore for many years recommended less trade union power, lower social benefits and wage moderation as measures against high unemployment. Unemployment is still high in the major countries of the European Monetary Union, although income distribution has changed considerably and especially the German competitive position has become somewhat stronger. The persistence of unemployment on the Continent has challenged the new consensus models, because the explanation of temporary inertia does not fit when the unemployment can stay high for more than a decade. Here the new-Keynesians, just like Pigou, seem to lack a convincing theoretical (and empirical) explanation.

In a history-of-theory perspective, there might therefore possibly be a point in renaming new-Keynesians (since the name is deceptive) 'pre-Keynesians'; and why not then go the whole way and call them 'new-Pigovians', since the methodological and theoretical similarities are so striking?

KEYNES AND POST-KEYNESIANS[14]

Introduction

> Professor Pigou's *Theory of Unemployment* seems to me to get out of the classical theory all that can be got out of it; with the result that the book becomes a striking demonstration that this theory has nothing to offer, when it is applied to the problem of what determines the volume of actual employment as a whole. (Keynes, 1936: 260)

I will now justify the claim that Keynes wished to be a methodological realist. The writing of *The General Theory* had been 'a struggle of escape from habitual modes of thought and expression' (Keynes, 1936: viii). Keynes knew better than most what he was talking about; he had got stuck six years earlier in his book *A Treatise on Money*. Here he discovered that it was not possible to explain long-term unemployment within the framework of a neoclassical equilibrium model. When Keynes had realized the epistemological mistake that occurs when model and reality are confused, he could have demonstrated with some practical examples from his own earlier book why the classical equilibrium theory cannot explain 'the economic society in which we actually live' (Keynes, 1936: 3).

As pointed out above, there are many common features between new-Keynesians and the modelling framework used by Pigou to justify why in the true meaning of the word there is a methodological gap between on the one hand Keynes (1936) and post-Keynesians, and on the other new-Keynesians and the entire (neo)classical tradition. One may wonder why it is the new-Keynesians' interpretation that today dominates mainstream macroeconomic teaching. The explanation is perhaps that they seem to have a foot in each camp, politically recommending a (not too) active economic policy, while theoretically using the general microeconomic-founded macro-theory, which is easily expressed in the terms of economic equilibrium: budget balance, supply = demand, saving = investment, fulfilled expectations and so on. These equilibrium conditions can be given a simple model presentation supported by calibrated parameters and simple empirical 'laboratory tests'.

Today post-Keynesians take inspiration from Keynes and therefore have given up the general equilibrium model and non-empirical laboratory experiments in favour of realism, resulting in more short-term and low-key political recommendations. But it does not explain why post-Keynesian theory is hardly mentioned in mainstream textbooks and survey articles, see for example Romer (1996) and Andersen (2000) and, if mentioned at all, it is often in connection with adjectives like 'extreme', 'fundamental' or 'Keynes's disciples' (Dasgupta, 2002).[15]

Post-Keynesians: The Macroeconomics of Uncertainty

Post-Keynesians are methodologically best defined by taking Keynes literally: uncertainty plays a crucial role in microeconomic behaviour. This insight Keynes already unfolded in his fellowship dissertation in 1909, published as *A Treatise on Probability* in 1921. When economic behaviour is partly determined by uncertainty, it cannot be described by a statistical probability distribution. The macroeconomic development is determined by the sum of millions of these decisions with only partially knowable consequences. Hence, individual uncertainty is transmitted into macroeconomic uncertainty, which epistemologically implies, among other things, that a relevant long-term equilibrium model cannot be formulated. Although this is a straightforward conclusion, one risks being labelled extreme and fundamentalist when voicing this methodological viewpoint, in spite of the fact that it is based on simple logic and supported by empirical observation.

Keynes died in 1946 with, to put it mildly, a lot of unfinished work to be done. He left behind a number of pieces which may be reconstructed into a coherent framework of macroeconomic methodology. Without that framework it is difficult to understand fully the originality of his theoretical approach and hence to comprehend his genuinely new analytical results: an equilibrium (a 'standstill', see Chapter 6) with persistent involuntary unemployment caused by lack of effective demand and not by 'inflexible prices and wages' (Skidelsky, 1992). The need for a more explicit method to analyse and fully understand this kind of long-term 'standstill' was evident but unresolved in *The General Theory*. Keynes's focus was upon systemic involuntary unemployment that could last for decades, as was the case in Britain between the world wars. It was not trade cycle theory,[16] but a long-lasting macroeconomic development, a possible situation of 'standstill' without any automatic change for the better (or worse), which Keynes had in focus in *The General Theory*. He had no intentions to separate trade cycle theory from the longer-term considerations. Trade cycles were an integrated part of his 'unemployment equilibrium', which of course could fluctuate through time without any tendency to disappear:

> In particular, it is an outstanding characteristic of the economic system in which we live that, whilst it is subject to severe fluctuations in respect of output and employment, it is not violently unstable. (Keynes, 1936: 249)

This state of affairs is determined by effective demand (see Chapter 8 in this volume), which among other things relies on long-term expectations as a part of 'the marginal efficiency of capital', about which we know little, because the future is uncertain, and as Keynes formulated it in his 1937 paper, 'we simply do not know' (CWK, XIV: 114).[17]

For his neoclassical colleagues the concept of 'involuntary unemployment equilibrium' defied understanding. Keynes had anticipated this reaction in the foreword to *The General Theory*. Here he wrote: 'those who are strongly wedded to what I shall call "the classical theory", will fluctuate, I expect, between a belief that I am quite wrong and a belief that I am saying nothing new' (Keynes, 1936: v). On this point his colleagues did not disappoint him. Most assumed that Keynes in his usual self-promoting fashion was reissuing the theory of employment disequilibrium based on friction in price–wage adjustment, including rigidity of the rate of interest causing disequilibrium between real investment and financial saving, and that aside from these price, wage and interest rigidities the content of *The General Theory* was 'old hat'. Furthermore, his colleagues would claim that 'unemployment equilibrium' was caused by Keynes being inconsistent in specifying his macro-model. According to the conventional wisdom every economist should know that the overall macro-budget constraint, that the sum of supply should equal the sum of demand on all markets in total (Walras' law), must be respected. How can a supply exist without a demand (see the Introduction to this volume) – and therefore he was 'quite wrong'.

With regard to interpreting the equilibrium concept, see Chapter 6 in this volume, the neoclassical economists and Keynes (and later the post-Keynesians) completely misunderstood each other. Keynes did not use the term 'equilibrium' in the sense of 'market clearing' but rather with the meaning of 'no change' in the endogenous macroeconomic variable, for example employment (Katzner, 2003). Equilibrium in the sense of stationary variables can be interpreted to mean the opposite of another analytical concept, *quaesitum*, which Keynes used in his summarizing Chapter 18 in *The General Theory*. In direct translation *quaesitum* means 'that which we seek'. What we seek depends on the analytical question, which could as well be the dynamic development of several endogenous variables as it could be a stationary state. It was much more difficult to describe that type of dynamic development, verbally and mathematically (back in the 1930s), but it has since been tried by post-Keynesians and also in a more formalized manner, which is called the 'path-dependency' method (see for example Cornwall and Cornwall, 2001). (I shall return to this in Chapter 6.)

The epistemological essence that separates Keynes from his predecessors (and his colleagues) was particularly the concept of 'uncertainty'. The fact is that we do not have, and cannot achieve, certain knowledge of what the future will bring. This insight was the basis of Keynes's theoretical development during the time between the world wars; it culminated with *The General Theory*, where neoclassical methodology is definitively given up. The concept of uncertainty is relevant when understanding how several of society's institutions work and have been organized. The 1936 book is filled with examples of uncertainty influencing all kinds of economic activity. The book is much less illuminating when it comes to defining the methodological consequences of this changed perception of reality that the emphasis on fundamental (that is to say not statistically measurable) uncertainty should lead to.

The concept of uncertainty has another and different epistemological meaning when a general equilibrium model is used as the (relevant) analytical framework. In this case uncertainty can be reduced to risk, and can be further reduced to certain (statistical) knowledge on the macro-level. This very different methodological limitation concerns the information which rational agents can be expected to have. If uncertainty can be reduced to statistical risk, then it is no longer rational to use money as a value-preserving object, as money does not give a rent, a fact which has troubled the neoclassical economists during all these years. But the future is analytically perceived to be (partially) unknowable, because we simply do not know. For example, when the volatility of the value of shares and bonds seems to be without limits, then money provides a yield which is less uncertain. On the other hand, when future consumer price inflation is unpredictable, it causes uncertainty of any financial assets in real terms and has an impact on the demand for both money and bonds.

Non-quantifiable or 'fundamental' uncertainty through its effects on money and interest cause changes in the effective demand for labour. Thus uncertainty unifies the elements in Keynes's title: *Employment, Interest and Money*.

POST-KEYNESIAN (I): GROWTH, PRICE THEORY AND INCOME DISTRIBUTION

Growth

When Keynes died in 1946 Richard Kahn, Nicholas Kaldor, Michal Kalecki and Joan Robinson were given the task to carry the Keynesian torch in Cambridge, with help from Roy Harrod in Oxford. They had the major problem that methodologically they were starting nearly from scratch, when the focus in economic discussion shifted in the post-war period from unemployment to growth.

Unemployment could be explained within the framework of the IS–LM model, where aggregate demand played the key role. Long-term growth perspectives were more difficult to explain. Keynes included a chapter in *The General Theory* entitled 'The State of Long-term Expectations', which concluded that investment demand was primarily determined by expected profits, the state of confidence, animal spirits and financial interest rates; on the other hand the capacity-increasing effects of investments were not explicitly analysed. There was quite a bit of unfinished work to be done, which will be described in the chapter about effective demand (Chapter 8).

Harrod (1939) formulated a growth model based upon a production function without substitution between capital and labour. The model's *quaesitum*, the dynamic development, was determined by the relationship between investment demand (the multiplier effect), and the effect on capacity (the accelerator effect). In Harrod's model investment demand was solely determined by the need for extra capacity; left out were convention, the state of confidence, animal spirits and the financial interest rate. In spite of this, Harrod achieved in this truncated model the result that the process of growth is truly unstable, because either the supply effect runs ahead of demand, which results in an increase in unemployment, or there will be a constant shortage of capital, implying a permanent inflationary pressure. The Harrod model is strictly analytical and completely lacks a realistic incorporation of uncertainty.

It was not until Solow's neoclassically-inspired growth model (1956), that the methodological differences between neoclassical theory and post-Keynesian theory were laid bare. The question whether the general equilibrium model is a relevant – in other words, realistic – framework for understanding macroeconomic growth was central. Joan Robinson and Nicholas Kaldor thought 'no', which led to the so-called 'capital controversy' (see Harcourt, 1972) that uncovered the crucial role played by the chosen method for the analytical conclusions reached concerning growth and functional income distribution. The methodological dispute centred upon the question of whether neoclassical analysis is valid when the macroeconomic system finds itself outside general equilibrium, as long as it is 'approaching' a new equilibrium. How do we uncover and describe an economic system where the microeconomic assumptions, which the theory is based upon, are not automatically fulfilled?[18] Robinson tried to defeat Solow (and Samuelson) on the fact that neoclassical theory was valid only when in equilibrium. What do we know about the determinants of the growth process outside of equilibrium? Joan Robinson asked this in Robinson (1962). This discussion between Cambridge (US) and Cambridge (UK) did not result in a unified outcome.[19] Neoclassical economists continued to use equilibrium theory (without uncertainty) to analyse economic growth paths outside of stock-holding equilibrium.

Within the post-Keynesian camp, there was not much unity on growth models. Harrod's model (Harrod, 1939) was not especially post-Keynesian, assuming investment equal to savings. Despite Kaldor's considerable wealth of ideas, he continued to use the general equilibrium model well into the 1960s, and therefore he did not have a constructive alternative to replace Solow's growth model. As mentioned above, no help was to be found in Keynes's writings, which primarily focused upon how to conquer unemployment, which in the 1960s seemed to belong to a distant past. Robinson and Kaldor realized, too late, that the actual point of dispute was methodology, entailing a complete dismissal of general equilibrium as a relevant analytical concept. This made them both, in an increasing degree towards the end of their careers, argue about the irrelevance of equilibrium concepts, especially in the long run: 'The first notion to be discarded, in such a process [of spring cleaning], must be the equilibrium of the long run' (Robinson, 1985: 160).

Kaldor published in 1985 the book *Economics without Equilibrium*, where in strong terms he criticized the use of general equilibrium models. He used as an example of the irrelevance of this framework a totally traditional neoclassical production function, where he merely exchanges the standard neoclassical assumption of constant returns to scale with parameters that imply permanent large-scale advantages, the so-called 'increasing returns to scale'. If this is the case there will be no convergence towards long-term equilibrium. The following year Kaldor asked the question: are there limits to growth? If exhaustible resources cannot be substituted with new technology in a continual process, then not only will growth cease, but it will also move into a Harrodian unstoppable stagnation process. This is a theoretical problem that cannot be answered in a meaningful way within the neoclassical growth theory framework, which allows the unlimited substitution of natural and produced capital.[20]

The Theory of Price and Income Distribution

Post-Keynesians are not only concerned with growth, employment and unemployment. They are also concerned with the distribution of income and consumption, conditions Keynes (1936) only touched upon in his concluding chapter with the title: 'Concluding Notes on the Social Philosophy towards which the General Theory might lead'. One point Keynes made was that distributional justice cannot be ascribed to the outcome of a market process:

> The outstanding faults of the economic society in which we live are its failure to provide for full employment and its arbitrary and inequitable distribution of wealth and incomes. (Keynes, 1936: 372)

This conclusion implies that a relevant macroeconomic analysis should also contain theories about what determines the economic distribution between production factors and households in the short and long period. Unfortunately, there was no explicitly expressed income distribution theory in *The General Theory*. The Polish economist Michal Kalecki focused more directly on the distributional consequences. He demonstrated that on the macro-level profits are determined by real investment which led to Joan Robinson (see Toporowski, 2003) coining the aphorism: 'workers spend what they earn, capitalists earn what they spend!' This aphorism can be explained as follows.

Start with the national income identity:

$$P + W = Cp + Cw + I$$

where: P = profit, C_w = consumption of workers, W = the wage bill, I = investment of capitalists, C_p = consumption of capitalists

If: $C_w = W/$'Workers spend what they earn'

Then: $P = C_p + I/$'Capitalists earn what they spend'

Profits are a source of continued growth if they are used for real investment and so increase the capital stock. In fact, Kalecki broke away from the Cambridge group of post-Keynesians by stating a theory of price formation which was not influenced by Marshall's marginalist principle of thinking. Kalecki thought that prices, partly due to monopoly power and partly due to lack of information, were predominantly determined by a mark-up on the average total cost. The wage rate was determined by the relative strength between employers and workers. In the final analysis income distribution is a complicated relationship between, on the one side, the wage rate and the demand for consumer products; and on the other side, costs and unit profit: if output is increased more than the margin of profit falls, then in the end total profits increase. This macroeconomic result is called the 'paradox of cost', where a higher wage rate leads to greater profits, when, as a consequence of a wage rise, demand increases sufficiently (see Chapter 7).[21]

Kalecki focused upon the functional distribution of income and its effect upon the macroeconomic dynamics. On the other hand post-Keynesian literature does not provide a theory about what determines individual income distribution. Even though Keynes had a few remarks about the relative wage for the individual wage-earner or trade group being at least as important as the absolute wage development, there is no substantial analysis of what determines relative wages and how wage-earners react to changes. This lack of theory can be explained by the dominant interest that post-Keynesians show in macroeconomic development. But it is not a satisfactory answer when the theory is applied to reality.

In the same way, post-Keynesians do not have a consistent dynamic analysis for the effect for example of the introduction of a minimum wage or a reduction in the length of the working week. In this case, a method that combines institutional reality with the macroeconomic landscape as a whole (see below) could form the basis for a post-Keynesian analysis that among other things would shield it against the risk of committing the fallacy of composition (atomic fallacy). This conclusion leads directly to the statement that post-Keynesian theory is completely blank regarding an analysis of the structural consequences of the welfare state. This absence has left a clear field for any alternatives to traditional neoclassical welfare theory rooted in Pigou's book of 1920.

New-Keynesians have built a bridge between short-term demand-management analysis and welfare economics, concluding that there is a trade-off between growth and distribution, which has become a part of the conventional wisdom of the 'third way' propagated by New Labour; see Matzner (2003).[22] The new-Keynesian conclusion regarding the coming decades' challenges to the financial foundation of the European welfare states in the light of globalization and changed demographic structure is that individual economic incentives to work longer hours have to be strengthened, because full employment is taken for granted within this time horizon. The welfare state is perceived as an expense on society, a kind of luxury good, which is costly because it twists the price structure compared to the ideal market model. Redistribution of income and consumption is paid for by a reduction in productivity, which in this part of the literature is called the dead-weight loss of the welfare state.

The coming post-Keynesian challenge consists in completing a fully integrated analysis of the welfare state, income distribution, public sector employment and macroeconomic performance. This analysis takes its departure in a realistic social ontology which goes far beyond the assumption of individual optimization, perfect foresight and a well-behaved market system.

POST-KEYNESIAN (II):[23] MONEY AND INFLATION

Keynes's assumption in *The General Theory*, that the money supply is a predetermined variable, has for some time been a brake on the development of post-Keynesian monetary theory.[24] Keynes criticized the neoclassical general equilibrium model for not providing a consistent framework for the analysis of the working of the monetary and financial sector, because money and financial activities are superfluous in a world without uncertainty. Money only has a meaning in an uncertain world, as Keynes correctly stated. If the equilibrium model is opened up for transaction costs and individual statistical uncertainty (see Chapter 4) one could argue that individuals, even in equilibrium, have a stock of transaction money (see for example Baumol, 1952). On the other hand, this argument did not change the qualitative nature of the equilibrium, because the money supply solely determines the level of prices.

Keynes remained in one sense a loyal student of Marshall, insisting that on the macroeconomic level economic development is driven by the interaction of supply and demand. But on both the money market and the labour market he was in *The General Theory* surprisingly uninterested in discussing the factors determining the supply. This theoretical gap was quickly filled by the economists behind neoclassical synthesis assuming the money supply to be exogenously determined and the supply of labour to be similar to the conventional neoclassical labour market supply function derived from aggregated microeconomic arguments.

The two missing macroeconomic supply functions have, in the post-war period, been the source for theoretical contemplations by the post-Keynesians because it became empirically more and more apparent that the money supply contained considerable endogenous elements, just as the supply of labour could not realistically be considered as uninfluenced by structural and institutional matters, like the welfare state for example.

Monetary Production Theory

Keynes's liquidity preference theory, where the demand for money is partially determined by transaction (and finance) motives and partly by uncertainty (the state of confidence), is relatively unproblematic from a realist point of view; but a given money supply did cause increasing difficulties in the post-war period, because the amount of bank money and the lending capacity within the private banking system have considerable endogenous elements. Furthermore, this endogenous element of the money supply has been immensely increased, as controls on international capital movements have been lifted, from the early 1970s onwards.

The assumption of a given money supply, controlled by the central bank, belongs to a distant past. Today, central banks have far less control.[25] Unfortunately, a given money supply fitted easily into an equilibrium analysis where the activities of the banking system were described by a constant credit multiplier, and this assumption was useful to demonstrate the working of the real balance effect as an equilibrium-creating mechanism. Neither central bank control nor the assumption of a constant multiplier is compatible with the post-Keynesian ambition to explain the specific historical development within the banking sector where uncertainty plays an important role.

Paul Davidson (1972), Hyman Minsky (1975), Victoria Chick (1983), Basil Moore (1988) and Sheila Dow (1996) have made a number of significant contributions to post-Keynesian monetary theory. They have worked on how to incorporate the theory of endogenous money supply. The relationship between uncertainty and liquidity preference theory dominated by fluctuating expectations has also been through a laborious scrutiny. Chapter 12 in *The General Theory* has been an important source of inspiration. In it Keynes described with insight, and in an entertaining way, how price-setting in the financial markets can be compared to gambling at a beauty contest. The condition of winning is not in any objective sense to detect the prettiest girl, but to figure out who the other players will judge the prettiest and then gamble on her.[26] The functioning of the financial sector as an integrated part of the economy as a whole was a theoretically underexposed area, which the post-Keynesians tackled at a time when monetarism (exogenous money supply) and the theory of efficient money markets (stock prices reflecting true values) were dominant in the main-stream literature. The improved understanding of the interplay of money demand and supply has brought the monetary circuit theory (Graziani, 2003) closer to a mutual understanding within post-Keynesian economics on a monetary theory of production (Jespersen, 2009).

The Phillips Curve[27]

Likewise it was shown by the second generation of post-Keynesian economists that the Phillips curve, not to mention the NAIRU (non-accelerating inflation rate of unemployment), instead of being a missing link uniting price development with demand and supply conditions on the labour market in *The General Theory*, became an analytically constraining factor in the understanding of the dynamic causal relations between price expectations, effective demand and employment. It became obvious that the development in inflation could not be explained by a simplistic and mechanical link between unemployment and inflation-determined expec-tations. The expectations-augmented Phillips curve had given equilibrium economists a theoretical platform to formulate the hypothesis concerning natural unemployment and a vertical Phillips curve, which was to stand unopposed for a long time despite lacking an empirical base. But given uncertainty and the macroeconomic context of path-dependence and hysteresis a theoretical case was made that no static NAIRU could be expected to be relevant for the understanding of the dynamics of prices and wages.

Hence, the absence of an elaborated post-Keynesian methodology was demonstrated in a number of theoretical areas. It became apparent how difficult it was to establish a convincing alternative to the dominant mainstream equilibrium theory without discussing methodology. The scattered methodological inheritance from Keynes had too often led post-Keynesians astray, into basing their theories on arguments surrounded by partial, market-clearing models and losing sight of 'the economy as a whole'. These partial models, for example the Phillips curve, lacked dynamics and an explicit consideration of uncertainty that according to Keynes should characterize a relevant macroeconomic model. At the same time the post-Keynesian approach was not fully geared to carry out macro-economic analyses caused by institutional changes in the labour market.

POST-KEYNESIAN (III): THE NEED FOR A METHODOLOGY TACKLING REALITY

Fifty years after the publication of *The General Theory*, the demand within post-Keynesian economics was to constitute a more explicit methodological foundation for realistic macroeconomic analysis. Too much time had been spent in arguing out how Keynes's (at the time) new and ground-breaking macroeconomic conclusions had been derailed by the neoclassical synthesis due to the lack of a methodology which could tackle reality. The neoclassical synthesis analysed the macroeconomy as a clockwork system which could easily adopt a logical-positivistic methodology.

Hence, post-Keynesian methodologists had to return to Keynes's specific comments on macroeconomic method and combine them with his earlier philosophically inspired theoretical work concerning decision-making under uncertainty. How to analyse a macroeconomy system heavily influenced by uncertainty?

> ... [E]conomics is essentially a moral science and not a natural science. ... [I]t deals with introspection and values ... [and] with motives, expectations, psychological uncertainties.
>
> It seems to me that economics is a branch of logic, a way of thinking; and that you do not repel sufficiently firmly attempts ... to turn it into a pseudo-natural-science. ... *Progress* in economics consists almost entirely in a progressive improvement in the choice of models. The grave fault of the later classical school, exemplified by Pigou, has been to overwork a too simple or out-of-date model ...
>
> Economics is a science of thinking in terms of models joined to the art of choosing models which are relevant to the contemporary world. (From two letters to Roy Harrod commenting upon Harrod's presidential address to the Royal Economic Society 'Scope and Method of Economics', July 1938, *CWK*, XIV: 296–7, 300)

The macroeconomic system is in other words assumed by Keynes to be open in the methodological sense. One cannot once and for all create a single general equilibrium model that with clockwork precision describes and predicts the macroeconomic development. Why not? To this the new generation of post-Keynesians answered: because macroeconomic epistemology must reflect the fact that human behaviour is not mechanical. Because the science of economics is basically a study of human behaviour (moral science) with the resulting uncertainties, which are arbitrarily understood as unexplained rather than unsystematic actions. Within this partly unexplainable system individual behaviour is also influenced by group behaviour, short-sightedness, altruism and impulsiveness. These are phenomena that are compatible with rational behaviour but that cannot be fully explained by individual utility-maximizing with complete knowledge. Quite the opposite: the future is uncertain on the micro- and the macro-level, so for that reason alone altruism and group bonding can be very rational, as they lessen the consequences when accidents happen. This is a condition, among others, that the development of the welfare state has changed, which of course is reflected in the macro-behavioural relations discussed in Chapter 3 of this volume.

A consequence of this changed perception of how the macroeconomic ontology should be described is that the science-theoretical base is turned in the direction of realism, but not only realism that is observable. Ontologically we know that other factors than just microeconomic behaviour determine macroeconomic development. Economic structures, information, credit and the labour market's structure, foreign competition, and expectations of economic policies all play an important role, but their appearance is not always directly observable. They are operating in an empirically grey zone that in the terminology of critical realism is called the 'deep stratum'. To include the impact of these unobservable factors, hypotheses must be formulated about their role in the macroeconomic development, which can be given some indirect verification through empirical testing. One thing is certain, though: that these economic structures, like microeconomic behaviour, are constantly changing. Therefore the analytical framework must be organized in such a way that these changes can be dealt with. Institutional changes, just like economic policy expectations, in the broadest sense, cannot possibly remain stationary. All these conditions run counter to the realism of the assumptions behind the general equilibrium model and point towards an open and much more flexible model structure that can continually be revised.

These are some of the methodological key points behind the new theories developed within post-Keynesian economists (III) starting in the middle of the 1980s, with important contributions from, among others, Anna Carabelli (1988), Athol Fitzgibbons (1988), Rod O'Donnell (1989), Sheila Dow (1996, 2002), Tony Lawson (1997, 2003) and the *Journal of Post Keynesian Economics* (1999), which will be given a thorough presentation and a critical assessment in the following chapter.

Macroeconomic Method in a Modern Context

It is important for me at this early stage of my exposition to specify that my intention is not to complete a historical analysis of Keynes's impact on macroeconomic theory and method. It is not my intention to give another possible interpretation of 'what Keynes really meant'. On the other hand, it is apparent that I have got so much inspiration from my reading of Keynes's major works that it would be wrong not to attribute my intellectual debt to him (and other post-Keynesian economists) whenever I think it relevant. It is beyond doubt that Keynes established a new methodological foundation for understanding the macroeconomic instability of the 1930s, especially concerning the sources of unemployment, and that this foundation is still relevant today.

I have no illusions about uncritically transferring Keynes's method to problems which we face at the beginning of the twenty-first century. As argued above, it is a challenging and still uncompleted research project to establish a post-Keynesian methodology which in a constructive way can contribute to a better understanding of the origins and consequences of present macroeconomic imbalances on a national, regional and global level. With this purpose a fresh reading of Keynes's own works and of other Keynes-inspired methods and macroeconomics can deliver new insights to this methodological project of establishing the groundwork for macroeconomic analysis.

The welfare state did not exist in Keynes's day.[28] A number of public and semi-public institutions play a more important role today than they did 70 years ago, not least vocational organizations on the labour market and public welfare services. The capital markets have been integrated across national borders and have a turnover that has surpassed real transactions many times over. This has changed the institutional framework for monetary and currency policy. The stagnating population in the rich countries and the population explosion in the poor nations have created global imbalances in a number of areas.

In the same manner environmental effects have had national, regional and global consequences. A methodology needs to deal with resource and pollution problems as yet another macroeconomic imbalance, which cannot be analysed independently of, say, the developments in growth, the balance of payments, distribution and inflation. The task for politicians is to prioritize and pursue policies based on realistic macroeconomic analysis, which sheds light upon and describes these connections in a relevant context.

SUMMARY

The various forms of macroeconomics inspired in one way or another by Keynes have in common the opinion that economic policy can make a difference, but they deviate markedly with regard to the applied method of analysis.

Employment and unemployment are included in the macroeconomic analysis. Influencing the employment level is central to Keynes-inspired macroeconomic analysis. It is also a widely accepted point that achieving full employment is an important goal that economic policy can, to varying degrees, contribute to achieving.

On these two points, Keynes-inspired macroeconomic theory differentiates itself from the new-classical theory formation, which actually uses the expression 'equilibrium business cycles'. As already mentioned, it is assumed in the new-classical macro-models that the labour market is always in equilibrium. There is only voluntary unemployment.[29] This modelling approach entails that a decrease in employment is an expression for changed preferences among workers and does not therefore represent a condition with involuntary unemployment. This also explains the new-classical conclusion that economic policy will (at best) be 'ineffective' if it is announced. However, if the policy comes as a surprise, it will disrupt an otherwise fully adjusted equilibrium. In a general equilibrium model, where the actors are assumed to have full knowledge of the future (the assumption of rational expectations) and where there are no market externalities, economic policy will serve no purpose with regard to establishing macroeconomic stability, much less efficiency. Under these assumptions the market mechanism will always be superior to the policies.

Keynes-inspired macroeconomists are in no doubt that involuntary unemployment is a real problem, but they disagree fundamentally about which methodology should be used to understand and analyse this macroeconomic phenomenon. Just like neoclassical economists, new-Keynesians use a general equilibrium model and accept the hypothesis of rational expectations. The fact that they reach different results compared to new-classical economists is explained by their focus on a number of market imperfections and externalities that can be given an individual (that is, microeconomic) rational explanation, and which among other things are caused by transaction costs, asymmetric information, moral hazard (for example among those who take out insurance), or the absence of well-defined ownership rights. These are conditions that create inertia or actually obstruct adjustment to the general equilibrium. This process of adjustment can be hurried along, through a well-designed economic policy; however, to the extent that policy is only aimed at aggregate demand, it will not alter the general equilibrium, because new-Keynesians, just like new-classical economists, methodologically use a closed, deterministic model.

As we will see in the next chapter, post-Keynesian theory and analysis uses a fundamentally different methodology. In the opinion of the post-Keynesians, macroeconomic reality has a qualitative social ontology which simply makes a closed equilibrium method inapplicable for the understanding of the development within the macroeconomic landscape (see Chapter 3 in this volume). In the short run, and perhaps especially in the long run, the macroeconomic process can only be perceived within an open framework that, among other things, is characterized by lack of full information and no terminal point, because uncertainty is a real and therefore also analytically inescapable phenomenon. Of course, people are expected to act rationally on the information available, with respect for the inherent uncertainty in the real world. In this ontological perspective, the macroeconomic process cannot be analysed within the framework of a closed model with a predetermined terminal point. A new method of analysis must be developed that can describe an economic process through time that is characterized by inherent uncertainty, lack of knowledge about macroeconomic structures and imbalances. To meet these methodological requirements, much inspiration can be gained not only from Keynes's and post-Keynesian economists' writings, but also from the philosophy of science based on (critical) realism.

NOTES

1. Particularly Friedman (1968).
2. Lucas and Sargent (1978) *After Keynesian Macroeconomics*, where 'Keynesian' specifically refers to the 'old-Keynesians' and especially their econometric models.
3. In that respect Snowdon and Vane (2005) is a more balanced presentation of different macroeconomic schools and their mutual similarities and differences.
4. I say 'the Anglo-Saxon tradition' because on the Continent, as early as the end of the nineteenth century, a theoretical framework had been produced for how the analysis of the individual markets could be linked to an overall model. This work was begun by the Frenchman Léon Walras and was continued by the Italian Vilfredo Pareto, who were both attached to the university in Lausanne. However, Walras's book (1874) was not translated into English until 1954. The work of Walras and Pareto was brought into Anglo-Saxon economies through John Hicks's *Value and Capital* (1939). Thus it was not until after the Second World War that the work of producing a general equilibrium theory (generalized micro-theory) was established in the Anglo-Saxon tradition.
5. Keynes's development from equilibrium economist to macroeconomist is a topic that I have discussed in Jespersen (2002a).
6. In many ways, it would be natural to place Friedman on this list of 'methodological economists', not least on the basis of his 1953 article. But I am hesitant because he concludes that economic theory is simply a form of instrumentalism – an abstraction, where the realism (or rather lack of realism) of assumptions is not important, as long as the 'theory' can predict. In my opinion, this is a problematic point of view, since it makes the choice of theory depend on such an instrumental basis. If we do not know why the theory has produced good predictions in the past, we are prevented from arguing that the theory can continue to produce good predictions in the future, unless we assume that the economic reality is stationary. As a consequence of this, Friedman's

theoretical work moved in the direction of general equilibrium theory, when he explained that the concept of 'natural unemployment' could be interpreted as the rate of unemployment that would be the outcome of a Walrasian equilibrium exercise.

Thus, Friedman moved away from the Keynesian camp, where he was an exponent of the view that a stabilization policy could and should be followed by manipulating the LM curve without surrendering the inflation goal, into the 'policy-ineffectiveness' camp, where a discretionary use of monetary policy only creates problems because of information lags and political opportunism (time inconsistency).

7. The methodological point of departure is presented in Appendix 2.1.
8. It is important not to confuse 'aggregated demand', 'aggregate demand' and 'effective demand'.
9. Hence, these two Keynesian schools are placed on different sides of the 'gulf' in 'the family tree' presented in Figure 0.1 in the previous chapter.
10. That it is not a question of a random lapse, but a conscious theory development, is evident from Modigliani (1999) where he confirms his Keynesian position in an interview.
11. The list of old-Keynesians is long. Here I will only mention Lawrence Klein, James Meade, Franco Modigliani, Paul Samuelson, James Tobin and of course John Hicks (all Nobel Prize winners).
12. We will return to the discussion of models, but it should be mentioned here that Denmark also had its macro-econometric model, ADAM, on the initiative of Professor Ellen Andersen at the end of the 1960s, that was later connected to Klein's world model project Link.
13. There is a degree of break-up in the new-Keynesian (and partly also in the monetarist) camp, because until a few years ago it was completely normal to assume that the microeconomic actors had rational expectations, which ensured the adjustment to general macroeconomic equilibrium. But because of the obvious lack of realism of these assumptions and of persistent and large imbalances in the labour market in Germany and France, a search has developed for a better and empirically grounded expectations-formation model. Giving up the hypothesis of rational expectations-formation only has the consequence that the laboratory model no longer ensures an automatic return to equilibrium after being hit by an external shock. As a replacement for the assumptions of rational expectations, the Taylor rule with regard to monetary policy is used instead. It is based on the assumption that it is the monetary policy authorities that have rational expectations and who have the responsibility for returning the economy to equilibrium after a shock. In other words, the central bank should act as a type of shepherd that it is rational to follow. This assumption contributes to supporting the effectiveness of a policy based on inflation targeting, see for example Sørensen and Whitta-Jakobsen (2005).
14. Should the reader wish for a more detailed assessment of the different post-Keynesian schools and their relationships, then J.E. King (2002), *A History of Post Keynesian Economics since 1936*, is warmly recommended.
15. In this case Snowdon and Vane (2005) is an exception, because it has a separate chapter on post-Keynesian macrotheory.
16. Within *The General Theory* there is only one chapter out of 24 which explicitly deals with trade cycle theory.
17. Characterizing Keynes's assessment of long-term prospects, his quip 'but in the long run we are all dead' is often quoted. But it is misplaced here, because this quotation comes from as far back as 1923 (*CWK*, IV: 65), and is an (early) criticism of the neoclassical theory, which claims that general equilibrium might be valid in the long run; but this 'long run' is so distant that we are all dead, and therefore it is without relevance.
18. Within welfare theory the equivalent problem is called 'the theory of the second-best solution', which in truth should be called 'the lack of a theory of the second-best solution'.
19. Judged in retrospect it seems apparent that the three 'old' post-Keynesian economists (Robinson, Kaldor and Sraffa) were unprepared to take the analytical debate of the long run on Keynes's methodological terms. They all had the idea that a long-run

equilibrium made analytical sense. At that time they mainly doubted – as Keynes did in 1923 – whether this long run was relevant. A couple of decades had to pass before Robinson and Kaldor protested against the very concept of a long-run equilibrium, which was expressed by Robinson when she titled a paper *History versus Equilibrium*. Kaldor questioned the relevance of equilibrium in an economy characterized by increasing returns to scale which led to the book called *Economics without Equilibrium* (1985). Sraffa was the leading figure within the neo-Ricardian school, which has continued to use the equilibrium method and therefore could more easily point to a number of theoretical inconsistencies within the neoclassical general equilibrium model; see King (2002), Chapter 4.

20. A discussion continued by among others Herman Daly (1997).

21. The wage paradox can also be interpreted as an example of the fallacy of composition.

22. The 'third way' has, as so many labels, changed content. The Scandinavian model was, in the 1960s and 1970s, the exponent for the third way between the liberal model on the right and economic planning on the left. In British economic literature it is termed the Keynesian welfare state. The third way had a specific Swedish example based upon the Rehn–Meidner model: it combined demand management, an active labour market policy, a compressed wage structure and universal welfare goods. These days it is British New Labour that is identified with the third way; see Giddens (1998). Demand management is preserved, but welfare goods are reduced, so in conjunction with a considerable increase in the wage structure spread the individual inducement to remain employed is strengthened.

23. Roman number refers to Figure 0.1

24. And, one can safely say, for the thousands of students that have had a supply–demand diagram for the money market forced upon them, where the money supply is vertical.

25. Keynes included a long passage in his penultimate chapter where he examines mercantilist policies aimed at increasing the money supply through a surplus on the balance of payments.

26. It is a very sophisticated metaphor. In a beauty contest there are no objective criteria for beauty. The results are due equally to rumour and convention. The judges of the contest will always try to guess where the majority are presumed to cast their ballot, and then do the same, in spite of what they think of the participants' qualities. Keynes's point in relation to the stock market was: forget what you think of the individual stock's potential. The prize is achieved by following the flock or, even better, leading it. The assumption that the best stock wins is a theoretical illusion.

27. Discussion of the Phillips curve's empirical and theoretical relevance is a chapter on its own, but since the Phillips curve was never a fully integrated part of the post-Keynesian theory, I will not go into the discussion here.

28. One of the many theoretical-historical paradoxes is the often-mentioned post-war 'Keynesian' social democratic welfare state model. The paradox is that Keynes was primarily connected to the Liberal Party for most of his life and was only interested in welfare state reforms to a very limited degree. For Keynes, understanding why unemployment was high, and contributing suggestions to alleviate this, was an important responsibility for all governments, regardless of party affiliation.

29. 'Involuntary unemployment is not a phenomenon which it is the task for theorists to explain' (Lucas, 1978: 353)

2. Macroeconomic methodology: from a critical realist perspective

> The coherence of Post Keynesian Economics lies principally at the methodological level. (Dunn, 2004: 34)

PROLOGUE

The purpose of this chapter is to give the theory-of-science background to the development of a realist-inspired, macroeconomic methodology that can serve as a foundation for post-Keynesian macroeconomic theory. It is crucial to clarify the methodological fundamentals before any theory is drawn up. Theories and models in economics cannot be plucked out of thin air; they will always be anchored to the chosen method, and therefore it is important to discover whether there is consistency between the employed scientific practice and the theoretical intention. If the goal of a macroeconomic analysis is to provide policy recommendations to improve real macroeconomic development, then the theory must be anchored to a realistic methodology. If on the contrary the goal is to investigate the existence of equilibrium in a theoretical model, then the method should be chosen accordingly to fit this problem. It is important that the aim of the analysis is recognized when the analytical models for policy recommendations are developed and selected.

In the previous chapter, the significant division of purposes between neo-classical general equilibrium theory and post-Keynesian macroeconomic theory was described. General equilibrium theory has the primary task of analysing and understanding the nature of the functioning of a perfect market system. Here, the existence of equilibrium is a core attribute. The ambition of post-Keynesian macroeconomic theory is to understand and explain trends in past macroeconomic development and to provide policy recommendations with relevance for the future. This clear division of tasks is naturally a determining factor for the choice of methodological foundation, which these two macroeconomic schools use to honour their very different analytical ambitions. It can be seen from Figure 2.1 that post-Keynesian macro-theory must have a foundation based on reality

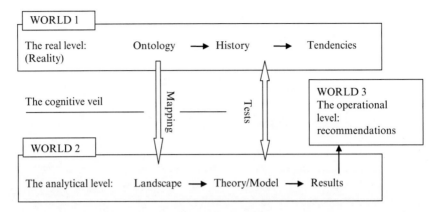

Figure 2.1   Critical realist methodology (retroduction)

and be formed through a reflection of reality. The general equilibrium model-builders, on the other hand, prefer primarily to build on a deductive methodology, where the starting point is a handful of axioms that determine the functioning of the economic system. In this way, the ground is laid for an analysis that can reveal the properties of the system. It is not the axioms' basis in reality, but rather their analytical precision, that is the deciding factor in their selection.[1] The focus on two quintessentially different macroeconomic issues that the two schools wish to analyse and understand also explains why two fundamentally different methodologies are employed. The importance of choosing the right methodology is illustrated in this chapter.

The chapter is also intended as a broader presentation of the theory of scientific method. It contains a number of more common methodological issues that are particularly relevant for interdisciplinary analyses within the social sciences. This approach has been chosen because it simultaneously substantiates the methodology behind post-Keynesian macroeconomic theory.

INTRODUCTION TO MACROECONOMIC METHODOLOGY: CENTRAL ISSUES

Economics is a science of thinking in terms of models joined to the art of choosing models which are relevant to the contemporary world ... because ... the material to which it is applied is, in too many respects, not homogenous through time. The object of a model is to segregate the semi-permanent or relatively constant factors from those which are transitory ... so as to develop a logical way of thinking about the latter ... (Keynes, 1938, *CWK*, XIV: 296–7)

The previous chapters included a short presentation of the central macroeconomic characteristics that must be taken into account when justifying the selection of methodology in relation to the theory of science. Macroeconomic theory differs from microeconomics in that it aims at a holistic analysis. Reality must be simplified in order to gain an overview of its entirety, and so a few, central variables (employment, balance of payments, growth, inflation and the national income, and so on) must be selected and described together. The next chapter describes how macroeconomic reality can be given an analytical representation in the form of a 'macroeconomic landscape'. The metaphor 'landscape' is used in order to emphasize that we are working with a simplification of reality, and that reality is in a state of constant flux because many other important conditions, in addition to the purely economic, exert influence over the shape of the landscape and the way in which it changes. Finally, this metaphor also highlights the fact that the part of the landscape which we are capable of observing is, figuratively speaking, just the tip of the iceberg, since all the important factors that lie hidden beneath the surface cannot be represented.

These are the conditions under which a macroeconomic analysis of reality must be performed; we must get to grips with the system as a whole. It is therefore not the actions of individuals that are of interest, but rather the interaction of countless individual transactions, conducted within given, yet evolving, structures, national as well as international, that serve as our focal point. For this reason alone methodological individualism is rejected as the starting point in macroeconomics.

The analytical ambition, on the other hand, is to explain the transformation of the macroeconomic landscape as represented by a few central macroeconomic variables. The aim of the analysis is to reach a better understanding of the causal relations constituting the macroeconomic reality that can be described in part through national accounting data and in part through the behaviour of important macroeconomic institutions, such as the government's economic policy.

The microeconomic foundation is not of particular interest. It is often the case within post-Keynesian macro-theory that model results could (in principle) be generated by various (and on the micro-level competing) behaviour models. It is therefore not possible to derive post-Keynesian macro-theory, much less the macro-model, exclusively from deductions based on theories of microeconomic behaviour. Fundamentally, the fallacy of composition serves as a barrier to this. On the other hand, a realistic macroeconomic theory requires that the model not be built upon assumptions that are clearly in conflict with observable microeconomic (institutional) behaviour.[2] For instance, there is no *a priori* reason why post-Keynesian macro-theory should accommodate the assumption of rational expectations – the condition that macroeconomic actors are assumed to have perfect foresight – as this assumption directly contradicts observable microeconomic behaviour. The reader can find a discussion of the meaning of 'unrealistic' assumption below.

However, it is a fundamental empirical fact that economic transactions are conducted in spite of an inherent uncertainty with regard to the future. It is methodologically challenging that the future is, to varying degrees, uncertain. Uncertainty exists on three levels. Firstly, the course of economic development is unknown when plans are laid for the future. Secondly, the consequences of economic actions are similarly uncertain. Thirdly, it is at least partly uncertain how macroeconomic actors will react, particularly in relation to this non-quantifiable uncertainty. It is precisely because uncertainty is such a dominating phenomenon that post-Keynesian macroeconomics has been designated the economics of fundamental uncertainty, as distinct from the economics of risk (Davidson, 1972). It will therefore have a major impact on the analytical results and their interpretation if it is assumed that all actors have perfect foresight, meaning that everyone knows the same future with (stochastic) certainty. The real methodological challenge in macroeconomic theory lies in the ontological condition that the future is, at least partially, unknown. Macroeconomic uncertainty exerts influence over both the present expectations and the consequences of present actions. This holds true for the microeconomic actors' actions as well as for macroeconomic policy.

The overarching aim of this chapter is to discuss the scientific-theoretical foundation for conducting a macroeconomic analysis based on reality. The post-Keynesian macroeconomic ambition is to understand macroeconomic reality. This requires ensuring a high level of communication between, on the one hand, 'reality', which I will call World 1, that always plays out in a historical context on the actual level, and on the other hand, the analytical level, which I call World 2, where 'theory and model' are formulated and confronted with reality through empirical tests. The more rigorous empirical testing the model can withstand, the greater is its ability to describe historical phenomena using a scientific method and the more faith we can have in the analytical results. These results will, on the other hand, always be both conditional and preliminary and will always be open for improvement. They are context-dependent and must be interpreted as such before they are used to form statements about a specific case, which I call World 3, of a likely macroeconomic development that always will be path-dependent.[3]

This method of alternation between reality and model, where the inductive and deductive methods supplement one another, is called retroduction (or abduction) by a number of methodologists practising critical realism (Lawson, 1997; Davidsen,[4] 2000; Downward and Mearman, 2002).

Critical realism, which will be thoroughly illustrated in the following sections, is based upon this retroductive methodology, developed and described by, among others, the American philosopher Charles Sanders Peirce in the nineteenth century; 'reinvented' within social sciences by, among others, Roy Bhaskar, Tony Lawson and Peter Lipton; and used within modern macroeconomics by Philip Arestis, Victoria Chick, Sheila Dow and many others. This methodology is characterized by explicitly including real phenomena like uncertainty and the historical context, and in using open-system modelling in its representation of reality.

Why Realism? With inspiration from Karl Popper

It is important that the concepts within the methodological discourse are used clearly and, as far as possible, consistently with common practice. There is a need to specify what we mean by the terms 'ontology' and 'idealism', which diverge somewhat from the common philosophical use of the words. Ontology usually means 'knowledge of that which exists', but when it is used here it means 'the nature of (what exists in) the world; that is, the nature of being' (Lewis, 2005: 26). 'Idealism' is used about a deductive methodology that is based on postulated axioms, which are not subject to empirical testing. The method employed by general equilibrium theorists is an example of an idealistic line of theory that must be understood in direct opposition to realism, based in empirics.

The school of scientific methodology called realism shares the assumption that a physical or material reality exists independently of social-scientific practice. This approach to social science has the task of creating new knowledge which is in some way independent of the researchers' worldview and thereby provides a less subjective understanding of the macroeconomic relationships etc. Any scientific practice, meaning the development of theories and analytical models, must necessarily include a reduction of reality which cannot be entirely objective. On the other hand, this quest for realism requires that assumptions of reality used in the simplification process are in accordance with empirical observations. One obvious methodological problem related to critical realism is that exact procedures for how these empirical requirements are best met cannot be formulated explicitly.[5]

Any model will to a certain degree be unrealistic; otherwise it would not be a model. The demand for realism complicates the leap from the real level to the analytical level. But this is the consequence of the fact that the analytical method cannot be independent of the domain under investigation. There is a difference between the methods of analysis used to describe how, for example, the strawberry market and the labour market function, respectively. The ontology of these markets differs significantly in so many ways that it would hardly be prudent to use the same analytical template on the two markets. An introductory ontological reflection would help uncover this issue and therefore ought to be a prelude to any realistic analysis. It is precisely the required correspondence between the ontological domain and the analytical method employed that characterises realism, as opposed to idealism and logical positivism. The requirement of an ontological reflection is represented in Figure 2.1 by the wide arrow from the real to the analytical level.

But even a thorough ontological reflection must, following scientific practice, be of an *a priori* nature and include a number of limitations. Stated simply, analytical results must always be unrealistic. As is often emphasized in the realist tradition from David Hume to Karl Popper, the absolute truth can never be found; still, more general theories will, through the scientific process, replace theories with a smaller domain. We naturally find ourselves on a slippery slope, in that the analytical results will always be influenced by unrealistic assumptions and the employed methods. There will often be a trade-off between realism in the selection of assumptions, and the clarity of the results, the so-called conflict of *Truth versus Precision in Economics* (Mayer, 1992).

With Inspiration from Popper's 'Three-Stage Methodology' and 'Three Worlds'

> I am totally on the side of *realism*. ... [W]e can draw conclusions about [the theory's] proximity to the truth only if we are realists. ...
> [To] be a 'positivist' is tantamount to being an opponent of all philosophical speculation and especially an opponent of *realism*. ...
> I think of myself, then, as a metaphysical realist. (Popper, 1999: 22–4)

Karl Popper stands as an exponent for methodological realism. It is reality (World 1) that we wish to understand. We seek 'the truth', meaning the complete explanation of the dynamic relationships that determine development, both physically and socially. Regardless of the fact that there are major differences between natural science and social science, the level of ambition is the same, yet the ambition is unreachable, as human understanding sets limits to what can be fathomed – not least in a world under constant change. This limitation exists also, at least partially, on the analytical level (World 2). There are simply limits to what the human brain can comprehend in an uncertain world that constantly changes. The growth of our knowledge must necessarily lag behind reality. The knowledge which we acquired about World 1 is finally reflected in World 3, which represents our interpretation of the analytical results obtained from World 2. Popper's important contribution to the discussion of the theory of scientific method was that he pointed out that knowledge will not become science until it has been subjected to empirical validity testing. If a theory cannot be tested against the material used to formulate a statement, then it is impossible to speak of its validity. According to Popper, the demarcation line for being able to attach the term 'science' to a hypothesis is that the hypothesis can withstand a falsification test.[6] It is important to acknowledge that falsification is a demarcation criterion for the theory's range of validity. On the other hand, no 'true' theories in the strictest sense of the word can ever be found. All theories are approximations of an unknown reality. Einstein's demonstration of the constant speed of light did not make Newton's theories more or less wrong, used within the theory's range of validity. The range of validity was merely more precisely defined, and outside of this range, Einstein presented a theory which demonstrated a better approximation of reality. If Einstein had not developed his theory of relativity, then Newton's theory would probably have continued to be used also outside of its own range of validity, though increasingly with the help of *ad hoc* supporting hypotheses, until another new and more general theory was developed. When the number of anomalies and their related supporting hypotheses increases, it is often a sign that the existing theory is being deployed outside of its range of validity. This was the case when the understanding of the solar system changed, a process which took more than 150 years. Similarly, it was the case within macro-theory when the term 'involuntary unemployment' arose in the period between the two world wars. And it is the case today with economic growth, where the explanation of the stagnant and even reverse growth trends, using neoclassical theory, requires a growing number of supporting hypotheses.

Popper's requirement of falsification has been criticized from many angles by Caldwell (1982), McCloskey (1986), Hausman (1992), Hands (1993; 2001) and others, yet the critique mainly targets Popper's position as a realist (and positivist) and, in the opinion of his critics, his exaggerated faith in empirical tests. But they seem to me to all fall short when alternative scientific criteria are to be formulated. If science is not to be eroded by relativism, or even more worrying, be decided by power relations, then it is difficult to find a more objective umpire than reality. But this can take a long time, particularly when strong economic or political interests are involved. Seen in a historical perspective, a number of competing theories can exist over long periods. This is not surprising, particularly within the social sciences where reality changes rapidly. These changes will themselves demand a continuous renewal of the knowledge base. Acknowledging this places greater focus on the importance of developing a robust methodology that can help social scientists – in this case macroeconomic theory – to keep up with the times. However, it will be possible to subject the realism of these theories and models to empirical testing against historic material, which can provide an indication of the degree of 'realism'. This testing is represented by the double-ended arrow in Figure 2.1.

Lakatos on Research Programmes

It is one thing to be a theoretician of science and lay down guidelines for how to perform good research, just as Popper formulated his scientific criteria. However, it is considerably more difficult to conform to these guidelines in practice. The sociology of science is an independent research area to which Imre Lakatos and many others have contributed. As described in the previous chapter, macroeconomics is divided into schools which increasingly reside in their own 'space'. Members attend different conferences and write in different journals, and their teachings are presented in separate courses. If these researchers meet by chance in the corridors of the university, they speak of other issues than economics. They have nothing to say to one another. These researchers are simply engaged in different research programmes.

Lakatos characterized a research programme as consisting of a 'hard core' and a 'protective belt'. A few indisputable axioms compose the hard core, while the belt consists of a number of supporting axioms, which can be modified along the way in the event that the results of the model encounter empirical difficulties. This construction gives research-significant inertia. Burned-out research programmes are rarely dismantled, because within an established research milieu it takes a generation to acknowledge the condition of exhaustion, particularly when the hard core is never subjected to real empirical testing. The hard core can consist of basic behaviour-related assumptions (for example rationality), assumptions of institutional conditions (for example market clearing), and/or a particular method (for example general equilibrium), which are considered as an indispensable part of the research programme. If the hard core cannot be confronted with falsification tests, then – according to Popper – the scientific programme remains speculative. In that case the hard core can easily become a creed rather than an empirically proven fact, and thereby push the research programme toward degeneration.[7] The lack of serious empirical testing might also hinder the unveiling of internal inconsistencies, because the hard core of the research programme does not become subject to scientific discussion.

This problem with the lack of empirical testing of hard-core assumptions is well known from neoclassical macro-theory, where axioms of rational actors, market clearing, rational expectations and perfect competition are used unchallenged by reality. Within the borders of general equilibrium macro-theory, these assumptions have not been subjected to a systematic falsification process and so it is impossible to define the theory's range of validity. With this comes the risk that the research programme will at some point begin to degenerate when the theory cannot explain a number of phenomena that lie outside of its range – a kind of indirect falsification. Such a fate befell the 'neoclassical synthesis' in the 1970s, when the coincidence of rising inflation and rising unemployment could not be explained within the model. The same process also characterized a period in the Marxist school when the breakdown and dilution of the production-determined class society in the West led to the 'meltdown' of the research programme's hard core in that part of the world.

It will become apparent in the following section that a number of the difficulties that these research programmes confronted could have been prevented if only the researchers involved had been more open to Popperian methodology. As has been stated above, Popper rejected the idea that any part of a research programme could be 'above the principle of falsification', meaning beyond the demarcation lines for scientific cognisance. He naturally acknowledged that the initial hypotheses, formulated in World 2, do not just appear from nowhere; they must be a product of *a priori* reflection. The fact that reflection is based on preconceived notions and often unsystematic empirics provides further encouragement to conduct a falsification test. For as Popper formulated the constructive element in his theory of science: 'we learn *only* through trial and error' (Popper, 1999: 47). In this way, Popper places the interaction between the real and the analytical levels at the heart of his theory of science and therefore of scientific progression.

Popper is not a Simple 'Falsificationalist'

As mentioned above, the requirement of falsification is regarded by a number of proponents (for example Lakatos and Blaug) and critics (including Caldwell and Hands) as Popper's most significant, though not only, contribution to the theory of science.[8] This view is hardly compatible with Popper's insistence upon his being primarily a critical realist, with the emphasis on 'critical' (Boland, 2003). Popper's approach to acquiring knowledge is characterized by Boland, a major admirer of Popper, as being that as a starting point we should admit that we hardly know anything, which is a rather Socratic view of science. In such circumstances, falsification can be a useful tool to delimit what we still do not know.

Furthermore, it is important to emphasize that Popper has an understanding of knowledge and the acquisition thereof as being an open and never-ending process:

> ... [S]cience is never stable but always in a state of constant revolution, ... [because] science [is] a social enterprise of coordinated criticism rather than coordinated agreement.
>
> Those readers with a Popperian background have always taken 'critical realism' for granted (Boland, 2003: 250)
>
> Basically, the main question is: do the model's assumptions truly represent reality, that is, represent the real, objective world? (*ibid.*: 284)

This question is reminiscent of that posed in relation to Figure 2.1: How can communication between the real and analytical levels be ensured? It is in its response to this question that critical realism can make a difference. The 'critical' element lies among other things in its continued insistence and discussion of the importance of ensuring an interaction between theory and reality.

CRITICAL REALISM WITH REFERENCE TO MACROECONOMICS

> There is an emerging consensus that the Post Keynesian approach is consistent with much of critical realism, with open-system theorizing applied to an economy understood as an organic, open system ... . Different forms of abstraction are relevant to different questions, and different economies; and indeed the study of actual economies required before abstraction can occur involves the application of different disciplines. (Dow, 1996: 79)

> Finally, since Post Keynesian theory starts with observation, the position on empirical matters must be discussed. First, [Post Keynesians reject] the subjective/objective dual ... . 'Facts' can be observed with some degree of objectivity ... . Since the group of theories includes formal models which are susceptible to empirical application, Post Keynesians do not ... reject econometrics. (Dow, 1996: 80)

Critical realism is not a well-defined theoretical-scientific direction. 'Critical' should be understood in this context as discussing or delimiting. When Popper calls himself a realist, where are the boundaries for his realism? As mentioned above, he uses the expression 'metaphysical realist'. Popper goes so far as to describe himself as a non-positivist (Popper, 1999: 24), since knowledge is a dynamic concept in World 3 based on the comprehension of results obtained in World 2 through speculation, deduction and empirical tests.

Roy Bhaskar (1975), one of the relatively new proponents of critical realism, even uses the expression 'transcendental realism' to describe his position within the theory of science. He notes especially the importance of real phenomena that are not readily observable. The term 'transcendental' is used in reference to unobservable structures at the 'deep' cognitive level. Bhaskar can at times present his theoretical discussion in such flowery language that it can give the reader a 'mystical' impression, which diverts attention away from the realist project – to understand reality.

Tony Lawson (1997) is heavily inspired by Bhaskar in his theoretical discussion of (mainstream) economics and reality. His book is primarily a theoretical criticism (in the common use of the word) of general equilibrium theory's split from the real level. He opens his book with the following ironic sentences: 'No reality, please. We're economists!' This divorce from reality is a development which he finds could be attributed to neoclassical economists' search for a microeconomic foundation on the basis of methodological individualism, the assumption of market clearing and the required method of formal deduction by means of mathematically formulated models. Lawson's critique (see Appendix 2.2) centres on the lack of a proper ontological reflection in this line of theory. The same basic analytical model is used regardless of its subject. The corn market, labour market and money market are modelled on the same template, based on the assumption of rational agents, individual optimization and potential market clearing.

The common denominator for the three theoretical contributions presented here under the title 'critical realism' – Bhaskar, Lawson and Popper – is the desire to achieve congruence between the ontology of the subject matter and the epistemology. This science-theoretical orientation should be understood as a reaction to the dominance of positivism within the natural and social sciences.

Critical Realism as Different from Positivism

Positivism has been with us for centuries. Its adherents claim that only objective, demonstrable phenomena can be made subject to scientific investigations. It is important therefore to develop methods and instruments that could be used independently of the investigator. Objective measurement and infrangible logic became the trademarks of positivism, which culminated in the Enlightenment; but it has confined itself to the natural sciences ever since (Favrholdt, 1998). Phenomena that cannot be sensed cannot be quantified. Positivism was thus originally a justified revolt against metaphysics, including the influence of religion on the natural sciences. But within the social and human sciences, positivism was influenced at an early stage in its development by Hume's scepticism, since 'human' values were contained within these sciences and these could neither be measured nor ranked. How can sense impressions that cannot be physically measured be 'objective'? They can only be objective if they are brought about by exercising mutual, interpersonal control (Schultzer, 1957). This scepticism helped push positivism in the direction of less empiricism and more deductive modelling that was not troubled by sub-jectivism. This development culminated in the logical positivist position from the turn of the twentieth century (associated with the Vienna Circle to which Popper belonged for a short period); this position sought a scien-tific method that was based on as few and as generally applicable empiri-cal 'facts' as possible, from which new conclusions could be deduced on 'objective' grounds.

This tendency can also be seen within economics. Here, utilitarianism, originally developed by Jeremy Bentham near the end of the eighteenth century, has been a particular variant of positivism. Bentham argued that human happiness, or 'utility', should be measured in 'utils', as the net sum of 'pain and pleasure'. The idea was to calculate the number of 'utils' that each person experienced. The problem was how these utils could be meas-ured. In the absence of something better, it was tempting to equate money (which can be measured) with utils. So, the greater the national product in money terms, the greater the level of measured happiness will be. However, the classical economists and the first generation of neoclassical economists (including Marshall, 1890 [1920], and Pigou, 1920) were aware that the marginal 'utility' of real income decreases when income increases; but they lacked an objective measurement of this income effect. Therefore the second generation of neoclassical equilibrium theory, introduced by Robbins (1932) and systematized by Hicks (1939) and Debreu (1959), abandoned the practice of conducting inter-subjective comparisons of utility values. They argued that such a comparison would be normative and therefore unscientific.

It is beyond doubt that this second generation of neoclassical theory, in the version that appears in the textbooks as 'economics', is marked by logical positivism, in that a very few axioms serve as the foundation for the deduction of economic laws, 'whose substantial accuracy and importance are open to question only by the ignorant or the perverse' (Robbins, 1932: 1). Robbins proclaimed himself a realist: 'It is a characteristic of scientific generalisations that they refer to *reality*' (Robbins, 1932: 104, emphasis added). One can almost draw a straight line through the history of eco-nomic theory, from Lausanne (Walras and Pareto), through the London School of Economics (Robbins and Hicks) to the Massachusetts Institute of Technology, MIT (Samuelson and Debreu), to track the development of general equilibrium models with microeconomic foundations based on logical positivism, that today constitutes mainstream macroeconomics,[9] particularly after the collapse of the neoclassical synthesis known as (old) Keynesian economics.

Critical realism was originally developed in an attempt to break positivism's dominance over the natural sciences. In contrast, macroeconomic theory was first truly dominated by logical positivism only within the last 20–30 years of the twentieth century, in the form of general equilibrium models with a so-called microeconomic foundation. In this way, methodological individualism, market equilibrium and deductive reasoning became dominant for macroeconomic theory development and analysis. At the same time, empirical testing came to play an ever decreasing role in the formation, much less the testing, of the models' power of explanation.

The methodological approach of critical realism, on the contrary, places decisive emphasis on the fact that it is reality that must be understood and explained, and so methodological practice should be determined by the concrete manifestation of the subject matter. And it is precisely the often complex character of economics that is one of the primary reasons why Lawson insists on the necessity of introducing critical realism into this discipline. In Lawson's words:

> In short, the world … is densely (if not exclusively) populated by totalities … [that are] complexly structured, open, intrinsically dynamic, characterised by emergence and so novelty, and inclusive of totalities and causally efficacious absences, amongst other things. (Lawson, 1997: 65)

These complexities and differences necessitate that every investigation should commence with a characterization of the social ontology – an 'ontological reflection', to use Lawson's terminology. The cognitive starting point for this ontological reflection should be a preliminary characterization of the subject matter as it can be observed in reality (World 1). This characterization forms the basis of the macroeconomic landscape which has to be understood subsequently through a retroductive analytical process conducted within World 2.

The theoretical starting point for critical realism is therefore the socio-economic relationships that are assumed to exist independently of the researcher, but which are undergoing constant change. The development of theory, therefore, does not consist of uncovering an eternal, unchangeable economic structure. Rather, the aim is to explain the causal mechanisms that connect macro-actors and macro-markets under the further premise that the actors' behaviour and the structures change and exert mutual influence on the macro-system's ontology over historical time.

Seen from a critical realist perspective, macroeconomic methodology does not merely consist of piecing together a jigsaw puzzle where the pieces are known in advance. The pieces are not known in advance. They become apparent through the scientific process of open system analysis in World 2; then results are interpreted and subsequently applied to World 3, where they will appear in a case- and context-specific way. Anyhow, the macroeconomic landscape is not static. On the contrary it changes continuously in an unpredictable way. Hence, new knowledge has to be constantly generated, just as the structures into which the pieces of knowledge will fit may also change through time. Critical realism, therefore, is open to methodological pluralism, naturally including the use of mathematics (at the analytical level) – which Lawson summarizes under the term 'epistemological relativism'.[10]

On the other hand, he rejects those methodologies that assume that the economic phenomena, including the macroeconomic reality, should simply be a social construction. This critical realist perspective has as its starting point that macroeconomic reality exists, where analysis of the causes of unemployment, for example, is not a relative question of which discourse is given the highest priority, but rather a matter of finding the most convincing empirically supported explanation.

The basis for realism (as opposed to idealism[11] and relativism) is that 'reality' does exist independently of which hypotheses the natural or social scientists develop. This view encapsulates a clear dissociation from the idea that it is a scientific task to analyse 'nature' or 'society' as just an ideological abstraction (idealism) or a social construction (relativism), whose existence and manifestations are determined only by the research traditions and their interpreters detached from reality, as might be the case when logical positivism or postmodernism is employed. In this respect, Lawson is in complete agreement with Arestis (1992) and Dow (1996) and stands clearly in a realist position.

Critical Realism Seeks Congruence between Ontology and Epistemology

As already described, Lawson does not attempt to hide the fact that he has taken significant elements of his ontological reorientation from the science-theory discussion among natural scientists. In particular, he often cites Bhaskar (1975), *A Realist Theory of Science*, where a research programme based upon transcendental realism in biology is presented as inspiration.[12]

The need to escape the restrictions of positivism and create a more accommodating methodology arose within the natural sciences as early as the end of the nineteenth century. To a certain extent, the need had always existed. But its necessity was made explicit through Einstein's observation of inexplicable phenomena which justified a renewed reflection of the nature of the physical world; ultimately extending the range of validity to include his theory of relativity. The research domain for classical physics was at that time limited to Newton's Laws of Motion,[13] which stood in the way of understanding a number of real phenomena. They simply could not be explained using 'Newton's method'. For example, classical physics could not explain the constant speed of light, much less the random motion of electrons. The classical model of analysis had to be supplemented with, and in some cases replaced by, broader theories and models that were in better communication with the 'new' knowledge in physics. This did not render classical physics superfluous, but rather uncovered a number of previously unknown ('deeper') structures of World 1 that could be incorporated into the analytical World 2 and give a richer understanding of World 3.

In Bhaskar's terminology, such a new discovery in the deep stratum is merely an example of the fact that behind the observable 'reality' exist structures, mechanisms and powers which play a significant role for macroeconomic development. Precisely for this reason, the framework for understanding reality (the interaction between the real and the analytical level), according to Bhaskar, ought to be established as an open system, capable of adapting new phenomena and producing new knowledge, under the influence of, among other things, these transcendent and, just as importantly, fluctuating real phenomena and structures. Here we confront a well-known 'classical' problem. Heraclitus is remembered, among other things, for his statement that you cannot step into the same river twice, for fresh waters are ever flowing upon you. The water is continuously renewed, the banks eroded and the landscape can be hit by an earthquake – the future is uncertain. Thus, even seemingly unchangeable 'physical circumstances' will undergo constant changes – some naturally faster than others. A deeper understanding of these physical and social processes requires the development of open research programmes, as has been demonstrated numerous times even throughout the history of natural science. This does not necessarily mean that the existing research programmes are not useful, but that their range of relevance is limited by the available knowledge. These conditions exist within all sciences, and therefore the theory of scientific methodology is important for our scientific understanding. Let me give an example.

The starting point for research programmes based on realism (including positivism) is that reality exists independently of the scientists' observations and interpretations. The earth does not change its orbit, and the sun continues to rise every morning, despite the fact that science's view of the solar system changed from revolving around the earth to revolving around the sun. Perspectives on the cosmos have since changed numerous times. Hawking (1988) and others have demonstrated that science will continuously change our understanding, in this case of the universe – without actually ever reaching a full understanding.[14] But – and this is an important addendum – following Newton's work, solar eclipses could already be predicted with astonishing precision, something Einstein's subsequent theories have changed very little. Within 'macro-natural science' there are some areas where the constancy of reality is so dominant that it is possible to establish analytical 'subsystems' which are approximately comparable to closed deductive systems where everything seemingly is predictable.

However, the social sciences do not share this constancy. As the macroeconomic system changes over time, individuals and institutions are influenced by the new events they experience. If a government or central bank governor demonstrates a systematic pattern of reaction over a number of years, then the economic actors will begin to calculate this economic policy into their expectations of the future. In this way, the effect of economic policy does change through time.

The Link between World 2 and World 3

According to Popper, scientific explanations are only approximations of the real world. Researchers are often inspired to use colourful images and metaphors when they translate their analytical results into descriptive explanations that can be utilized in World 3; World 1's true nature remains (partially) unexplained. Gravity is an example of one such metaphor from the world of physics. It seems to provide an explanation of the planetary orbits, and in this respect, predictions have had an emphatic influence; but if we ask for the causal relations behind gravitation, then the answers of researchers fall short. It is a similar case with electricity, described as the 'movement of electrons', or with the DNA molecules that carry our genes. These metaphors are best understood as a creative use of language, rather than the expression of the true understanding of a number of physical phenomena.

There has also been a great deal of linguistic ingenuity in the social sciences, including macroeconomics. Terms such as 'voluntary unemployment', 'natural and structural unemployment' and 'cyclical unemployment' came into fashion in the 1980s, when unemployment peaked and mainstream theorists were unable to provide a convincing analytical explanation of its causes. When it became necessary to offer some advice on a possible reduction of unemployment in World 3, these metaphors were used to establish a causal relationship that could legitimate a reduction of the wage level.

In fact, social researchers may develop metaphors or adopt concepts from other research areas in natural sciences or humanities that may lead the interpretation of the analytical results astray and confuse the political implications of the results when applied to World 3. Take for instance the metaphor of 'sound finance' applied to a public sector surplus, which in a recession might actually be an inappropriate fiscal policy. Using the term 'sound' however gives a signal of something beneficial, which depending on the context might or might not be so.

Another example is the assumption of 'rational expectations', which sounds like a reasonable behavioural practice. Who would ever assume that economic agents form 'irrational expectations'? But the concept of rational expectations could easily, for linguistic reasons, be misleading, because in neoclassical theory a 'rational' expectation does not mean the 'best possible' expectation based on available information, but an expectation based on full and correct information about the future. The wording may have flair, but it obscures the far more important methodo-logical issue, that the analytical results are based on the assumption that the future can be known with certainty. This is an idealistic assumption far from reality, which influences the analytical results. Hence, rational expectations could much better be called 'ideal' expectations, which would clearly communicate an analytical difference from 'realistic' expectations.

Linguistic metaphors may cause unnecessary misperception when ana-lytical results are to be transferred to World 3.[15] They might give rise to a net of miscommunication between the 'actual' reality and the political reality. It is important that linguistic barriers, and thereby cognitive barri-ers, are not erected between the analytical and the political domain on the basis of such misleading metaphors.

I will later, in Chapter 7, return to further analytical implications of using ideal assumptions, especially when they constitute a part of the hard core of the research programme and hide behind a veil of linguistic meta-phors such as 'sound finance' and 'rational expectations'. It is sufficient to mention here that any assumptions ought to be tested empirically, and the outcome of these tests should have an influence on how the analytical results are passed on as policy advice in World 3.

The analytical level (World 2) will always be different from World 1. That is the whole meaning of constructing an analytical model. But if it happens that clearly unrealistic assumptions are introduced, perhaps for a practical purpose, and a subsequent falsification test of this assumption or its implications is omitted – perhaps with an argument that we are in any case looking at a hypothetical long-term model that requires observations of 20 or 30 years into the future before it can be empirically tested – in that case any theory is as good as any other. Without a firm grounding in reality, World 2 can take any hypothetical shape, and the normative considerations associated with the chosen but untested axioms can be difficult for anyone working outside the hard core of the research programme to detect and assess.

Andersen (2000) (see Appendix 2.1) goes one step further when he compares a neoclassical analysis in World 2 with laboratory trials, where the whole macroeconomic system is made ready for experiments. The laboratory outcome is treated as the best possible description of reality, which is accordingly offered as the best advice regarding the real world. Lawson would claim that an epistemological error is made when World 1 is being equated to World 2. Even if the laboratory were the very best presentation of our (limited) knowledge of World 1, it would be a misrepresentation of the analytical results to conclude that they represent reality. In other words, World 2 will always be a logical construction which reproduces elements of World 1 in stylized form and can, of course, never be a 1:1 projection. Therefore, policy advice should always be made conditional and modifications clearly expressed.

There is a significant distinction in the theory of science between whether it is the epistemology that analytically determines the target field or whether, on the contrary, it is the target field's ontology that sets the (quite often very demanding) requirements on the epistemology.

Critical realism is a coherent argumentation that explains why it is most relevant, particularly within the field of macroeconomics, to adopt the latter position. This is done despite the fact that full correspondence between the three worlds can never be achieved, since the macroeconomic reality, on the basis of its ontology alone, is both open and indeterminate.[16] This circumstance must be taken into account for the subsequent presentation in World 3 of the analytical results obtained.

A methodology based on critical realism is therefore a possible solution for achieving a more general[17] macroeconomic understanding.

Critical Realism: Understanding the Complex and Stratified Reality

Tony Lawson (1997: 15)[18] defines ontology as an 'enquiry into the nature of being, of existence, including the nature, constitution and structure of the objects of study'. He follows up the definition with a number of examples of how the analytical tools have to be adapted to the ontology. Surprisingly, almost all of these examples have a background in natural science. He suggests, for example, that a pneumatic drill can be a handy tool if we need to drill a hole in material made out of concrete – given the ontology of concrete. However, if we attempted to use the same drill to make a hole in a glass window, things would certainly go wrong. Why?

Because we have not made the window's 'nature of being', or ontology, clear to ourselves – with catastrophic results.

Understanding the object's ontology is of great importance for acquiring relevant knowledge for any subsequent analysis. This conclusion also applies to the work of discovering causal macroeconomic mechanisms. Lawson points out that it is important to differentiate between the target field's ontology and the knowledge that it is possible to obtain about the macroeconomic landscape. Lawson (1997: 33) quotes Bhaskar's warning, mentioned above, against the erroneous epistemological conclusion that is reached if a statement about the target field's ontology is reduced to (and actually equated with) a statement about the epistemological knowledge that we can gather exclusively on the analytical level (see above and Appendix 2.2). On the contrary, it is the nature of the target field that determines the type of macroeconomic knowledge that can be acquired at all (the epistemology is limited by the target field's 'being') – and so it also determines which questions can be answered meaningfully. The connection between 'what is' and 'the knowledge of what is' is established through adapting the epistemology to the ontology, which if done correctly can produce reliable results that constitute new, though still uncertain, knowledge of macroeconomic relationships. This means that it is important for the selection of the analytical method whether it is the labour market, the banking system, the exchange rate or the energy supply that is the subject of analysis. This will be discussed in more detail in the following chapters. These four macroeconomic institutions have different characteristics in the form of formal power relations (legislative action), formal and informal agreements (for example wage negotiations, changes of interest and exchange rates) and the organization of the market(s) being analysed. To the extent that a common 'drill' can be used to investigate and devise theories about the macroeconomic importance of these four very different institutions, the drill's size and shape must be adapted to the social ontology of the target field.

Following this introductory and relatively general discussion of the importance of understanding the target field's social ontology, it is now possible to make the presentation more concrete. Lawson argues that our knowledge of reality can be advantageously depicted in stratified form. He works with three different levels of cognitive data organized in three different levels: the empirical, the factual, and the deep stratum (see Figure 2.2).

The empirical stratum is the surface of the macroeconomic landscape. Here we have a number of observations from the national accounts, labour market statistics and so on. But we know that all macro-data are only estimates and, for that reason alone, there must be a certain amount

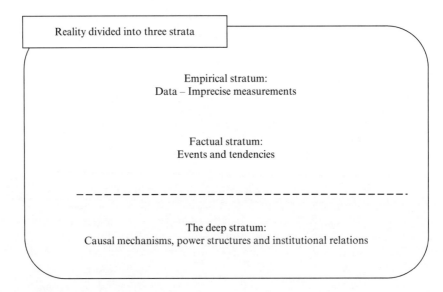

Reality divided into three strata

Empirical stratum:
Data – Imprecise measurements

Factual stratum:
Events and tendencies

The deep stratum:
Causal mechanisms, power structures and institutional relations

Source: Based on Lawson (2001)

Figure 2.2   Stratified reality grounded in critical realism

of (statistical) uncertainty associated with all these numbers. In addition
to this, we should remember that the definitions of data have to correspond with the prevailing theory. The classic example is the division
of the demand components in the national accounts – here the influence
of Keynes is unmistakeable. These data are the immediate empirical
representation of the landscape's appearance.

The next question in describing the landscape's appearance is whether
there is a detectable pattern within these data. Can any tendencies be
established that statistically demonstrate a robust significance, that goes
beyond ordinary statistical randomness? Such tendencies cannot immediately be observed but can be said to exist in the factual stratum. These
tendencies will appear as postulates, until they have been subjected to
a retroductive scientific process in which the formulation of hypotheses
interacts with the empirical observations and are substantiated through a
statistical testing procedure. In this way, an effort is made to discover the
causal mechanisms that are the specific scientific result of macroeconomic
analyses.

The empirical and factual strata are a part of both positivist as well as
critical-realistic reasoning. But critical realism differentiates itself from
positivism by contending that more general knowledge can be reached

by discovering the causal mechanisms which are rooted in the deep stratum and not directly observable. In Chapter 3 I will characterize these causal mechanisms within macroeconomics as macro-behaviour functions, grounded in empirically tested and stable relations, but not directly observable. These macro-behaviour functions (causal mechanisms) cannot be analytically deduced as micro-behaviour on a grand scale. They are aggregate items to which, in the majority of cases, no specific aggregated micro-activity is associated. On the contrary one single macro-number is caused by a myriad of individual and interrelated activities.

However, a few of the so-called macro-institutions stand out as dominated by individual activities. For example, the decision of the central bank to change the discount rate can be directly referred to as one specific activity. In fact, such a change will usually be followed by an 'official' explanation. In this case, the causal mechanism is apparently observable. But it is only 'apparently': for what lies behind the central bank's decision? This brings us to the important question about the macroeconomic method: how to uncover the causal mechanisms that lie behind a macro-behavioural relationship? and how to detect the relationship between cause and effect within macroeconomics, for instance between an external influence (for example the discount rate) and an observed trend in a data stream (for example private consumption)? Similar questions can also be posed concerning the decisions taken by a finance minister with regard to a change in the tax rate, expenditure, welfare payments, and so on. Why did he do it and what effects are likely to be expected on, for example, employment, income distribution and public finance? Here we are down at the 'deeper' stratum of the macroeconomic landscape, that which Bhaskar aptly describes as the transcendental level. It is the part of the landscape's topology which we cannot readily observe as it lies buried beneath the surface.[19]

It is important that the researcher be aware of the meaning of the three ontological strata outlined in Figure 2.2 and of the relationship between them in order to be able to formulate relevant hypotheses. The empirical and factual strata can (to varying degrees) be observed, while phenomena in the 'deep' stratum, by virtue of its nature, must remain largely hidden. Knowledge about the deep-stratum phenomena will always be limited by the uncertainty that is related to its unobservable character, which can only be uncovered by indirect methods and empirical falsification trials.

It is a challenge to do research on phenomena that are not readily observable. In the deep stratum, we cannot even give a preliminary answer. In this case, unexpected observations might be a source of inspiration for new discoveries. But we can only proceed by inference.

Within the framework of an open system, 'inexplicable' events will lead to a search for more general hypotheses within the existing research programme. For example, Keynes considered persistent involuntary unemployment as a kind of inexplicable phenomenon within the neoclassical macroeconomic theory. Throughout the 1920s he tried to reformulate the existing framework to make it capable of explaining this new tendency. But in the end he had to acknowledge that the neoclassical research paradigm could not give a satisfactory explanation, that is, an explanation that corresponded with empirical observations. Hence, he had to search for a new methodological paradigm to explain the hitherto inexplicable. At that stage the scientist will find himself in the speculative domain with a genuinely open research agenda, where his method of research, his understanding of the social ontology, has to be reformulated before new scientific knowledge can be established.

This is the *raison d'être* of following a critical realist scientific procedure in an attempt to understand the apparently inexplicable. For Keynes the explicit inclusion of uncertainty became the challenge and the key to a more realistic understanding of macroeconomic development. Uncertainty is present in social systems for many reasons, but in one respect social science is especially different from natural science, namely, people's ability to learn from previous experiences. Social behaviour is (partly) self-correcting through a cognitive process, which by itself makes it impossible – contrary to laboratory trials – to repeat the experiments in an unchanged form. Every macroeconomic study must therefore be evaluated in light of the present context and people's past experiences. An assessment of the context as well as past experiences is crucial for determining the generality of the conclusion being drawn from the study in question.

In a macroeconomic research programme based on critical realism the researchers set themselves the task of understanding the 'external' reality and describing the structures and causal relationships that can substantiate (and explain) observed developments within the macroeconomic landscape. This scientific work can most advantageously be conducted in cooperation between a number of social science disciplines. Concepts such as power, institutions and social structures are fully understood in a concrete, historical context where economic, political, legal, physical and cultural factors are intertwined. The search for universally valid, context-independent macroeconomic 'laws' is therefore doomed to fail (Hoover, 2001).

It is here that methodology enters the picture. However, before we begin this discussion, it is important to round off the section on ontology by emphasizing that it is the open, stratified and holistic perception of reality, and the science-theory implications that derive from it, that are the distinct trademark of critical realism. The true science-theory challenge then consists of developing a theory and method that can bind these three substantial strata together; see Figure 2.2. This is a prerequisite for uncovering the causal mechanisms resident in the macroeconomic landscape that is manifested in observed events – perhaps even in the form of a statistical trend.

The level of ambition within macroeconomic science should be high, but the results concerning the understanding of the deep stratum will rarely be able to live up to such a high level of ambition. The ontology of the target field is often too fluid and our understanding of the deep stratum too diffuse for this. So it is all the more important to employ a science-theory strategy that is based on a continuous, open and critical discussion. There are no preprogrammed answers here and therefore no easy answers to macroeconomic questions. To sum up in brief: there can be no 'critical realism' without ontological reflection.

Critical Realism: Ontology + Epistemology Lead to Causal Relationships

Lawson's methodological reflections based on critical realism are the basis for the three elements of the above heading: ontology, epistemology and causal relationships. The methodology sets up a logical sequence: (1) describe the characteristic structures of the target field assessed in relation to the cardinal question: 'What are we looking at?' (2) move to the more practical approach: 'Given the social ontology, how do we organize the analysis in a consistent way?' (3) the answers to (1) and (2) constitute what kind of new knowledge can be achieved from the analysis.

On the analytical level, we are looking for a method of theory-construction that can form the basis for developing hypotheses about causal mechanisms that can substantiate and explain tendencies in the factual stratum, which in practice means the most robust empirical relationships. As Lawson emphasized (1997), we are not looking for theoretical consistencies of the type 'whenever x, then y, without exception'. The actual social ontology is usually an obstacle to the discovery of such precise predictions. In this way, critical realism challenges Friedman's methodological conclusion that the accuracy of predictions is the best criterion for assessing the quality of analytical models.[20] So instrumentalism is rejected, since it does not attach importance to the matter of securing congruence between ontology and epistemology.

The idea that a laboratory experiment can be used in macroeconomics is, as explained above, for similar reasons regarded as methodologically misleading from the perspective of critical realism, when there is little congruence between the open ontology of the macroeconomic landscape and the epistemology of employing unrealistic assumptions unconditionally

(Mäki, 2002). Critical realists would say that the methodological notion that a laboratory trial can be used as a general macroeconomic method is 'misplaced concreteness' (Daly, 1997). The ontological basis for controlled experiments is rarely, if ever, present when the macroeconomic landscape is researched (see below on the difference between open and closed system analysis). In addition, for practical reasons it would be impossible to conduct a series of identical macroeconomic experiments that would be numerically sufficient to reduce the statistical randomness related to any laboratory experiment. Instead, macroeconomists must work with observations from time series. This is problematic in itself because of the changing macroeconomic landscape. This will be discussed separately in Chapter 6.

On the practical level, therefore, it is trivial that predictions will seldom be fulfilled. The crucial criterion, therefore, is not the precision of the prediction, but its relevance to the work in World 3 at the 'political' level. It is of vital importance, in this connection, to understand the qualitative difference between working with open and closed systems, respectively. It was the failure to acknowledge this important difference that helped to bring about the collapse of the 'great macro-econometric models' in the early 1970s. However, it was not a critique of the closed and mechanical nature of these models that was prevalent at the time, but rather, as described in Chapter 1, a critique from the neoclassical economists that the models lacked a basis in axiomatic micro-theory. From this perspective, one could say that the macro-econometric models were not closed enough. They were accused of being specified in too *ad hoc* a manner, which reduced their range of validity in a forward-looking perspective. This was the core of the so-called 'Lucas critique' (see Lucas and Sargent, 1978). Lucas and Sargent claimed that the most stable socio-economic parameters could be found in microeconomic behaviour, in the form of constant consumption preferences and production conditions.

The critique by Lucas and Sargent presented here can be directed at every form of scientific work that bases itself on simple verification of the past and of theories that are limited to the factual level. The Lucas critique is correct on this methodological point: that empirical regularities should be explained by stable causal mechanisms that are rooted in the deep stratum and referred to in neoclassical terminology as 'deep parameters of individual preferences'.

Seen from the perspective of a critical realist methodology, it is equally important to recommend that phenomena from the 'deep stratum' are included at both the real and the analytical levels, recognizing that the observed surface phenomena must necessarily be dependent on the underlying structures. These structures can be of a behavioural or an institutional nature. However, there is a tricky methodological problem associated with pinpointing these causal mechanisms: they are often non-observable and under constant change. The empirical material that we have readily available is macro-data of varying quality. The statistical correlations uncovered are in any case contextual and often characterized by random occurrences, since the underlying 'mechanisms' are not necessarily constant over time, as there were changes in the river of Heraclitus. The main reason for the sceptical attitude towards statistically established correlations, as seen in for example Lawson (1997), is their ontologically superficial and analytically random characters. So, statistical correlations cannot stand alone. They are only meaningful when supplemented with a theoretical, explanatory model that corresponds to the concrete macroeconomic ontology. However, statistical tests, if interpreted with respect to the underlying statistical material, can be a bridge between the analytical and the factual levels, inspiring further work to discover the causal mechanisms in the deeper stratum. In this way they can become an important input as part of a retroductive working method.

Retroduction

We are now ready to assess the science-theory working method, which is a combination of induction and deduction, so-called 'retroduction', that Lawson recommends (see also Nielsen and Buch-Hansen, 2004) as a procedure of the critical realist methodology in developing social science theories. Retroduction starts with an ontological reflection; but where do the organizing categories for this reflection come from? Here of necessity a significant amount of previously acquired experience and convention is used. This is a preliminary characteristic of the target field, that should subsequently be investigated with the aim of improving the knowledge base. This reflection, at the very least, should not be in direct empirical conflict with observable data.

It is possible to deduce (preliminary) theories on this (preliminary) empirical base, preferably by including bold hypotheses concerning the structures in the deep stratum. These theories must then be confronted with reality through a constructive falsification test that can be quantitative and/or qualitative. An indication of the theory's range of validity can be achieved in this way. Not least, the limits of the range of validity can inspire clarification and further development of our understanding of the causal mechanisms. This empirical testing is of an inductive nature. Should the same phenomenon appear repeatedly, then the macroeconomist, with inspiration from Hume as well as Lawson (2003: 145–6), should ask: 'Are there reasons to believe that all swans are white?' Which underlying mechanisms could have brought about this seeming regularity? It is questions such as these that must be answered through a retroductive practice so that we can obtain new knowledge, rather than merely observing a statistical correlation.

The retroductive practice is based on an interaction between 'common sense', deduction, observation and induction. It is especially important to have this interchange when uncovering causal relationships in open systems. This will also help to ensure correspondence between the real level and the analytical level, and thereby prevent the occurrence of epistemological errors.

> It is important to recognise, therefore, that the essential mode of inference sponsored by transcendental realism is neither induction nor deduction but one that can be styled *retroduction* or *abduction* or 'as if' reasoning. (Lawson, 1997: 24)
>
>   This consists in the movement, on the basis of analogy and metaphor amongst other things, from a conception of some phenomenon of interest to a conception of some totally different type of thing, mechanism, structure or condition that is responsible for the given phenomenon. (Lawson, 2003: 145)

Instead of seeing induction and deduction as polar opposites and therefore mutually exclusive practices, Lawson encourages us to consider these two very different principles for design of hypotheses as being complementary. Retroduction can be described as a method that includes the main elements of induction (observations and apparent regularities), which are subsequently given a (hypothetical deductive) theoretical foundation in respect for the ontological character of the target field.[21]

In this respect, retroduction is clearly distinguishable from pure deduction, which is briefly outlined in Appendix 2.1, as an axiomatic logic without real empirical testing of the selected axioms. Retroduction[22] on the other hand, combines the observed regularities (induction) with hypothetical deduction (conditional inference), which can, for example, be stochastic. Induction helps to ensure correspondence with 'the reality of life', while deduction can maintain a logical consistency in the development of theory. There is not one particular approach that is correct, but the selection of the method of analysis is of critical importance and should therefore be given adequate attention. It should be the character of the 'problem area' that (co-)determines how the analysis is conducted in practice; see Lawson's metaphor of the pneumatic drill.

Lawson often uses metaphors to suggest phenomena in the deep stratum, which by their nature cannot be subjected to direct observation. This gives an apparent parallel to Friedman's instrumentalism; but it is an illusion, since the ambition of critical realism is to replace metaphors with actual, realistic explanations of causal mechanisms. The better (more realistic) the theories of 'macroeconomic behaviour' that can be established, the more the use of 'as if' metaphors can be forced into the background. It is unlikely that they can be completely removed, however, since a lack of knowledge (and observations) forces us to work with an open (and therefore partially underdetermined, not to mention non-ergodic) explanatory model of the underlying (and presumably open) structures. As a part of the critical realist methodology, there will always be the speculative 'as if' element serving as a hypothetical explanatory element.[23]

Pålsson Syll (2001b), one of Sweden's most enthusiastic advocates for the use of critical realism in socio-economics, introduces a section in his book on economic method with the title 'Vad är en relevant förklaring' ('What is a relevant explanation') in the following way:

> No clear criteria can be found for what a satisfactory explanation should be. ... [On the contrary] a relevant explanation should be correct in the observation, that it is in accordance with reality and that it should be useful. (Pålsson Syll, 2001b: 112)[24] (My translation)

FROM THEORY TO PRACTICE

Until now I have discussed the methodological criteria for obtaining relevant knowledge about macroeconomic reality, including a lengthy discussion of the importance of ensuring correspondence between the real level and the analytical level. These two levels cannot be separated within macroeconomic science, which ought to be reflected in the methodological practice. This argumentation can, without difficulty, be developed to include all social sciences, since the methodological levels are interlinked, just as the various disciplines are difficult to separate completely. Economics, politics, sociology and law are artificial divisions when one paints with a broad brush. The disciplines are socially embedded and exercise mutual influences. Yet, to make this book more specific, I have decided to focus on the macroeconomic domain, which can help give the methodological considerations a more concrete and, consequently, operational character.

There is also the fact that macroeconomic analyses must be context-dependent. What field of socio-economics are we looking at, and how can the general socio-economic relationships be described? A contextually embedded macroeconomic landscape will therefore be presented in the next chapter, not as a fixed, unchanging framework for analysis – quite the opposite. I would rather call it a type of reality checklist.

Reality: The Round Trip

In the above argumentation, the idea has been put forth that when realism serves as the basis for macroeconomic methodology, the analytical level cannot be viewed in isolation. It is from our image of reality – the onto-logical reflection – that the activating questions must spring. These ques-tions should be answered on the analytical level in a constant interaction between theory, model formulation and empirical testing – the so-called retroductive process. The result of such a contextual analysis must finally be brought back to reality where it is intended to be utilized (World 3). What can we social scientists conclude as an answer to the introductory question, and with what (un)certainty and limitations can the answers be formulated? The model of analysis is not reality, so the results of the model – the new knowledge – must, to a certain extent, be brought back to reality. There is a methodological gap here which can easily be over-looked. It occurs (too) often that there are just two lines drawn under the analytical results. This is 'the most qualified answer' to the question posed. In this way, the analytical level and the operational level are equated, so that the analytical results are left unmodified. The absolutely necessary, yet often unanswered, question is: How do we get from the analytical level to policy recommendations while maintaining a scientific basis? Let me illustrate this problem with Figure 2.3.

The Analytical Level (World 2): Axioms, Analysis and Results

As is shown in Figure 2.3, the activities in World 2 (the analytical level) play a dominant role within general equilibrium macroeconomics.[25] The analysis centres on the mathematical formulation of the axiomatic basis with maximizing individual behaviour, full predictability, market clear-ing and long-term equilibrium, all of which are predetermined axioms. In Lakatos's terminology, these axioms constitute the 'hard core' of this research programme which cannot be challenged and therefore have never been subjected to actual falsification. It is upon this analytical basis that the mathematically formulated general equilibrium model has been devel-oped and discussed. And this shared axiomatic foundation must be the basis for Andersen's (2000) statement that 'there are practically no meth-odological differences within macroeconomic theory', which is why 'the method is not the message'; only one research programme is recognized by the 'mainstream'. As long as the axiomatic foundation and the hypo-thetical-deductive method are not challenged, there is simply no methodo-logical difference that can be questioned. The discussion of methodology plays out within a narrowly defined World 2. Consider also Andersen's

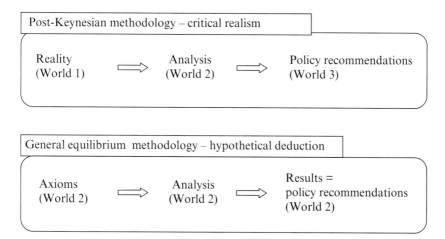

Figure 2.3   Two different methodologies

remark about the lack of realism behind the assumption of, for example, rational expectations (which, however, does not make him hesitate to give policy recommendations directly derived from the analysis). A mathematical, deductive model cannot be 'wrong' if the mathematical operators are used correctly. The postulated theoretical relationship and the dynamic structure can be given various mathematical representations, as long as the solution of the model converges towards general equilibrium. The last condition is of course also axiomatically determined. The general equilibrium models, therefore, rarely overstep the boundary separating the analytical level from the real level. The analysis consists primarily in finding the solution to the closed model under different structural conditions. The analytical outcome is quite often a demonstration of the 'distortions' caused by external effects and government regulations compared to the perfect competitive market model, and policy recommendation consists of the so-called welfare gains which can be obtained if these distortions were eliminated.

The post-Keynesian school, on the other hand, maintains that it is necessary to include fundamental uncertainty, that characterizes the real world, at the analytical level. It is not the question of individual rationality that is debated, but rather how the macroeconomic representation of individual behaviour, subject to uncertainty, can be given a realistic, operational and rational representation. The ontological reflection does not provide any immediate justification for assuming that individuals do not behave rationally on the basis of the knowledge they possess, and the norms and habits that make up their social and historical reality. The core of this post-Keynesian discussion of methodology is rather about how individual, rational behaviour can be represented within the framework of an adequate macroeconomic model so that the existence of fundamental uncertainty is attributed the analytical importance it requires. I will address this question below and assess to what extent a mathematical formulation of macroeconomic behaviour under uncertainty is a relevant method of analysis (see Chick, 1998).

Precisely because the post-Keynesian school gives decisive significance to uncertainty in its ontological description, it has been a challenge to the theory of science to achieve correspondence between the ontology and the choice of a method that can analytically include fundamental uncertainty on both the individual and the structural levels. It is precisely on this point that critical realism has caught the attention of post-Keynesian researchers, since this school of the theory of science, as already mentioned, strives for congruence between ontology and epistemology.

The post-Keynesian macroeconomic landscape is therefore assumed to be populated with rational actors equipped with limited (and uncertain) knowledge. These actors act within a structure of macro-institutions, norms and habits in which explicit and implicit individual and social contracts are established. Through these contracts, a varying level of regulation, redistribution and limitation of macroeconomic uncertainty is achieved. These structures co-determine the causal mechanisms that drive macroeconomic development. But as Keynes pointed out in his 1934 paper on methodology, there is no empirical support to the view point that the causal mechanisms will interact as to justify the existence of a long-term equilibrium, much less a long-term equilibrium with full utilization of resources; and even if such an equilibrium did exist, there was no real probability of it ever being reached at the macro-level through the market mechanism. Nothing can be stated *a priori* on this subject. Therefore, in *The General Theory*, Keynes changed his stance on analytical method in relation to his earlier books and abandoned the assumption that long-term market-clearing equilibrium was empirically relevant. He did so on the basis of an intensive ontological reflection, which at the beginning of the 1930s brought him to the preliminary conclusion that even a well-organized market-economic structure did not necessarily include the realization of a long-term general equilibrium. But, as already mentioned, the altered macroeconomic reflection was still based on the assumption that the individual actors behave rationally, given the knowledge they have about present macroeconomic developments and about future individual behaviour (see Chapter 4).

Building Bridges between the Real and Analytical Levels

A theory-of-science orientation that calls itself critical realism must naturally have a theory for how 'reality' can be included as a part of the overall methodology. The real level and the analytical level cannot be kept separate. Critical realism is characterized by the existence of a constant interaction between observations and analysis that provides opportunities for new and 'deeper' understandings of the basic causal mechanisms. Although we never achieve a complete understanding of reality, the ambition is to improve our understanding. Let us briefly include the Popperian perspective. Scientific results should be characterized by the fact that the underlying, analytical proposition as a part of the research process has been confronted with the part of reality that is observable in one way or another. This research procedure is a part of embedding the analytical level into the real level. If the hypothetical statements cannot be rejected on the basis of the available empirical data, then we have expanded our knowledge of reality.

Methodologically, it is a serious challenge to cross the divide between reality and analysis, since here the researcher moves from being an observer to being an operator. Here, stylized observations are combined with theoretical models so that a broader, yet also more abstract, cognition can be reached in the form of analytical results.

I have called the initial operation of this retroductive process for an ontological reflection in the form of drawing up a sketch of a macroeconomic landscape, a kind of 'mapping'.

Next follows the formulation of hypotheses and empirical testing, which will later often be followed by necessary reformulations and more testing. These results must then be brought into harmony with reality, taking the most demanding assumptions into consideration. To what extent do they compromise the generality of the analytical results? Are the results relevant for the formulation of policy recommendations at the real level of World 3, where they will form part of the basis for decision-making? Some relevance could eventually be achieved through conditional, path-dependent projections of a limited scale.

If the ambition is to reach results that contain relevant statements about reality, it is important that the analysis is not begun with clearly unrealistic axiomatic foundations. For such assumptions cannot avoid distorting the results in relation to reality, whereby they lose their generality. This was for example the background to Keynes calling his book *The General Theory*, as the theory developed there included neoclassical general equilibrium (full employment) as a special case.[26]

The design of an analytical model is an important issue, although in the broader methodological perspective it is limited. It is only included here to show that the disagreement does not lie exclusively in whether, but also in how the divide between the real level and the analytical level (where some theoreticians are exclusively located) can be crossed.

The analytical level is subordinate to the real level, in more ways than one. The important assumptions on the analytical level – not least the axioms – should also be evaluated on whether they are 'realistic'. All assumptions are to varying degrees unrealistic. A classic example of such an unrealistic assumption is 'perfect foresight' or permanent 'market clearing', which on the other hand has a crucial impact on the analytical result.

It is here that Popper's scientific method comes into the picture. His requirement for falsification testing should be taken seriously, as it is the most important demarcation between science and ideology. This requirement is relatively easy to formulate, but as Blaug (1980 [1992]) pointed out, it is often more difficult to perform in practice. The consequence of a positive outcome from a falsification test (that the hypothesis in its current form must be rejected) should not be overinterpreted, since all hypotheses and analytical results are 'false' in a theory-of-science perspective. A demand for full agreement between reality, theory and empirical tests would inevitably lead to scientific nihilism. This is a view that a number of Popper's critics have attributed to him, while Popper himself is more concerned with the strength of empirical corroboration that can be attributed to the theory based on the available evidence.

Critical realism seeks to unite reality (World 1), analysis (World 2) and practice (World 3) through the acquisition of new knowledge that is constantly confronted with reality. It is a methodology that should be used in a complex world with conflicting interests and an incomplete understanding of reality.

This is also the macroeconomic methodological challenge.

APPENDIX 2.1:   AN EXAMPLE OF THE HYPOTHETICAL-DEDUCTIVE METHOD, LIMITED TO THE ANALYTICAL LEVEL WITHIN 'MODERN' MACROECONOMIC THEORY: THE GENERAL EQUILIBRIUM MODEL

One of Denmark's most acknowledged macroeconomists, Torben M. Andersen, stands as an exponent of hypothetical-deductive methodology. Here the analytical model is represented by idealized macroeconomics. In 2000, he wrote a review article on the status of modern macro-theory. On that occasion he presented the methodological foundation as follows:

> The purpose of theoretical analyses is to construct a laboratory for testing various hypotheses.
> Modern macro-theory has the following methodological similarities:
>
> > ... [it is] focusing on optimizing behaviour, that is systematically driven by economic incentives. (If this were not the case, then the problem falls outside of the economist's realm of expertise.)
> > ... the analytical framework consists of general equilibrium models.
> > ... individuals have an infinite timeline (or an overlapping generations model for identical agents).
> > ... individuals maintain rational (model-consistent) expectations.
>
> The aspects of method enumerated here serve the purpose of giving the analysis consistency and discipline, insofar as we wish to discover if a given problem can be described as a variation in the systematic economic behaviour. In some parts of the newer macroeconomic literature, there is a tendency to say that 'the method is the message'. This is misleading. The selection of method gives the analysis discipline and consistency, and thereby demarcates a 'laboratory' for the analysis. (Andersen, 2000: 21–2, my translation)

The methodological foundation for so-called 'modern macroeconomics' is described in an admirably precise way. The mathematically formulated general equilibrium model constitutes the practical device for developing and testing hypotheses concerning the understanding of macroeconomic development. In the laboratory of the thought experiment, the social ontology plays no direct part; all results are measured according to the ideal. The connection with reality is conveniently replaced by a non-existent ideal. It is, in the true meaning of the word, a closed model, where everything is under control. It could not be written any clearer than here, that the method defines the practice upon which the analytical results depend.

In short, the neoclassical school has opted to place its main emphasis on the hypothetical-deductive method, with its theoretical-scientific roots in the tradition of logical positivism. Neoclassical macro-theory is built on a foundation of a few fundamental hypotheses and axioms concerning: (1) individual rational behaviour; (2) market clearing; and (3) a stable long-term equilibrium. Work is conducted within the method-related confines that Léon Walras established in the 1870s, to be later perfected in the Arrow–Debreu models in the 1950s. The model-related foundation is a deductively derived general equilibrium model from which the subsequent macroeconomic analyses are conducted (see Andersen, 2000). This research strategy means that already, in the background, a dissonance exits between the subject's ontology, characterized by macroeconomic uncertainty, and the practised epistemology, seen in the founding method of analysing by means of a deterministic (closed) system. The laboratory model is, in a scientific-theoretical perspective, intended to be closed, again because the intention is to conduct controlled experiments. The degree to which macroeconomic uncertainty can be explicitly included in such 'laboratory trials' is discussed in Chapter 5. Is a deterministic model relevant for analyses where ontological uncertainty plays such a dominating role? The degree to which the basic axioms and the method employed can limit the generality of the results in relation to reality will similarly be discussed in a later chapter in relation to the meaning of the so-called 'fallacy of composition' in macroeconomic theory. This particular discussion requires that an alternative scientific-theoretical methodology is made explicit.

APPENDIX 2.2: LAWSON'S FOUR CRITICAL THESES AGAINST 'MODERN ECONOMICS' PRACTISED WITHIN THE FRAMEWORK OF 'THE LABORATORY MODEL'

Lawson's four theses are quickly stated:

> 1: Academic economics is currently dominated to a very significant degree by a mainstream tradition or orthodoxy, the essence of which is an insistence on methods of mathematical-deductivist modelling.
> 2: This mainstream project is not in too healthy a condition.
> 3: A major reason why the mainstream project performs so poorly is that mathematical-deductivist methods are being applied in conditions for which they are not appropriate.
> 4: Despite ambitions to the contrary, the modern mainstream project mostly serves to constrain economics from realising its (nevertheless real) potential to be not only explanatorily powerful, but scientific in the sense of natural science.
> (Lawson, 2003: 3)

As has been put forth in the four theses stated above, Lawson is sceptical (to put it mildly) in his assessment of the relevance of the work being conducted within the four walls of the economic laboratory. His main objection is the exaggerated use of mathematics on a social ontology that is not suited to analysis by means of mathematically formulated models. It requires that the elements and reciprocal relationships included in the analysis are deterministically defined, that 'the area is closed off' from further influences, and agents act individually and repetitively. These are conditions that are poorly reflected in the ontological reality, which Lawson hopes to be able to observe:

> My concern at this stage, though, is to emphasise that with mathematical methods being insisted upon by the mainstream but regarded as *in*essential by heterodox traditions and others, we can see that the various strands of orthodoxy have not only a common, but also a distinguishing, feature after all. This, as I say, just is the *insistence* that the mathematical-deductivist methods be used in just about all endeavour to advance knowledge of phenomena regarded as economic ... (Lawson, 2003: 8)

Lawson focuses on the use of mathematics and the precedence of the deductive method as the demarcation line for whether mainstream economists observe a theory, a method and an analysis for 'economics' – see for example Varian (1999), cited in the introductory chapter.

Although I (in line with Lawson and a number of internationally renowned economists – including Nobel Prize winners quoted by Lawson) often feel that the requirement to use mathematical deduction has gone too far, not least because its use goes beyond the relevant and valid domain of deductive method in economics, it is, in the end, up to each and every researcher to ensure congruence between ontology and method. So long as one specific method is not forced upon the whole of macroeconomic reasoning the use of mathematics is not controversial by itself. This point is aptly described in Chick's work (1998), 'On knowing one's place: formalism in economics'.

I would rather see the requirement of correspondence between ontology and epistemology formulated in a more explicit way, by developing macroeconomic theory and models used as a basis for the eventual categorization of macroeconomic theory. I am here influenced by Keynes's clear distinction between economics which has an explicit ontological assumption that the market is self-regulating, and economics where the social ontology is under constant change and the development is path-dependent without being self-regulating. However, in his 1936 book, Keynes portrays the equilibrium model as an integrated special case, as a part of a new, open-system ontology. The open system is thus an overarching term, wherein closed equilibrium economics can be used, where a number of quite often rather unrealistic assumptions must be fulfilled. I find this to be a better explanation than giving a very formal analysis of why 'closed equilibrium economics', in the best-case scenario, has such a limited usefulness (at least within macroeconomic theory). I will expand upon the issues surrounding the use of formalized analysis in macroeconomics in Appendix 6.1, Chapter 6.

NOTES

1. It is in this perspective that the assumption of 'rational expectations' can be understood. Originally, in Muth (1961), the basic assumption of rational expectations-formation entailed that actors were assumed to utilize all available information as best they could. This assumption at first glance seems realistic and plausible. It only becomes indisputably unrealistic when its content is altered to an assumption that actors have full knowledge of the model's long-term outcome (meaning they can foretell the future). The assumption of full information implies a number of simplifications in the analysis, not least its technical nature, but prevents the model's results from being applicable to reality.
2. It was explained in the previous chapter that the so-called second neoclassical labour market postulate, which concerns firms' microeconomically-based demand for labour, was not in conflict with Keynes's macroeconomic model.
3. The inspiration for this three-worlds metaphor is from Popper (1999); but my use of World 3 as a semi-reality, where analytical results is applied, deviates from Popper's definition of World 3.
4. A Norwegian post-Keynesian methodologist.
5. Friedman (1953) cuts through this issue with ease by looking away from the realism of the assumptions. For him, it is enough that the model is good at making predictions, but not why it is good at making predictions. For me, it is a perspective that hinders

the understanding of the kinds of causal mechanisms that are at play behind the predictions. In this way, it is made impossible to assess the validity of the theory beyond the limited field of prediction where it has been tested. This fundamental weakness with Friedman's instrumental approach is due to the fact that the validity of the results is somewhat doubtful when the realism of the model's empirical basis is not evaluated.

6. The problem is known from, for example, neoclassical consumption theory, where it is impossible to test the hypothesis of 'utility maximization' on the basis of observed consumption data alone, except for inconsistencies. One cannot disprove the hypothesis that the consumer had maximized his expected benefit. To do so demands experimental attempts such as Richard Layard (2005) and others have described. Popper names Freud's psychoanalysis as an example of a hypothesis that must remain a hypothesis as it cannot be falsified, because neuroses are attributed to unknown traumas. This does not exclude the possibility that Freud's theories are apt descriptions – only that they cannot be tested, and until they can, the results cannot be called scientific.

7. The so-called 'stylized facts', an expression that is associated with Kaldor, involve a development whereby empirically-backed statements risk gradually becoming indisputable axioms.

8. Blaug (1980 [1992]) uses the name 'critical rationalist' to describe Popper's theoretical approach, as he narrowly attributes the name 'critical realist' to the limited approach represented by Bhaskar and Lawson described below. Surprisingly, Blaug (2002) later characterizes the latter as 'postmodern', using the argumentation extending from the expression 'transcendental realism'.

9. Beautifully described in Weintraub (1985).

10. The attachment of epistemological relativism to ontological realism facilitates a judgemental rationality (Lawson, 1997: 59).

11. A purely ideological system is without an empirical foundation.

12. It is a well-known problem within the natural sciences that whole entities cannot always be analysed on the basis of smaller entities (atoms). Biological organisms are not wholly described by their chemical structure, for example. Medical analyses must include both the biological and the human and social factors if they want to claim to be complete. F. Capra has written an important book about this subject, *The Turning Point* (*Vendepunktet*) (1986).

13. One should not underestimate how great a leap in the direction of a realistic explanation of natural phenomena Newton's theories were in their day, which only underlines that the critical perspective, in all scientific research, should never slip out of view.

14. Hawking (1988) is a fascinating book about the history of the natural sciences, whereby unexpected observations, when first seen, were pushed aside, understood as the result of analytical or observational mistakes, and only much later became the foundation for a reorientation of the dominant theories. Such examples can also be found within macroeconomics: a number of 'inexplicable' phenomena during the crisis in the 1930s were a source of inspiration for establishing the Keynesian research programme, whereby the domain of the previously closed model was reduced to that of a special case.

15. There is a notable example from the Danish political debate. A group of neoclassical economists were asked to make a report on the economic development in the Danish economy for the next 35 years. They used a general equilibrium model, DREAM, where agents were assumed to form rational expectations. The concluding policy recommendations were delivered to World 3 without reservations related to the unrealistic assumptions underlying the calculations made by the DREAM model.

16. As will be described later in the chapter, an open system is not only understood as a negation of a closed system; it is not either/or. The word 'open' is used in the sense that within the selected cognitive frame there is openness to everything that is possible – also the unforeseeable. An open model can include a closed model as a special case. In the same way, determinate should not merely be understood as the duality of indeterminate, rather as one possibility in an indeterminate (and therefore open) system.

17. Once again we run into semantic ambiguity. Keynes, in the title of his masterpiece, *The*

General Theory, gave the word 'general' an ontological meaning, in that his new theory could explain a greater number of real phenomena than the existing theory. In connection with general equilibrium theory, the term 'general' indicates that the analytical model deals with a greater number of markets, in contrast to partial equilibrium of just one market.

18. His books are by no means light reading. They are quite clear in their critique of neo-classical, mainstream economics; but, though they are both over 300 pages long, it is surprisingly difficult to grasp 'critical realism' as a scientific-theoretical tool.

19. I have in another context used the iceberg as an image of the ontological stratification. The empirical top can be observed above the surface, but it is the 90 per cent under the surface that is critical for shipping.

20. Described in *Essays in Positive Economics* (Friedman, 1953).

21. It is acceptable that the explanation is counter-intuitive (cf. for example the savings paradox) but impermissible that it be in conflict with empirical observation. The theory may conclude that the sun is the solar system's gravitational centre, as long as the theory also can explain why 'the sun moves across the celestial sphere'.

22. The more I work with these terms, the more I find that the word 'reason', or in Latin *ratio*, covers this methodological practice, which bases itself on applied sense (that which we in generally refer to as 'common sense'): 'Are there reasons to believe that x has been caused by a mechanism (let us call it 'f') mainly depending on $y, \ldots, z$? Are there reasons to believe that the tendency behind $f(y, \ldots, z)$ also will be valid in the future taking properly into consideration that (a) the system is open, (b) the structure is uncertain and (c) causal relationships are stochastic (with a hardly known mean and variance)' Lawson (1997).

23. The use of 'as if' assumptions, the somewhat archaic use of language and the assumption of a transcendent level have together contributed to giving critical realism linguistic trappings that upon a superficial reading point in the direction of rhetoric, as used within the postmodern tradition. It is possible that this led to Blaug's (2002) aforementioned confusion, and consequent rejection, of critical realism as an irrelevant economic methodology.

24. Here Pålsson Syll refers to Sheila Dow (1996: 18) and others as supporters of this view, and thereby underlines the affinity with post-Keynesian methodology.

25. Note that I constantly underline that it is macroeconomics that is the object of my analysis. For me, one of the more dangerous generalizations can be seen in Lawson. He is largely concerned with microeconomics but unconditionally calls his books *Economics and Reality* (1997) and *Reorienting Economics* (2003).

26. Keynes writes near the end of *The General Theory*: 'Our criticism of the accepted classical theory of economics has consisted not so much in finding logical flaws in its analysis as in pointing out that its tacit assumptions are seldom or never satisfied, with the result that it cannot solve the economic problems of the actual world' (Keynes, 1936: 378).

3. The macroeconomic landscape: an example of an ontological reflection

The general [Post-Keynesian] methodological approach is an open system approach, involving collections of partial analyses that aim to build up a (fallible) knowledge of different aspects of socioeconomic systems. Rather than relying on a single, formal method, a range of methods are employed (formal, institutional, and historical for example) that draw on different types of evidence. (Dow, 2001: 16–17)

THE SOCIALLY EMBEDDED MACROECONOMIC VISION

The subject of this book is macroeconomic methodology as a means of understanding 'the economy as a whole', an expression often used by Keynes to demarcate his field of research. No macroeconomic phenomenon can be analysed in a state of isolation. The macroeconomic system is an interconnected whole. A realistic macroeconomic approach requires the development of a macroeconomic theory and method that correspond to the social reality. It is the relevance of the theory and method that determines the quality of the knowledge we are able to acquire. For this reason I will first illustrate the macroeconomic perspective in a context that comprises society as a whole. I will then review a series of simplifications of reality, which will provide a basis for a realistic macroeconomic analysis.

The overall dynamics of society has to be considered as an interconnected process. In this perspective, the macroeconomic phenomena are connected with the other social sciences in a common 'social reality'. They are, in the words of Karl Polanyi, 'socially embedded'. The division into disciplines such as economics, law, politics and sociology tends to create a set of artificial barriers that hinder interdisciplinary analyses.

It is particularly difficult to distinguish the disciplines when the purpose is to understand the evolution of the welfare state. 'Welfare' is by itself a multidisciplinary concept where numerous individual activities and social structures and institutions interfere: for example, a well-functioning, representative democracy, the rule of law, employment, access to basic social goods, a social community, protection of the environment and so on. In addition to personal abilities, these conditions determine the quality of life of every individual. The framework conditions created by the welfare state should be perceived analytically in the perspective of society as a whole, because the common institutions are factors of great importance for the quality of life considered as a multidimensional phenomenon. Such a total analysis of society is a challenge on a scale far beyond the ambitions of this book.

My ambition is of a more limited character. I attempt to develop an adequate methodology for understanding the driving forces behind the macroeconomic development, understood as just one dimension of the welfare system. As we know, Keynes focused on employment and 'output as a whole', especially on how to create full employment. This choice of focus was first and foremost because full employment is an important condition for obtaining individual freedom. In this sense, Keynes was a liberal. To him, collective regulation could be a remedy for increased individual freedom – to the extent that these two phenomena can even be viewed separately. A title such as that of his 1926 essay 'The end of laissez-faire' (*CWK*, IX: 272–94) is characteristic of the economic philosophy of Keynes, since a *laissez-faire* policy – by way of totally market-based economic development – will restrict individual freedom, due to the risk of involuntary unemployment and poverty (see also Keynes, 1936: Chapter 24).

In Figure 3.1, I have made an attempt to illustrate this point of social embeddedness, that a macroeconomic analysis cannot be carried out independently of the social context in which it operates. Instead, the starting point of such an analysis has to be the social totality. Ideally, an interdisciplinary analysis should be conducted of the essential societal

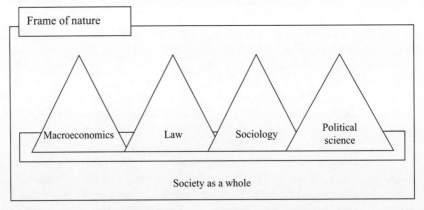

Figure 3.1   Macroeconomics as a subdiscipline of social sciences

circumstances that constitute the welfare society. As mentioned, an analysis of such scope would require a comprehensive process, which would entail a multitude of simplifying assumptions that could undermine the realism of the analysis. Conversely, a narrow focus on a single discipline would mean that relevant aspects would be omitted and the realism would thereby be constrained. There is no theoretical answer to this problem.

For practical reasons, the macroeconomic researcher is left with no other option than to set up boundaries for the societal totality. This can be done as part of the ontological reflection, where the researcher creates a preliminary division of the totality into a number of submodels that each consist of one well-defined social-scientific discipline. In the area of each discipline, an even more partial analysis can be conducted, which will ensure a deeper understanding of, in our case, the macroeconomic perspective. These partial analyses are by no means uncomplicated. To begin with, they must be conducted in accordance with the assumption that the sociological, legal and environmental circumstances maintain the *status quo*. Since it is an analytical violation to freeze parts of the research field, it is vitally important to consider this circumstance when the macroeconomic results are interpreted in the social context. It is for example hard to imagine that a high and persistent level of unemployment will not have an impact upon the general attitude towards being unemployed or on labour market legislation, which will change the way the labour market functions. Likewise, a strong growth rate will change the work and production conditions, for example through a degradation of the environment.

Differences within Macroeconomic Ontology

As described in the introductory chapter, several macroeconomic schools exist, each with their own perception of the theory of science. These divergent perceptions make communication about macroeconomic issues within the discipline difficult. There is, especially, one dividing line that creates a gulf of disagreement: the question of whether the macroeconomic system is self-stabilizing. The neoclassical tradition relies on the axiom that a perfectly functioning, atomistic market economy will, if left to itself, establish a general equilibrium.

The post-Keynesian macroeconomic school represents the opposite viewpoint in this analytical question. It is argued that given the macroeconomic system's embeddedness in the entire societal totality – not least including the fundamental uncertainty that applies to future development, both on the micro- and macro-levels, it would be unrealistic *a priori* to assume that this system should be self-regulating towards a social optimum. Within post-Keynesian theory, the societal reality is under analytical focus. Here individual behaviour is characterized by uncertainty, partly caused by the systemic macro-uncertainty, which primarily relates to the unknowable macroeconomic development because no predetermined centre of gravitation is assumed to exist.

It is evident from this short description of the ontological ambition of these two macroeconomic schools that the two approaches, one based on an ideal market system and methodological individualism and the other based on an 'economy as a whole' methodology with explicit emphasis on uncertainty, could hardly be more different.

Epistemology defines the boundaries of our knowledge. It is important therefore that theory and method are adapted to reflect the ontology of the field of study. In post-Keynesian macroeconomic research, the methodological criteria are dictated by the requirement of realism, in the sense of faithful reflection of uncertainty. Hence, macroeconomic theory and method must be realistic in order to meet the criterion of relevance, a requirement that can be tested on an empirical basis, for example. Theory, method of analysis and empirical material should be viewed as comprising an integrated whole that constitutes the methodology.

However, the requirement for realism should not get in the way of the equally important requirement that macroeconomic theory should be 'operational'. In the development of relevant theories to fill in the framework of the chosen model, it is inevitable that the complexity of the macroeconomic reality is reduced through both simplification and abstraction. This cannot be avoided if the macro-theory is to be used for analytical purposes, but finding a balance between simplification and abstraction on the one hand, and empirical relevance on the other, requires a considerable insight into the practice of scientific research.

This balancing act has given rise to the establishment of the scientific school called critical realism within the social sciences, presented in Chapter 2 (see especially, Lawson, 1997). One of the main premises of critical realism is the philosophical axiom that, in the social sciences, social reality exists independently of the scientific research undertaken.[1] One of the purposes of this research is to provide political decision-makers with a deeper insight into causalities and correlations in the macroeconomic processes. Thus, research can (indirectly) be the cause of changes in social reality.

In the social sciences, it is an epistemological problem that many social structures are not readily observable. The methodology of critical realism differs from positivism, for example, by including factors such as market forces, competitive power and institutional relations as explanatory factors of causality, although these do not readily allow observation, not to mention quantification. Social reality is affected by underlying structures, institutions and sets of rules of conduct, which also have a bearing on economic behaviour. An important justification for using the term 'critical realism' for this theoretical school is that it seeks to include relevant economic and societal factors, even though they may not be readily observable.

Thus, an effort has been made to ensure that the macroeconomic methodology used here is solidly anchored in reality. Accordingly, it should not contradict empirical observations without explanation, but may, on the other hand, accept arguments that are not directly observable. Herein lies the real theoretical challenge that critical realism can help to solve. The recommended procedure for meeting the methodological requirements of critical realism can be summarized in a number of points:

1. Initial ontological reflection. For instance, this could be an overall mapping of the topography of the field of study – a so-called macroeconomic landscape.
2. With this landscape as a starting point, the formulation of macroeconomic theories and hypotheses can be undertaken. This is performed on the basis of a retroductive procedure that aims to create correspondence between ontology and epistemology, which in turn will contribute to the fulfilment of the criterion of relevance.
3. Concrete hypotheses of causal relations ('macro-behaviour' functions) are evaluated in relation to the macroeconomic reality in order to discover whether they are consistent, realistic, empirically confirmed and relevant.
4. Results from a macroeconomic analysis should in the end be evaluated against the background of the imposed and often rather controversial (and unrealistic) assumptions, before any policy recommendations are issued with regard to employment, inflation, balance of payments and so on. In any case, results are always open to interpretation and it will be difficult, if not impossible, to reach an unambiguous conclusion.

Each and every macroeconomic analysis cannot start completely from scratch. It is useful to have a kind of macroeconomic framework. Here, the macroeconomic landscape could be a relevant starting point, also for macroeconomic research with a more limited scope. The structure of the landscape should be grounded in reality, but could also build upon an existing theoretical understanding created through previous post-Keynesian macroeconomic research and disseminated via post-Keynesian textbooks, for instance Arestis (1992), Jespersen (2005) and Godley and Lavoie (2007).

AN ONTOLOGICAL REFLECTION: A SKETCH OF A MACROECONOMIC LANDSCAPE

As described in the previous chapter, there are two parallel traditions of methodology within macroeconomic research:

1. Methodological individualism and closed system reasoning, including the axiom of the individual's rational behaviour and the requirement of general equilibrium. It is theoretically rooted in deductivism and logical positivism.
2. Socially embedded macroeconomic theory based on open system reasoning with a deliberate affinity to reality (the economy as a whole).

As already mentioned, this book will generally keep within the boundaries of Keynes-inspired macroeconomic theory. The main purpose is to provide a presentation that can be used for realistic analyses of concrete, historical development patterns. Therefore, this chapter contains a short description of the main structures in the suggested 'macroeconomic landscape'. One could say that setting up this sketch of a macroeconomic landscape is a first step into World 2. The three following chapters will discuss how an analysis, within the framework of an open system, can be undertaken within macroeconomics.

The structure of the macroeconomic system is highly complex. This complexity is due to the fact that macroeconomic variables do not develop independently – not even when viewed in a short-term perspective. In other words: everything is interrelated. In addition, the macroeconomic landscape is not stationary. If a 'landslide' takes place somewhere, it will inevitably have related consequences elsewhere. Any introductory, ontological description of the macroeconomic landscape, therefore, will necessarily be superficial; the presentation in this chapter merely covers the most important market structures, institutions and 'macro-actors' and aims at being 'neutral' in terms of methodology. Similarly with the categories of the national accounting system; these ought to be independent of whichever theoretical school is subsequently used as the basis for the macroeconomic analysis. The theoretical danger zone lies in the postulated hypotheses as to how the landscape's component parts mutually affect each other and to what degree they are interconnected by the shared underlying structures.

The macroeconomic landscape viewed as a whole is important because, as already mentioned, no macroeconomic phenomenon can be analysed independently of the context. Once the contours of the overall picture of the macroeconomic landscape have been drawn up, it becomes possible to zoom in on the specific markets and institutions, the labour market for instance. Here, more specific theories can be developed, for example with regard to the interconnection between labour supply and the welfare system. Next, these labour market theories will – if they are empirically substantiated – be incorporated into the macroeconomic landscape in the form of elaborated labour market relations. It is necessary to study the economy as a whole if we wish to avoid what are known as 'fallacies of composition' within macroeconomics. The purpose of creating a preliminary analytical, macroeconomic landscape is that it may function as a relevant, initial representation of the 'whole', which can then be used as inspiration for creating more detailed hypotheses combined with the use of an adequate method.

In a metaphoric sense, what is directly observed of the macroeconomic landscape is merely the tip of an iceberg.[2] The genuine macroeconomic task is to develop a theory for how the whole of the iceberg changes over time and to develop a corresponding method for this purpose. Together, theory and method should provide an understanding of the workings of the whole of the macroeconomic landscape, as well as of the causal relations and structures determining the way in which it changes through time. We retain the iceberg metaphor for a moment, for it illustrates that only 10 per cent of the macroeconomic system can be directly observed. In this case, it is reasonable to claim that it is largely the underlying structures, which cannot be observed, that determine the appearance of the tip of the iceberg, as well as how it changes through time.

Thus, a full understanding of the landscape's topology requires that a comprehensive and dynamic macroeconomic theory is developed, one which operates within the framework of an open model of analysis, since the 'iceberg' is in a state of constant change. This theoretical construct must provide a set of the causal relations that can explain the macroeconomic events that are manifest in, for example, the national accounting statistics.

So, macroeconomic theory differs significantly from microeconomic theory in having to explain aggregate statistical entities, which as a rule are not directly observable. Who can claim, for instance, to have seen a consumer price index, a balance of payments deficit or a gross domestic product? Unemployment is also a statistical concept that can be defined in a number of different ways. We do not doubt that unemployment is a real phenomenon, since real people are without work in the labour market. In cases where the unemployment figure stays unchanged from one month to the next, the composition of individuals adding up to that number is under continuous change. This movement in and out of unemployment is of course crucial to the individuals, but it does not change the macroeconomic landscape. The purpose of this chapter is to outline a framework that can serve to explain and elucidate a few central, macroeconomic variables, thereby providing an understanding of their development. This can be used to shed light on society's prosperity, significant imbalances that are central in the planning of macroeconomic policy, and investors' overall evaluation of the soundness of the economic development.

SOME STRUCTURES IN THE MACROECONOMIC LANDSCAPE

The macroeconomic landscape consists of a few discrete macro-markets. Each of these 'markets' constitutes a structurally determined framework for the exchange of a specific type of economic commodity, for instance the labour market, the money and capital market, and the market for goods and services. For analytical purposes, the trade on these markets can be split into an aggregate macro-amount and an aggregate macro-price, determined by the aggregate macro-behaviour and macro-institutions that together shape the causal relations.

Macro-markets are connected by these 'causal relations' – represented in Figure 3.2 by 'flow arrows'. They represent significant, empirically supported tendencies based on theories about macro-actors' behaviour. Together, macro-markets, macro-actors and macro-behaviour relations constitute a macroeconomic system as illustrated in Figure 3.2.

A macro-market constitutes the institutional framework of a specific, macroeconomic activity that can be viewed as a separate organization or organism in the overall macroeconomic ontology. In other words, it can be singled out. A certain amount of exchange takes place on these macro-markets in terms of volume. This exchange takes place on the basis of contracts, which can be of a very different nature, depending on how the market in question is organized.

The organization of the macro-market will be partially determined historically and partially determined by the type of economic transaction. As we shall see in the following sections, it makes a difference whether services, physical goods or financial assets are under consideration. Production conditions, the physical properties and the economic lifespan of the commodity are crucial factors. In addition to the above, the amount of information available on the quality of the product and on cancellation costs are all factors that influence the content of contracts linked to the transaction. There is a difference between a job contract (even more so in the case of a wage contract that covers a whole section of the labour market) and a contract for the trade of foreign currency. The latter can be

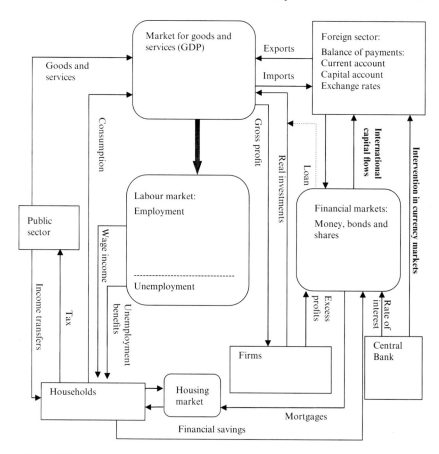

Figure 3.2   A macroeconomic landscape

a spot transaction (delivery of the currency on the spot), but more often a forward contract is used, where the currency is to be delivered at some specified time in the future, which makes the contract more resemble an insurance agreement. The organization of the market will also depend on the other characteristics of the traded goods – what is being traded: labour, houses, shares or foreign currency? Here, norms, traditions and conventions also play an important role.

The total turnover on a macro-market (for instance measured by the expected change in gross domestic product, GDP) can be split into two macro-variables: a volume index measured in aggregate physical units, and a corresponding aggregate price index. These two indexes are not directly observable at the aggregate level, but rather are a statistical

---

MACRO-MARKETS

Goods and services market (production)
Labour market
Money, bonds and shares markets (financial sector)
Foreign currency market
Housing market

MACRO-AMOUNTS (INDEXES)

Production and economic growth
Employment and unemployment
Financial intermediation
The current account on the balance of payments and capital flows
Private wealth (for example in houses and flats)

MACRO-PRICES (INDEXES)

Price level and price inflation
Money wage and income distribution
Long- and short-term interest rate
Effective exchange rate
Real-estate price and rent

---

construction of the historical development. However, the observed values of macro-variables reveal nothing about whether there has been equilibrium – so-called market clearing – on the markets in question. For this we need a macroeconomic theory that describes the expected demand, the desired supply, how price and volume adjust to imbalances, and the interactions with the rest of the macroeconomic system.

Will a completely flexible wage, price and interest rate development ensure a macroeconomic 'market clearing' on these markets? According to macroeconomic logic, this question cannot be answered unless a complete macroeconomic analysis is carried out, which includes the macro-markets' reciprocal interaction. Wages are an expense for firms, but they also finance wage-earners' demand for consumption goods and housing. Real investment also constitutes a simultaneous demand for physical goods and a supply of financial assets for financing. Imports are a demand for goods and services from abroad, as well as being demand for foreign currency to pay for the foreign products.

Using only one macro-market for the entire exchange of all goods and services is quite an abstraction. Figuratively speaking, this amounts to saying that all firms produce identical items of GDP. This premise is not acceptable if the composition of production in terms of product categories and services is important. On the other hand, if the purpose is merely to describe the overall tendency in the growth rate in production viewed as a whole, and thus in income development and employment, operating with a single market for the entire GDP does indeed make sense.

As described in Chapter 1, market structures can vary considerably. Some markets are organized as flex-price and fix-price markets respectively. The reasons for this are partly historical and partly structural. On a flex-price market, a change in demand will register primarily as a change in prices, which is an indication to manufacturers to adjust the level of output. On fix-price markets, on the other hand, a change in demand will result in a change in the volume of turnover, which in turn will result in an adjustment of production and prices.

Flex-price is most common in the so-called 'bulk markets', where raw materials, manufactured products or financial assets of a standardized nature are traded and where production is continuously adjusted according to the total supply. Examples are the trade in raw materials, semi-conductors and agricultural produce, where prices can vary considerably according to expectations of the supply the following day, month or next year. News of frost in Brazil or conflict in the Middle East immediately pushes up prices of coffee and oil respectively.

Fix-price markets can be found in most markets for finished goods and services. In fix-price markets, most production is contract work or work to order, where the volume of output is determined by the expected final sales. The less uncertainty there is regarding the market price of the finished product, the easier it is to convert expected demand to a specific physical volume of production and thus determine the appropriate number of orders. Many manufacturers of goods can, if there is spare capacity, regulate the level of output more easily than can farmers and producers of raw materials. For this reason, in fix-price markets, supply follows demand (in terms of volume) at a semi-constant price, which ensures profit on the entire production.

Larger investment contracts can neither be classified as flex-price or

fix-price. These are usually put up for sale by public tender, where the final
contract depends on a number of economic factors.

The market for services is dominated by employment in the public
sector, where wages are normally fixed according to the current wage
agreement. Conditions are similar in large areas of the private service
sector – the retail trade, transport, and the hotel and restaurant business –
where prices do not whiz up and down with minor fluctuations in demand.
However, if the actual labour market were entirely unorganized, there
would be a risk that wage determination governed by the flex-price principle would vary quite considerably. As labour cannot be stored, supply will
be quite inelastic, especially for people without private wealth or unemployment insurance. This would mean that minor fluctuations in effective
demand[3] would be reflected as changes in wage levels, which would cause
instability in the whole fix-price sector and on the labour market. Both
employers and employees are interested in having predictable costs and
income. For this reason, wage determination in the organized part of the
labour market moved towards longer-term contracts with a considerable
fix-price element in the late nineteenth century, a development which
continued until the 1980s in most countries. Since there has been a change
in direction towards more flexibility in labour contracts, elements of individual wage adjustment have come to play an increasingly important role
in collective agreements.

The currency market is another example of a market where the institutional conditions play a crucial role in procedure of price determination.
Some countries have chosen to have a floating exchange rate, a flex-
price, while other countries have a fixed but adjustable exchange rate. In
Denmark and several other EU countries, it has been decided to keep the
exchange rate fixed in relation to the euro within a limit of ±2.25 per cent
around the central exchange rate. Other countries within the European
Union have given up their own currency. Whichever form of currency
management is chosen, it will have far-reaching consequences for how the
macroeconomy as a whole functions, especially under the current, increasing rate of internationalization.

The macro-price on the property and housing market plays an important role in the development of the private sector's wealth, and also affects
activity in the construction sector. Existing houses and flats constitute
the bulk of the supply. However, the demand from the actual owners is
largely unaffected by prices, since they have a home and need a home and
it is pretty costly to move from one house to another. So, prices in the
housing market are determined by the balance between the supply of new
properties and the net demand from newly established households, determined by demographic factors in combination with expected income and

interest rates. At any rate, in a longer-term perspective, the macro-price on the housing market cannot deviate much from the cost of building a new house.

The financial macro-market has a structure similar to that of the flex-price market described above. Here, government bonds, mortgage bonds and shares are traded on a transparent market, where the price continuously changes so that supply and demand are in tune. The banking system, on the other hand, has more of a fix-price structure, where the 'price', banks' interest rates on loans, follows the rate of interest set by the central bank. Accordingly, bank customers may experience varying degrees of credit rationing together with changing interest on bank loans.

Macroeconomic transactions are 'carried out' and contracts are 'entered into' by 'macro-actors'. A macro-actor is merely an analytical construction. Macro-households, macro-firms, macro-wage-earners and macro-consumers are all phantoms used analytically to visualize the basic, causal relations that knit the macroeconomy together. Naturally, these phantoms are not to be found in the real world; they are used to demonstrate the fact that macro-behaviour relations cannot be exhaustively accounted for by a single, representative micro-agent's 'optimal behaviour'. Here we are moving along the fine borderline between, on the one hand, the requirement of realism and on the other hand, the recognition of the fact that some phenomena are analytical constructions that do not exist literally.

This is an important point, since it maintains that there is no explicit assumption concerning the 'correct' microeconomic behaviour in this analytical representation of the macroeconomic system. There is not necessarily any theoretical contradiction between an assumption of individual optimizing behaviour, as we know it from traditional microeconomic theory, and the macroeconomic behaviour relations suggested in the landscape. On the other hand, it is just as important to emphasize that, even if the individual agents' behaviour is in accordance with neoclassical microeconomic theory, relevant aggregate macroeconomic behaviour relations cannot, except for very unrealistic cases, be consistently described by the behaviour of a single representative micro-agent; see Kirman (1992), Hartley (1997) and others.

The apparently intrinsic dispute between micro- and macro-theory stems from the fundamental assumption in microeconomic theory that the optimal, individual behaviour can be determined according to the *ceteris paribus* condition – meaning, subject to the prerequisite that all other factors remain unchanged. This can be a relevant and realistic assumption on the micro-level, but it has little validity on the macro-level, where everything is interrelated. The *ceteris paribus* condition has the consequence for microeconomic theory that optimal behaviour can be determined under the assumption that market prices and output are unaffected by the individual agents' behaviour, that is, that they remain unchanged. The individual is characterized as an 'atom' that has no ability to affect the whole. The behaviour of the atom can be analysed as not having any noticeable effect on the economy.[4]

The behaviour of macroeconomic actors, on the other hand, has a direct effect on both the market price and the volume traded on the market where the transactions take place. This invariably affects macro-actors' expectations, and at the same time it has an effect on the behaviour of other macro-actors. Consequently, in the macroeconomic landscape *ceteris* is never *paribus*. When that is understood, the fallacy of composition is more easily avoided (see Chapter 7).

It is convenient to distinguish between three different types of macro-actors. Firstly, a group of private individuals, aggregated to form a 'macro-actor'. This could typically be the entire household sector or all private firms, where this delimitation is relevant. These macro-actors perform clearly distinctive activities in the macroeconomic landscape. Households have the mixed roles of being consumers, workers, home-owners and accumulators of savings (see Figure 3.2). The role of firms is primarily to determine the volume of production, the extent of real investment and external financing. In reality, these groups of macro-actors are not homogeneous of course, since they are comprised of a large number of individual units, each with their own unique characteristics. Therefore, the behaviour of macro-actors depends on both group-internal circumstances, for example distribution, credit rationing and behavioural norms, and exogenous events and structures. So, macro-behaviour is always context-dependent and influenced by how the rest of the macroeconomic landscape is structured and organized.

Secondly, we have to deal with private organizations: in the labour market they could be employers' associations, trade unions, and in the goods market we find wholesale societies and larger national and transnational firms. The outcome of labour market negotiations cannot be understood without a thorough description of labour market organizations and their power structures. The credit market is dominated by the banking system and related legislation. These kinds of macro-actors are of such a size that, when planning their behaviour, they have to take account of the effects of their behaviour on the rest of the economy, even though they have to work in the best interests of their members. Employers' organizations and trade unions cannot agree, for instance, on a 10 per cent pay rise without considering the consequences for the international competitive position, total production and employment, as well as possible political reactions.

Thirdly, public institutions are considered. The government and other public authorities play a particularly important role. The government has legislative powers to change both its own behaviour and the structural framework of the private (macro-) behaviour.

These macro-actors are ascribed a macro-behaviour which underlies the causal relations that create the macroeconomic interrelationships and thus the inherent dynamics.

MACROECONOMIC CAUSAL RELATIONS: 'MACRO-BEHAVIOUR RELATIONS'

The macroeconomic consumption function is a well-known example of such a macro-behaviour relation – where for example households' disposable income, the distribution of income and wealth and expectations related to future events play an important role. The macro-investment function is also an often-used macro-behaviour relation, but this is considerably less stable because the uncertainty of future outcomes is such a strong factor.

The consumption and investment behaviour functions (and several other macro-behaviour functions) are based on the assumption that the microeconomic actors, taken as a group, behave in a way that justifies operating with a largely stable, macroeconomic causal relation which contributes to the uncovering of some of the systematic elements in the macroeconomic dynamics. Because there is such a large number of consumers, the macro-relation will be purged of the arbitrary (stochastic) elements in the individual behaviour patterns. We are then left with the more solid correlations which comprise causal relations between macroeconomic variables, but where uncertainty, group behaviour and context-specific circumstances, of course, make these relations 'open' in a theoretical sense, as well as historically contingent. Therefore, a full description of the behaviour relations of macro-individuals cannot be given; the ubiquitous uncertainty is far too great for this.

Similarly, the effect of the behaviour relations of other macro-actors is also subject to uncertainty. This applies for instance to labour market organisations, since they do not have dictatorial power over their members. Agreements may not be approved, feedback effects are often unknown and the institutional framework is constantly changing (the number of members varies considerably, both over time and between different trades). The central bank endeavours to maintain price stability but has few instruments (a short-term interest rate and loans to banks) with which to pursue this goal. The causal relations are weak and their determination subject to arbitrariness and uncertainty. The government can pursue both demand and structural policies, which are both subject to varying degrees of uncertainty. Increased public spending would be expected to increase total employment, but this is not necessarily the case since, for example, public production could substitute private employment in similar occupations.

The macro-behaviour relationships cannot be considered as causal relations lasting for ever. They are established under the conditions of genuinely uncertain and constantly changing environments. In this light, one may detect provisionally stable elements as a part of these macro-behaviour relations by studying the way in which structural conditions and macroeconomic (aggregate) phenomena mutually influence each other.

SUMMARY

Macroeconomic theory comprises systematized knowledge about the economic correlations that determine domestic product, employment, unemployment and inflation. These correlations have been briefly sketched in the so-called macroeconomic landscape. Central to macroeconomic theory is the interaction between macro-actors' 'behaviour', macro-markets and structural factors. This interaction involves a number of causal relations – represented in Figure 3.2 by flow arrows. It is these causal relations, known as macro-behaviour relations, that describe the workings of the landscape. Macro-behaviour, economic policy and exogenous factors work together to determine the strength and composition of effective demand, which is the driving force behind macroeconomic dynamics (see Chapter 8).

As already mentioned in Chapter 1, the relative importance of supply and demand factors in the description of the economic landscape is a matter of considerable dispute in macroeconomic literature. When the landscape is viewed as being essentially stable, a closed (that is, predetermined) equilibrium model will be well suited for analysing these predictable conditions. If, on the other hand, the macroeconomic landscape is viewed as being in a state of constant flux, changes in supply and demand and the interaction between them will have consequences for growth, employment and inflation. What is needed here is an open analytical structure where the destination of the macroeconomy is not predetermined. Rather, the macroeconomic development should be considered context- and path-dependent, which furthermore makes the future generally unknown to macro-actors (and to macroeconomists). In that case the preliminary landscape serves mainly as a list of points to remember when conducting relevant macroeconomic analyses, since 'everything is interrelated'. Hence, no macroeconomic entity can be fully analysed as detached from the economy as a whole. The landscape is constantly reminding the researcher that the whole of the macroeconomy is analytically different from the sum of its parts, which might help prevent the fallacy of composition. Such fallacies occur, for example, if a goal is set for the public sector's budget without taking the corresponding changes in the private sector's budget and in the balance of payments into consideration.

Although the landscape is an abstract framework, one must be careful to avoid viewing the real macroeconomy, with its open structures consisting of markets, actors and causal relations, as a clockwork system. There is no predetermined answer to the question of which analytical framework is the most appropriate. At the end of the day it must be a matter of judgement as to which method best matches the perceived ontology. This matching process is dependent on the initial, ontological reflection on the shape of the landscape, as it helps to suggest some of the underlying, structural conditions that are difficult to observe. Thus, this procedure can contribute to a better understanding of the macroeconomic substrata that play a part in determining the macroeconomic development. The lack of direct knowledge about these underlying factors makes it necessary to give the macro-behaviour functions an open interpretation that allows incorporation of new findings into the deeper structures and allows for the influence of the unknown future, which might be analysed using an open system analysis with a path-dependent approach.

APPENDIX 3.1:   ANALYTICAL ELEMENTS WITHIN A MACROECONOMIC LANDSCAPE: A SUPPLEMENT TO FIGURE 3.2

Table 3A.1   Macro-markets, macro-actors and causal relations

Markets	Macro-actors and causal relations
A. Markets for goods and services	
1) Government consumption (of goods and services) and real investment (G)	Government (fiscal policy)
2) Exports (E)	Foreign sector (demand for goods and services, profitability)
3) Imports (M)	Households and firms (demand for foreign goods and services, profitability)
4) Private consumption (C)	Households (demand for goods and services)
5) Private real investment (I)	Households and firms (demand for real capital and new homes)
B. Labour market (employment and nominal wages)	
6) Output (GDP=C+I+G+E-M)	Firms and government decide on effective demand for labour Wage level (and distribution) is negotiated by the labour market organizations
C. Financial markets: (bonds/shares, bank loans, foreign exchange and the 'rate of interest')	
7) International capital flows	Foreign sector and firms' cross-border financial transactions – b-o-p capital account items
8) Exchange market interventions	Central bank buying or selling foreign exchange to manipulate the exchange rate
9) Central bank: short term rate of interest	Central bank lending rate paid by private banks (monetary policy)
10) Bank lending	Households' and firms' borrowing
11) Mortgage lending	Home-owner long-term borrowing on real-estate collateral
12) Household financial savings	Households' disposable income – private consumption
13) Excess profits	Firms' gross income minus real investment

Table 3A.1   (continued)

Income distribution	Macro-actors and causal relations
D. Disposable private income	
14) Wage income (labour)	Labour market organizations negotiate wage rates
15) Gross profits (capitalists)	Residual: GDP minus wage income and sales taxes
16) Taxes	Government sets tax rates (fiscal policy and income distribution)
17) Income transfers (households)	Government (fiscal policy and income distribution)
18) Unemployment benefits (unemployed labour)	Government sets benefit rates (labour supply and income distribution)

NOTES

1. This is what is known as philosophical realism, which contrasts with idealism, where the ontology is viewed as being socially constructed (merely an idea).
2. This is a metaphor I have elaborated upon in Jespersen, 2004.
3. The meaning of 'effective demand' is discussed thoroughly in Chapter 8.
4. Often, microeconomic market analyses are carried out using the *ceteris paribus* assumption in the form of a partial analysis, where prices and volumes on all other markets are unaffected by the turnover on the market being analysed. This method is evidently not applicable when the focus is on macro-markets, for instance the labour market.

4. About uncertainty, risk and limited knowledge

[Keynes's] perception [was] that economies did not behave in the way economists said they did, that something vital had been left out of their accounts, and
it was this missing element which explained their malfunctioning. ... Keynes
accused economists of his day of abstracting from the existence of uncertainty
[;] ... human beings take decisions in ignorance of the future. (Skidelsky, 1992:
538–9)

INTRODUCTION

In this chapter I will explore some of the consequences of the specific
assumption related to aggregate behaviour and the formation of expectations at the macro-level. While doing this I will concentrate on the difference between *risk* and *uncertainty*.[1] This will be done firstly through
an analysis of the individual decision-maker's situation, which can be
characterized by a kind of double uncertainty related to both the micro-
and the macro-level. To begin with, the future conditions are uncertain on
the individual level (health, income and family situation), which has to be
combined with the overall macroeconomic uncertainty related to unemployment, inflation, interest rates, and so on. Individual uncertainties
can, due to the 'law of large numbers', in varying degrees be transformed
to risk, which can be handled through different kinds of insurance policies (private companies or through welfare state institutions). Secondly,
there will always be uncertainty associated with the consequences of an
individual action for two reasons: we do not know the future and we do
not know the outcome of other people's reactions. The macroeconomy
outcome when many actors act even under the condition of identical macroeconomic signals is uncertain, because we literally do not know. The
further into the future the consequences reach, the greater the role played
by the uncertain expectations, which further contributes to the overall
macroeconomic uncertainty.

Macroeconomic uncertainty will be addressed in Chapter 5, where the
interaction between uncertain knowledge and the economy as a whole
will be discussed in the light of analyses using closed and open systems

(including semi-closures) respectively. These differences in the interpretation of the ontology[2] of the subject matter are decisive in their influence on the relevance of formalizing the applied models, which furthermore has significance for the analytical outcome of using an equilibrium or a path-dependency method.

Chapter 6 will conclude these three chapters on analytical methods in a macroeconomic perspective, where the relevance of the equilibrium method and the path-dependency method respectively will be evaluated in the light of the achieved conclusions regarding micro- and macro-uncertainties and the dependency of these uncertainties on a specific historical context. The possibilities for separating trend and business cycle in macroeconomic analysis will also be explored at the end of this chapter.

As stated previously, particularly in Chapter 1, macroeconomic theory can be divided into two distinct schools. They utilize two different macroeconomic landscapes, which lead to two very different analytical models and methods. The differences will be central to the discussion in this chapter and Chapters 5 and 6 dealing with macroeconomic behaviour, the macroeconomic model and, finally, macroeconomic methods.

The difference between neoclassical and post-Keynesian analysis can be summarized as follows. Neoclassical macroeconomic analysis in its basic form stems from the following assumptions:

1. Individual decisions are made on the basis of full information.
2. Macroeconomic reality is viewed as the result of individual choices.
3. There is a well-defined, long-term equilibrium.
4. The macroeconomic system is self-regulating, although with some inertia.

Post-Keynesian macroeconomic theory was presented in Chapter 1 and the specific methodology summarized in Chapter 2. It was shown that this school of thought has a number of distinct ontological presuppositions:

1. Individual decisions are made under circumstances of uncertainty.
2. Macroeconomic reality mirrors these inherent uncertainties and should be considered as an interrelated unity.
3. The dynamic development is regarded as being without an inherent, long-term equilibrium.
4. The historical context is a deciding factor for macroeconomic development.

The approach applied on the analytical level must be given a form that ensures that the significance of the four characteristics mentioned above

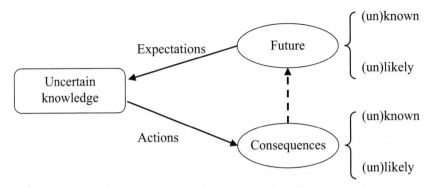

Figure 4.1   The anatomy of uncertain individual knowledge

appears in the production of a macroeconomic analysis for each of the schools of theory.

The contents of this chapter will primarily be a characterization of the concepts of uncertainty and risk as they are used within the two schools of theory. The problem for scientific methodology is illustrated in Figure 4.1. In this chapter, we find ourselves at the analytical level, where the macroeconomic landscape should be given an actual model-like representation. This will entail, among other things, that the four ontological characteristics mentioned above should be incorporated into the analytical model's design and dynamic structures of each school of thought.

ABOUT UNCERTAINTY, RISK, LIMITED KNOWLEDGE AND EXPECTATIONS-FORMATION

Uncertainty is a condition of life. Decisions are made on the basis of uncertain knowledge about the future and about the consequences of the actions that are decided upon. The analytical implications of this issue will be described in this section.

Figure 4.1 represents an outline of the basic problem. As already mentioned, Keynes distinguished between 'ignorance' and 'improbability'. Ignorance in its extreme form is like looking into a dark hole; you know that there must be something down there, but have no (or only a vague) idea of what it can be. This is the fundamental uncertainty that results from the fact that we simply do not know.

If, on the other hand, an event is considered to be unlikely, then at least we know which outcomes we are talking about, for example an increase in interest rates. This can be more or less unlikely, especially if we are a little bit more specific; for example an increase of five percentage points within the next year. A specific probability cannot be attached to this statement, but we can at least say that it is probably less likely than an increase of one percentage point. In some cases, we can be so specific that it makes analytical sense to put a figure on the probability. There will be more about this below.

Next, we are to varying degrees unsure of which consequences our actions have for ourselves and for our surroundings. And not only are the consequences uncertain, but they also depend on both the uncertain and the (un)likely future. These connections are also illustrated in Figure 4.1.

A Brief Note on the Difference between Uncertainty and Risk

Risk is often defined as the kind of uncertainty that you can insure against. Insuring assumes that the proposed activity is carried out a large number of times independently of each other and that the statistical parameters in the underlying, stable but stochastic process are known. In order for this requirement to be fulfilled, the following information about the process must be empirically determined:

1. all possible outcomes must be known;
2. the probability of the outcome occurring is known and constant;
3. there is independence between activities and outcomes.

If the activities under consideration can be carried out a large number of times under unchanged conditions (whereby the variance of results are minimized) risk will be reduced to stochastic certainty. These empirical requirements determine which consequences can be insured against for example fire, theft, traffic accidents and disease – circumstances which by assumption the individual insurance-taker experiences as uncertain and does not have direct influence on. (Since this is not always the case, it has been necessary to pass quite a strict law against insurance fraud.)

Note, however, that on the individual level, even processes that are fully described statistically will continue to include elements of uncertainty (the outcome is not known with certainty) unless the individual agent can repeat the activity in question a large number of times under constant conditions, which will rarely be the case (an appendix operation is a classic example of such an action that cannot be repeated). The establishment of insurance companies can remove individual uncertainty in those cases where there are reversible processes, particularly where there is only material damage. If on the other hand it is a matter of a non-reversible event, for example a fatal accident during an operation, insurance will not remove the uncertainty for something irreversible on an individual level – regardless of how well the risk is known.

Keynes's Contribution to the Understanding of Risk and Uncertainty

By 'very uncertain' I do not mean the same thing as 'very improbable'. (Keynes, 1936: 148)

If one single important phenomenon is to be pointed out that marks the difference between general equilibrium theory and Keynes's and post-Keynesian theory, it would be natural to mention the distinction between risk and uncertainty.

For Keynes, however, the emphasis in 1936 on uncertainty as an essential behaviour-determining factor at the micro-level was not in itself an expression of a new realization. He had addressed the question of how a theory of rational decision-making under uncertainty can be formulated during his work on his fellowship dissertation presented to King's College, Cambridge as far back as 1907 (Carabelli, 1988: 5). The dissertation was first published as an actual book in 1921 under the title *A Treatise on Probability*. Even the fact that Keynes, despite being engaged in many other activities, still made time to rework this thesis, which by that time was over ten years old, indicates that he must have regarded the thesis as more than merely an entrance ticket to the academic world. It was also seen at the time as an original contribution to the understanding of how rational decisions can be made under conditions of uncertainty, that is, without certain knowledge about the basis for the decision and of the consequences of the actions.

A Treatise on Probability was not specifically aimed at an analysis of economic decisions. It was to a greater degree a thesis on moral philosophy, where Keynes tried to address the question of how one should act when the consequences of one's actions are uncertain. Keynes had not only the economic consequences in mind, but also the moral consequences of an action, for example that it is not irrelevant how someone earns their money. If credibility is compromised, then the conditions for carrying out financial transactions have changed. The easiest solution for the actors to the problem of which actions, in this perspective, are 'right' or 'wrong', is to follow convention: simply do the same as all the others when there is not a (morally) certain basis for decision-making. But, says Keynes, merely to follow the rules is not rationally based behaviour, partly because the individual decision-maker can have knowledge that the other decision-makers in the area do not have, but equally importantly, the individual decision-maker can ascribe a significance to the different outcomes that deviates from the convention, not least because the convention will by definition be conservative.

The individual, rational answer to (in England) a trivial question about whether you should take along an umbrella depends not only on the probability of rain, but also on the subjective discomfort of getting wet compared to carrying around an umbrella. It is possible to set up an objective frequency function for the probability of rain, but the discomfort must be subjective. In other words, the rational action will always have a greater or lesser subjective element.

Uncertainty is inherent in every single action that reaches into the future, and is not deterministically decided. In this way, we move into a broad range of varying uncertainties. In some areas, ignorance is total because we cannot know which outcome the future will bring, be it long term or short term. One extreme is therefore the situation where the future is simply completely unknowable (Popper, 1996). The other extreme is the situation where everything is insured and all actions are reversible. The latter is equivalent to having bought all the tickets in a lottery so that we can know with complete certainty exactly how much we will lose.[3] For the individual decision-maker, however, precise knowledge of the probability distribution for the individual outcomes is not sufficient to remove the perception of uncertainty, since it rarely happens that you can 'buy all the tickets' or that the consequences of negative and positive results, respectively, are known, let alone reversibility related to, for example, an appendix operation or a bankruptcy. Even if you know that the mathematical probability of rolling a six in a throw of a die is 1:6, the next roll of the die is perceived as uncertain. If the individual actor has only a limited number of tries, the statistical risk on the individual level cannot be removed and the activity in question will be correctly perceived as having an element of uncertainty. For the individual actor there is something unique associated with every action. Almost all decisions on an individual level, therefore, will be perceived as uncertain to varying degrees, unless insurance can be taken out to cover all possible outcomes, which is impossible in practice.

This is the inherent uncertainty that is associated with every activity at the micro-level. Social institutions in the form of insurance companies and the welfare state can contribute to the reduction of uncertainty, but they cannot remove it, since far from all activities are reversible on the individual level, let alone that the outcomes have an objective probability. We can include here other institutional relationships (summed up in the economic literature and elsewhere by the terms 'adverse selection' and 'asymmetric information') that can also be obstacles to the establishment of traditional insurance markets.

Another equally important source of uncertainty is macroeconomic reality's lack of predictability. No one can say with complete certainty whether unemployment will increase or decrease in the coming year. Since expectations for the macroeconomic future co-determine the actors' dispositions, this is also a significant source of uncertainty.

> The sense in which I am using the term [uncertainty] is that in which the prospect of a European war is uncertain, or the price of copper and the rate of interest twenty years hence, or the obsolescence of a new invention, or the position of private wealth owners in the social system in 1970. About these matters there is no scientific basis on which to form any calculable probability whatever. We simply do not know. (Keynes, 1937, *CWK*, XIV: 113–14)

Macroeconomic uncertainty is an unavoidable element in decision-making also at the micro-level and is therefore a part of social reality that consumers, producers and investors must take into account through their expectations-formation and social behaviour. It is this fact that lies behind the new trend in macroeconomic theory that works with 'the macroeconomic foundation' for microeconomic theory. On what macroeconomic knowledge-base are the expectations of the various categories of actors formed? (Hahn, 2001.)

Macroeconomic uncertainty is thus both a cause (through exogenous events) and a consequence (manifest in endogenous events) which manifests itself by making the macroeconomic system open. This demonstration makes it apparent that one cannot speak meaningfully about a general equilibrium solution to an indeterminate system, where the future by definition is not knowable. I will return to this topic in the chapter on equilibrium and path-dependency.

To summarize: the macroeconomic landscape is open and undergoes constant change. It is therefore shaped by a partially endogenous macro-dynamic process which, at the same time, is anchored in historic time. Macroeconomic models must reflect the inherent uncertainties, and the analytical results must subsequently be interpreted from this perspective.

INHERENT MACROECONOMIC UNCERTAINTY

As mentioned above, 'uncertainty' and 'risk' in insurance theory have two separate meanings. Somewhat paradoxically, risk can be associated with random – unsystematic – behaviour. It is precisely the random, the unsystematic, that can be reduced, even removed, on the macro-level, where the law of large numbers may apply. One of the paradoxes of planning theory is thus that life's 'randomness', which creates uncertainty and perhaps even inability to act on an individual level, could be factored in at the macro-level.

Activities where the outcome is influenced by randomness will, as described above, make the individual event uncertain. We cannot know in advance which possible events will be realized. However, if the activity is repeated many times with many people engaged in the same activity under unchanged conditions, then the element of chance disappears at the macro-level. This means that, for example, the consumption of a number of daily products on the macro-level will be very stable, regardless of the fact that every individual household in the entire country makes individual decisions every day about the purchase of milk, bread, butter and so on. Just as we can hope that we survive the traffic every day (and hope is just about all we can do), it is also partly a random event generator that decides who will be an accident victim. On the other hand, the emergency rooms can anticipate with great accuracy the number of accident victims that will have to be treated in normal circumstances during one day with, of course, minor variations depending on the weather and road conditions. The number of traffic victims can be reduced through improved traffic planning, legislation and an altered driving culture, but such a reduction of the likelihood at the macro-level will not be cost-free in the form of changed public expenses and changed transport times – conditions that the macroeconomic landscape can help to evaluate. But the macroeconomic landscape cannot show how individual behaviour, determined by irreducible uncertainty, is influenced.[4]

If Macroeconomics Were Like a Game of Dice

We know with certainty that an average number of sixes from many rolls of the die is 1:6. So a game of dice where the prize exceeds six times the stake will give a profit if you have the time and liquidity to continue, even if 'bad luck' occurs temporarily. The individual person rarely has these requirements, so playing dice is perceived as uncertain on the individual level. Anyhow, a statistician would not call the game uncertain, because all the parameters are known, although they do entail risk.

Let us next characterize the dice game as a macroeconomic process:

1. The outcome range is given and the macro-outcomes are known.
2. The mathematical probability is known and is the same for all individuals. It is also constant; there is no 'learning by doing'. (We have assumed that there is no cheating with the dice and that the probability does not change.[5])

3. We can roll the dice an endless number of times under constant conditions and the outcome of each roll is independent of previous outcomes.

If all economic activity met these three requirements, and all actors were pure calculating machines in the sense that they repeated the actions an infinite number of times, and the prize corresponded to the mathematical probability, then it would be a pure amusement to engage in macroeconomic research (where an inspection of whether the dice really are 'honest' would have considerable importance). However, macroeconomic processes cannot be analytically described in this manner because reality deviates from these ideal assumptions.

Ad 3): One may wonder why in a world with rational agents these obviously money-losing games are so popular. Something is missing. It could be that limited uncertainty for some people is experienced as a welfare gain. One is willing to pay for the excitement and the dream that you might get lucky. If you have decided in advance to play only *x* times, the outcome will always be uncertain, but the maximum loss is controlled. With regard to any systematic activity which is only undertaken a finite number of times, there cannot be full correspondence between the stake and the expected return.[6] In other words, the outcome of the game is not known with certainty when it is not repeated an infinite number of times under unchanged conditions. This means that even the most organized of all activities (a game with known frequencies) is subject to a form of individual uncertainty. Hence, it becomes obvious that any individual economic activity in everyday life has an element of uncertainty with regard to outcome. To remove this element would require, among other things, that one has access to unlimited credit and/or an unlimited welfare state, which could compensate one if 'unlucky'.

In the post-Keynesian literature, the uncertainty that results from item 3 above is summed up under the label 'non-ergodicity', which refers to non-stationary, not-infinitely-repeatable events. The meaning of these everyday events is, as Paul Davidson in particular has stressed, that all individual actions are subject to uncertainty, since the mathematical probability only applies as an average of (infinitely) many identical actions. The statistical average (probability frequency) cannot be the only clue for the individual actor, who in the nature of things has his own specific characteristics and preferences. As will be shown elsewhere, the setting up of insurance firms, mutual credit associations, and so on is one of the ways in which groups of rather similar individuals have sought to limit the influence of individual dissimilarity.[7] The organization of the society according to universal welfare-state principles has the extra advantage that the number of 'insurance takers' is the largest possible, which reduces the variation on the total insurance sum that is paid out. In addition there are favourable distribution considerations, since adverse selection[8] is avoided.

Ad 2): Next we are struck by the question of whether the statistical probability (frequency) is: (1) well defined and identical; or (2) varies from player to player. We know that just as we can be hit by illness, so we can also be hit by unemployment, but we do not know what part of the frequency is primarily caused by a 'system failure' and what can be attributed to 'person-specific' conditions and what can be caused by gender, education or geographic location. If we, the researchers, want to answer the question about how high the level of involuntary unemployment is expected to be next year, then the answer and the margin of uncertainty will depend on the character of the analysis carried out within the framework of an (open) macroeconomic landscape. If the question is posed to an individual, he or she is exposed to the overall macro-unemployment in addition to a number of more person-specific characteristics related to occupation, gender, education, health, and so on – abilities which are not randomly distributed among people within the labour force. Knowledge about the existence of an uncertain macroeconomic development of unemployment influences the individuals' perception of uncertainty (see Figure 4.1). No society can insure itself against unemployment, though macroeconomic policy can possibly reduce it. On the other hand, the individual person can insure himself against the economic consequences of unemployment; but, partly because of the inherent macroeconomic uncertainty (which the law of large numbers cannot remove even if instances of unemployment were independent), it is impossible to predict the exact number of unemployed people, and partly because of the contribution made by the presence of asymmetrical information and adverse selection, a privately organized market for unemployment insurance will function rather badly and be costly for those (few) who take up insurance. There is an institutional barrier here that can only be overcome through a collective initiative in the form of establishing publicly subsidized unemployment insurance (to reduce the macroeconomic part) and perhaps making it compulsory, to circumvent some of the individual incentives (low income, low 'risk', optimistic attitude to life, and so on) not to take up such insurance (Barr, 2004). Public subsidies and legislation can both contribute, by increasing the number of people taking up insurance, to a reduction in individual uncertainty. In real life we cannot know if, let alone when, unemployment will hit, which in any case causes uncertainty.

This inescapable uncertainty at the individual level is the functional basis for establishing insurance companies and the institutions related to the welfare state – both initiatives require collective action and legislation to prevent unintended individual behaviour. Uncertainty is a welfare-reducing phenomenon. In the 'old days' it was characterized as an act of God, because it has serious consequences if you become unemployed or sick and no insurance is available. Without welfare state organizations and/or insurance-like institutions (perhaps relying on the family), the individual would instead have to base their survival on individual savings as a safeguard against destitution. If all individuals take precautions to prepare themselves for the worst-case scenario, then the sum of individual rational actions will lead to an exaggerated macro-behaviour, because all people will not get sick (or become unemployed). Hence, due to uncertainty the macroeconomic effect of individually rational actions is suboptimal. Welfare state legislation has a specific *raison d'être* as an uncertainty-reducing entity, making society function more rationally. This outcome of reducing the consequences of individual uncertainty is not only related to welfare state considerations or insurance companies. Organized credit markets in many ways undertake the same role of reducing individual uncertainty. If a firm (or wage-earner) experiences a minor setback in revenue, one goes to the bank to get a bridging loan. It is legal to set up companies with limited liability to reduce the economic uncertainty related to major investments. It is thus ensured that an economic loss resulting from a bankruptcy will be limited to the equity capital. Naturally, the firms' creditors know this too, which is why it is more difficult, especially for a newly established limited liability company, to raise capital without further personal collateral. Here we again find the problem of individuals often being too tight-fisted due to individual uncertainty, whereas at the macro-level only a limited number of investment projects will fail – but individuals cannot know in advance which ones. Furthermore the number of failed projects also depends on the macroeconomic uncertainty in general with regard to how the cyclical trend will develop in the coming years, in addition to the more industry-specific uncertainty. Some industries will be harder hit than others and within each industry there is greater uncertainty attached to some firms rather than others due, among other things, to the size of the equity capital.

Ad (1): What does it mean for the analysis of uncertainty that the range of outcomes is unknown? That will be the situation when the macroeconomic system is assumed not to converge towards a known equilibrium state. This means that the macroeconomic development is indeterminate, not only in the short term but also and especially in the long term, and that the amount of unemployment, for example, is therefore unknown. These macroeconomic conditions were described by Keynes as 'irreducible uncertainty'. The individual wage-earner does not even have the possibility of knowing the expected level of overall unemployment and therefore also

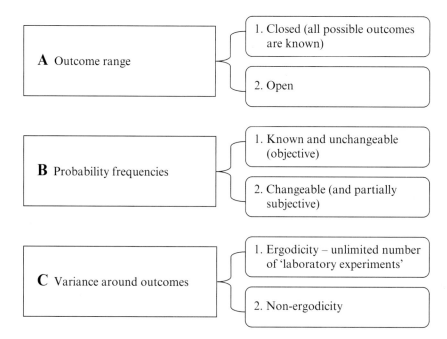

Figure 4.2   The statistical challenge of the macro-model

does not know his or her own risk of unemployment. The entrepreneur who makes decisions about real investment does not have the possibility of knowing the level of future sales or the price of oil, let alone the level of competition from China, and so on.

Short Summary: Risk Versus Uncertainty Theory

The purpose of this summary is to provide an illustration of how great a distance there is between the macroeconomic reality and the statistical requirements that must be fulfilled in order to reduce uncertainty to risk, which is the necessary assumption for a deterministic formulation of the microeconomic behaviour functions.

If there is to be congruence between microeconomic and macroeconomic behaviour and the statistical requirements that reduce uncertainty to statistical determinism, A1, B1 and C1 in Figure 4.2 must be fulfilled. The economic reality in which the individual actor finds himself is the exact opposite, where A2, B2 and C2 apply. It was this apparent conflict that was exposed at the beginning of the 1930s and that Keynes regarded as essentially being a question of using a realistic methodology, which lay behind his sometimes harsh comments about the lack of relevance of the A1, B1, C1 models: 'Walras's theory and all others along those lines are little better than nonsense' (from a letter to Hicks, December 1934; Skidelsky, 1992: 615).[9]

MICROECONOMIC UNCERTAINTY AS A BASIS FOR MACROECONOMIC BEHAVIOURAL RELATIONS

The purpose of this section is to explore the meaning of the concept of uncertainty for the design of macroeconomic behavioural relations within post-Keynesian theory.

Macroeconomic Uncertainty: An Ontological Fact

Macroeconomic conditions exert influence on the macroeconomic formation of expectations and thus on the decision-making process. Within the post-Keynesian tradition, it is an unavoidable characteristic of reality that future macroeconomic development is uncertain.

Keynes's ambition in *The General Theory* was precisely to give a theoretically relevant account of the macroeconomic reality in which the concept of uncertainty played a central role. For Keynes, uncertainty was an unavoidable condition for the understanding – especially with regard to the future – of economic actors' expectations and therefore their dispositions:

> Keynes's vision, which one can trace back to his youth, has to do with the logic of choice, not under scarcity, but under uncertainty. (Skidelsky, 1992: 539)

Microeconomic decisions have to be made, regardless of the fact that the consequences of these decisions cannot be subjected to anything that even resembles a classical probability-theory calculation: the range of outcomes is not completely described; probability frequencies, let alone the probability distribution, are rarely quantifiable; and, furthermore, many projects, especially real investments, cannot be repeated. They are irreversible. The macroeconomic challenge lies in formulating theories that can systematize the analysis of a large number of individual decisions that are made under conditions of uncertainty. Macroeconomic uncertainty especially influences investors' state of confidence, which is a non-quantifiable consequence of the fact that we simply do not know the future. Uncertainty also exerts influence on household savings: the more uncertain expectations of the future are perceived to be (on a macro- as well as micro-level), the larger the savings.

Expectations-formation is associated with considerable uncertainty on the actor level and there will also be considerable difference in expectations-formation from actor to actor when the future is unknown. The actors do not have a common fixed point in the form of a long-term equilibrium that they can take a bearing from. They must feel their way forward. Similarly, the consequences of uncertainty and ignorance vary. One of the decisive challenges for post-Keynesian macro-theory is to systematize the diffuse macroeconomic expectation formation for an operational theory for macroeconomic behaviour. Keynes's practical experiences encouraged him to propose the hypothesis that expectations are especially controlled by conventions: 'the existing state of affairs will continue indefinitely, except in so far as we have specific reasons to expect a change' (Keynes, 1936: 152).

But in a modern society we have good reason to expect changes, since macroeconomic development is a dynamic process driven forward by thousands of microeconomic dispositions based on uncertain expectations. These decisions cannot entirely rely on the law of large numbers and our understanding of them must therefore be continuously subjected to revision. Reality and expectations of reality are under constant change because economic transactions leave their mark. For example, it is unavoidable that every investment decision will exert an influence on the size and character of the capital apparatus of the future.

The passage of historical time is irreversible. Hence, the analytical model should reflect the fact that institutions, structures, conventions and, thereby, also expectations change over time. The continuous change of macroeconomic reality will happen partially independently of the macroeconomic development because of exogenous factors, and partially as a consequence of the development of the endogenous factors. A relevant model-like description of such a dynamic process must therefore be open in its demarcation of the surrounding world and at the same time path-dependent, since current and former transactions shape the future. We have reached an important conclusion: individual behaviour will always be dominated by uncertainty about the future. Individual expectations of the future cannot be reduced to risk, much less to certain knowledge.

How can the ontological conclusion be handled analytically in order also to ensure continued correspondence between the microeconomic basis (characterized by uncertainty) and the macroeconomic behavioural relations?

Microeconomic theory must also be compatible with the inherent macroeconomic uncertainty, using insight from the teachings on individual choice under uncertainty (as distinct from risk). The work of Kahneman and Tversky (1979), who formulated 'prospect theory', can provide inspiration here concerning individuals' reaction to uncertainty.[10]

Macroeconomic behaviour relations may, in contrast to microeconomic behaviour, reflect the interaction within the open macroeconomic landscape between the labour, goods, finance and currency markets and between macro-actor groups. For the sake of simplicity, I have used the term 'macro-actors' in order to differentiate from the concept of a representative micro-agent. Macroeconomic theory is, as already mentioned several times, an abstraction in itself: a way of summarizing the thousands of underlying microeconomic dispositions. It is the individual economic actor that is the macroeconomic grain of sand: households and firms in all their diversity. Households and firms make individual decisions, but they do not do it in a void. Here it is experience and convention that exert influence. In addition, individuals organize themselves in clubs, associations, firms and professional organizations so that their common behaviour has more weight. Macro-behaviour relations become 'building blocks', that can be used in macroeconomic analysis. In addition to this there are public institutions and the judicial framework for market and transaction structures (for example, there was a time when paying interest on debt was not allowed and attempts to form trade unions were forbidden). These are all conditions that can be given an introductory description in the design of the macroeconomic landscape and later on be included in an analytical macro-model, where macro-behaviour relations are formulated on the basis of uncertain expectations.

These macro-analytical aspects explain why the representative agent theory, based on a simple generalization of traditional microeconomic theory where individuals are assumed to know all prices with certainty, does not provide a consistent theory of macro-behaviour relations. Uncertainty also rules out the assumption of 'rational expectation-formation' at the macro level; see for example Sonnenschein (1972) and Kirman (1992). Next, no realistic attempt is made within this representative agent macro-tradition to operationalize the phenomenon of 'fundamental uncertainty'. This concept simply falls outside the beam of light that general equilibrium models cast on macroeconomic reality. A closed model is methodologically unsuitable for analysing an open ontology (see Chapter 5).

But it is primarily the methodologically-oriented post-Keynesian economists (III) who have carried out a consistent, theory-of-science based argumentation for this conclusion (cf. Chapter 1). These post-Keynesians provide an important new insight by explicitly discussing the consequences of macroeconomic uncertainty for aggregate macroeconomic behaviour and its influence on macroeconomic development described within the framework of a path-dependent analysis.

There are divided opinions, to put it mildly, about the extent to which post-Keynesian economists have understood the analytical significance of this change away from using fully informed individual behaviour as the foundation for macroeconomics (King, 2002). This discussion will be made evident in the next chapter. The full epistemological significance of this change was not made clear by the first generation (Kahn, Kaldor, Kalecki and Robinson) or by the second generation (Chick (II),[11] Davidson and Minsky). It was only with the third generation (Carabelli, Chick (III) & Dow, Fitzgibbons, O'Donnell),[12] with some inspiration from critical realist methodology, that this methodological shift of paradigm was explicitly recognized (among post-Keynesians); see Skidelsky (1992), see also Pålsson Syll (2006) and King (2002).

SUMMARY

The macroeconomic reality is ontologically open. This creates an inescapable and fundamental uncertainty of knowledge. We do not know the future – not even the future range of outcomes. This is a microeconomic condition: that the future is uncertain and that expectations for the consequences of our actions likewise, although to varying degrees, must be based on uncertain knowledge. A number of society's organizations and institutions should therefore be seen as a rational attempt to limit the extent of the microeconomic uncertainty caused by the open and unknown macroeconomic reality.

In *A Treatise on Probability* Keynes especially analysed the possibilities for making rationally based choices under conditions of an uncertain future. In *The General Theory*, he analysed the conditions for describing macroeconomic development under conditions of microeconomic and macroeconomic uncertainty.

Summed up in theory-of-science terms, the conclusion is that the acknowledgement of the fact that macroeconomics by its nature is open, and therefore unpredictable, will influence microeconomic behaviour in such a way that expectations-formation will be context-dependent. This rules out the possibility that a closed model can provide an adequate analytical framework. However, if uncertainty could be reduced in some segments of the macroeconomic landscape, perhaps by institutional arrangements, then an open-system model temporarily closed by a *ceteris paribus* assumption might possibly be analytically relevant; see Chapter 6.

APPENDIX 4.1: POSSIBLE LINES OF DEVELOPMENT FROM *A TREATISE ON PROBABILITY* TO *THE GENERAL THEORY*, AND A THEORY-HISTORICAL NOTE CONCERNING THE POST-KEYNESIAN INTERPRETATION

How to Analyse Rational, Individual Action under Conditions of Uncertainty

Keynes wrote the major part of *A Treatise on Probability* before the world turned topsy-turvy, in the brief interregnum of quiet optimism that was prevalent in Britain between the death of Queen Victoria and the outbreak of the First World War. This period was characterized by a marked growth in prosperity supported by a budding social-liberal welfare policy.[13] *The General Theory*, on the other hand, is fundamentally influenced by the deep economic crisis between the two world wars and the increasing social tensions that resulted from it. Here it is the macroeconomic uncertainty and its analysis that is central. What did macroeconomic uncertainty mean for individual behaviour considered at the aggregate level, and thus for understanding how the macroeconomic system functioned? The conclusion that Keynes arrived at in the 1930s was that it must be the government's, and especially the statesman's, responsibility to achieve macroeconomic balance with full employment. They had the power (and knowledge) to reduce uncertainty and re-establish optimism.

It is discussed within the post-Keynesian literature (see for example Runde and Mizuhara, 2003) whether the probability concept that Keynes worked with in *A Treatise on Probability* for describing various outcomes is of an objective or a subjective nature. When a single individual makes a decision, can it be reconstructed on a rational, albeit subjective, basis? Keynes's intention was to develop a logical theory of the probability concept appropriate to individual action under uncertainty: he asked under what circumstances it would be reasonable to act on the basis of partial information given the individual's preferences. As they differ from person to person nothing can be said in general, that is, encompassing all individuals, about what in an objective sense constitutes rational behaviour. On the other hand, there is no basis for assuming that individuals do not act rationally, given the information that they have available.

In *A Treatise on Probability*, Keynes uses the expression 'rational belief' to cover the individual assessment of the partially unknown probability that, for example, it will rain tomorrow. This 'rational belief' is based in principle on all accessible information, which is not always quantifiable, however. But the lack of quantification does not make expectations-formation 100 per cent subjective as long as it is partly based on objective data and a systemization of prior experience. On the other hand, the 'true' explanation of the weather tomorrow can never be fully recognized. The only explanations that can be fully recognized are the causal mechanisms that can be derived within the analytical model and have not been falsified by experience. It is therefore not the assessment of the (partially) stochastically dependent process that is subjective, but the perception of outside events and, not least, our knowledge of the underlying processes that will have subjective elements, as we discussed. Naturally, in the context of reactions to the prospect of rain, reactions will differ from individual to individual.

However, according to Skidelsky (1992: 86–92), Keynes's objective in writing *A Treatise on Probability* was not primarily to discuss the influence of the weather forecast on the behaviour of rational individuals, but on the contrary to produce an ethically based argumentation for 'good conduct'. 'The good life' was a personal responsibility that could not just be left to convention and good taste. To 'be good' could not be identified with 'doing good'. Individuals are obliged to adopt a personal opinion, not least because, in *A Treatise on Probability*, Keynes offered a logical justification for a personal attitude to 'good conduct'. But precisely because many qualitative assessments had to be included, the relevant decision model could not be presented as a rational calculation of optimal behaviour. Keynes was rather sceptical of these rational-calculation models where it is assumed that the individual can calculate the correct behaviour. On the contrary, the individual assessment should also accommodate intuition. According to Skidelsky's interpretation, good conduct in practice was an individual responsibility but based on a realistic social philosophy, with inspiration from the challenge by the Cambridge philosophers G.E. Moore and B. Russell to the dominant idealism that was still current in Cambridge at the turn of the twentieth century. *A Treatise on Probability* can therefore be read as a theory of individual behaviour which is based on reason and at the same time also has a moral foundation. This basis for behaviour bypasses utilitarianism and its mechanical calculation, and instead appears as an extension of Adam Smith's moral teachings (*The Theory of Moral Sentiments*, 1759), see Estrup *et al.* (2004). Smith is concerned that self-interest not come into conflict with self-respect, which can happen if respect for community interests are disregarded for the sake of personal gain.[14]

A Treatise on Probability is not a textbook of economic theory. It is a moral-philosophical treatise that discusses which beliefs the individual ought to base his actions on, if he wishes to be rational in a broader (human) sense.[15] As emphasized by Lawson (2003), Keynes employs a realistic ontology where uncertainty is acknowledged. In attempting on this basis to develop a theory of 'good conduct' under uncertainty, Keynes could be said to have provided early examples of critical realism applied to individual behaviour.

A heated discussion has broken out among post-Keynesians, however, about the degree to which there is a direct line from *A Treatise on Probability* to *The General Theory*. Elsewhere (Jespersen, 2002a), I have argued that Keynes's economic authorship can be interpreted as one coherent development story within macroeconomic theory based on realism. *A Treatise on Probability* does not fit into that story, because it focuses on rational *individual* behaviour under conditions of uncertainty. Important parts of *A Treatise on Probability* were written in the period 1906–07, in other words, before Keynes became macroeconomically 'aware'. However, it contributes to a more comprehensive understanding of the individual aspects of theory construction that lie behind the macroeconomic behaviour relations that Keynes used later on in his macroeconomic analysis.

Macroeconomic, Implications of Aggregate Individual Actions under Conditions of Uncertainty

The General Theory was mostly written in the period 1932–35 (published in February 1936). Keynes's ambition was to be a thoroughbred macroeconomist, at least from the time that *A Tract on Monetary Reform* was published in 1923, but it was not until 1934 (*CWK*, XIII: 485–92) that he drew the theory-of-science conclusion that microeconomic behaviour under conditions of uncertainty leads to an analytical macroeconomic system that does not automatically adjust to a general equilibrium. It could have been a macroeconomic landscape like the one presented in Chapter 3 that he had in mind. The crucial difference, however, is Keynes's realization in 1936 that it is impossible to construct a meaningful, long-term, general equilibrium within macroeconomics. It is no longer a question of whether market forces, more or less automatically, converge towards a general equilibrium, because there is nothing to converge towards. This is the crucial difference between *A Treatise on Money* and *The General Theory*. The microeconomic behaviour prevents general equilibrium from being a meaningful analytical framework; see Rogers (1997) who quotes Keynes as writing: 'I should, I think, be prepared to argue, that, in a world ruled by uncertainty with an uncertain future linked to an actual present, a final position, such as one deals with in static economics, does not properly exist' (*CWK*, XXIX: 222).

In short, this means that the long-run macroeconomic outcome is indeterminate. The future in the macroeconomic system is unknown for the individual actor, as if the die being used had an unknown number of sides and the probabilities attaching to the individual sides are indeterminate. It is this condition of fundamental or irreducible uncertainty that is a part of the knowledge background that the actors must accept as a part of the economic reality about which they form their rational beliefs.

In addition, the subject matter has been changed. In *A Treatise on Probability*, it was the behaviour of the individual actor that was discussed. In *The General Theory*, it is the understanding of which causal mechanisms co-determine the development of the macroeconomic system that is the subject of investigation. In *A Treatise on Probability*, the examples that Keynes used to illustrate his theories were typically about whether to take an umbrella, cast a die, the lottery and bookmaking and insurance firms. In *The General Theory*, it is aggregate consumer and investment relationships, liquidity preference and price formation on the financial markets that are the main elements for understanding the functioning of a macroeconomic system that can explain persistent unemployment. According to Skidelsky, the historical factor should also be added to this transformation of focus, in that many of the social norms that had provided social stability were undergoing radical change, partly as a consequence of the war and partly as a consequence of increased industrialization, both of which were development processes that led to increased rootlessness and uncertainty. Even the fluctuations in inflation and unemployment were dramatic in the period between the wars.

For Keynes it was important to demonstrate that not even the assumptions of correct, microeconomic expectations-formation and fully flexible price- and wage-formation could guarantee adjustment to general equilibrium. One important reason behind this conclusion is that individual expectations are formed under radical uncertainty: the outcome range is open, the probability frequencies are unknown and it is difficult, if not impossible, to repeat identical experiments. The macroeconomy changes and the individuals go through a learning process where they grope their way forward, if not blindly, then at least in near darkness. What would you do if you were groping your way around in near darkness? I would consider it to be rational to:

- take small steps – (trial and error to the extent that actions can be reversed);
- do as I usually do, if it has gone well previously (tradition or convention);
- follow norms and see what the others do.

When describing the macroeconomic behaviour relations, individual 'trial and error' will cancel out if the individuals' behaviour is stochastically independent. In that case, the first two items, following tradition or convention and 'doing like the others', will come to play a greater role at the macro-level than in standard micro-theory. This is also reflected in Keynes's explanation of why group psychology is an important factor when formulating the macro-behaviour relations. Here, the herd mentality easily gains a strong position. Waves of systematic, but partially unexplained, optimism and pessimism will spread, because when you do what the others do, your own position will be no worse or better than for them. In addition, a group that is marching in step can more easily generate self-fulfilling expectations. If a majority of actors believe that the price of oil will increase and act accordingly, the price will increase. If they are thereby confirmed in their expectations, the ground has been laid for yet another wave of price increases because there is no ceiling on the price of oil. Similarly, the price on the financial markets will increase as long as there is a majority who believe that the price will also increase tomorrow. This leads to overshoots that contribute to the feeling of uncertainty.

As will be demonstrated in Chapter 8, Keynes was, on precisely this basis, more than hesitant about the idea that it should be possible empirically to uncover stable, macroeconomic behaviour relations exclusively based on microeconomic arguments. The macroeconomic landscape will always be dependent on the specific context, which also explains Keynes's sceptical attitude to Tinbergen's econometric work. This was scepticism that the old-Keynesians unfortunately disregarded in the 1950s and 1960s, which then opened the gateway for the monetarists and later the new-classical criticism of so-called *ad hoc* macroeconometric models with Keynesian inspiration (see Chapter 1).

NOTES

1.　'Uncertainty' is a methodological minefield. It is difficult to propose a clear criterion for how a 'correct' ontological reflection should be carried out under conditions of uncertain knowledge. With inspiration from Keynes (see O'Donnell, 1989), concepts such as 'intuition' and '*a priori* reasoning' can be employed. These temporary explorations should be based on a realistic foundation, but this is no guarantee that the ontological reflection can subsequently be confirmed. For example, everyone can see that the sun during the day is moving from East to West in the sky; hence, it became quite a challenge to put up a theory which assumed that the sun was the fixed point and the earth was moving – contrary to the immediately observable facts.

2.　Here I use the term 'ontology' in the sense that critical realism uses it, that is: 'the fundamental nature of being and reality'; see Chapter 2 for further discussion. It refers to the characteristics of the object field. The ontological reflection thus becomes a preliminary description of how the object field appears, based on empirical observations and 'emerging properties', partly constituted in the 'deep' stratum. Hence, our knowledge about the 'ontology' of the object field will always be uncertain.

3. I must refer to my father's often-stated view of the national lottery and similar games: the more you play, the more certain you are of losing. He therefore played rarely, but had great pleasure from it.

4. We all know how easily the supply of energy can be cut off. Auckland was without power for more than a month at the end of the 1990s; California has regularly been blacked out; New York experienced a power failure for more than 24 hours in 2003; and so on.

5. This condition is discussed in the new-Keynesian literature as the problem of avoiding 'time-inconsistency'.

6. Furthermore, the practical consideration that the bookmaker must also have payment for his work suggests that the prize will always be less than the mathematical probability would suggest.

7. For example, you cannot automatically become a member of a pension fund. It requires a medical examination. If it turns out negatively, then the best-case scenario is that you can be accepted under more rigorous terms.

8. People in high-risk groups (possibly because of a dangerous occupation) cannot get private insurance coverage on normal terms, and low-risk groups get together and form their own exclusive insurance groups with a significantly lower average risk (for example the teaching profession's fire insurance).

9. In 1937, Keynes explained why the Walrasian system is little better than nonsense: '[because] in a system in which the level of money income is capable of fluctuating, the orthodox theory is one equation short of what is required to give a solution' (*CWK*, XIV: 122. This is primarily a critique of the Walras model evaluated on the premise of its being a closed mathematical system.

10. It is paradoxical in this connection that in the title of their groundbreaking article 'Prospect theory: an analysis of decision under risk', there is no sharp distinction between uncertainty and risk.

11. The number following the name of Chick indicates that she has made important contributions to post-Keynesian economics mark II and mark III.

12. King (2003: 182) describes this group as 'the philosophers', because they emphasize the significance of using an explicit theory-of-science approach for a better understanding of macroeconomic phenomena.

13. In many ways it is difficult to understand that Keynes could continue to work on *A Treatise of Probability* after his experiences during the First World War, where foolishness had been given free rein, not least in the design of the peace treaty with Germany. These events made Keynes even more sceptical of political prudence, which in his opinion was based on an increasing degree of populist democracy.

14. In an autobiographical reflection from 1938, however, Keynes (*CWK*, X: 433–50) expresses some doubts about this almost superhuman common sense, to which he had appealed 30 years earlier with regard to the individual's ability (and perhaps commitment) to understand sufficiently and thus make allowance for the collective interest. In the meantime, he became aware of how complicated macroeconomic relationships appear and therefore how difficult it can be for the individual person to act responsibly from a macroeconomic point of view.

15. That is, not in the narrow sense of rational which presumes full knowledge.

5. Uncertainty and 'the economy as a whole'

INTRODUCTION

The previous chapter dealt with how expectations-formation is subject to various forms of uncertainty at the level of individual behaviour. The point of the chapter was to study how microeconomic behaviour can be given as a systematic presentation, even though it is characterized by genuine uncertainty. It then becomes possible to introduce the concept of macroeconomic behaviour which is analytically applicable to the macroeconomic landscape.

In this chapter we discuss another basic problem, also founded in science theory. It is how to shape the analytical model that summarizes the economy as a whole, based upon the macroeconomic landscape. As seen in Figure 3.2, the macroeconomic landscape gives us a representation which makes it clear that the landscape is made up of parts and aggregates. The parts will represent the macro-actors, institutions and the macro-markets. The separation of the different parts will be determined by the structure and the character of interaction within the macroeconomy together with the overall point of the investigation. The resulting aggregates are somewhat abstract; they may have no clear-cut empirical counterpart. An aggregate is analytically relevant in cases where it appears that the sum of the parts is different from the whole.

An aggregate can for example be the whole financial sector, the whole Danish economy, the whole EU or even the global economy. As the 'whole' changes, the focus of the investigation, combined with the result of the ontological reflection, also determines the framework for what is relevant.

The central methodological question is therefore still how to build a bridge from ontological reflection (represented by the macroeconomic landscape) to the relevant analytical model[1] without committing excessive manipulation of reality. The analytical modelling based upon the macroeconomic landscape will be influenced, among other things, by:

- The microeconomic formation of expectations of macroeconomic phenomena.

- The exposition of 'the economy as a whole' as consisting of macro-actors and macro-markets, of causal relations and of the institutional framework of the complete macroeconomic landscape.
- The distinction between open and closed landscapes: each implies an important methodological choice.

In the next chapter the implications for the form of the complete model of the specific analytical method, either general equilibrium or path-dependency, will be discussed. In that discussion the following questions will be included:

- The equilibrium concept as a central analytical tool, which can be interpreted differently depending upon the specific context of the model: as a gravity centre, general market clearing or a state without tendency to change, for example with continued involuntary unemployment (Ingrao and Israel, 1990).
- The macro-dynamics: an open macroeconomic landscape will continually change, partially because expectations are disappointed and revised, partially because of structural reasons: increased productivity, innovations, competition and sector realignment. The further away the analytical horizon, the greater the changes to be expected (see for example Keynes's list in Chapter 18 of *The General Theory* of given factors including demography; Keynes, 1936: 245), and the importance of learning by doing which was emphasized by Popper.
- Path-dependency: the macroeconomic development process in historical time, where among other things trends and business cycles are difficult to separate analytically (Cornwall and Cornwall, 2001).

The present chapter will primarily contain a study of the difference between open and closed analytical models. This choice is important in determining how 'wholes' can be analysed, which the following chapters will illustrate in referring to the theory of effective demand (Chapter 8) and studying in depth the implications of the fallacy of composition (Chapter 7).

Open and Closed Macroeconomic Systems and Models[2]

In the methodological literature dealing with macroeconomic analysis the term 'system' is often used. The ontological speculation must be analytically organized within a 'system'. It can be 'tamed' by retroduction, that is to say, a methodological procedure of shifting between induction (based on experience) and deduction (based on a systematic logic), when hypotheses about reality are formed.

Within science theory there exists a sharp distinction between analysis completed in closed and open systems. To begin with it is important to state that they are not necessarily polar opposites, because parts of the macroeconomic landscape, in certain instances, are best analysed as a semi-closed system. As we shall see, the landscape can at certain times have an appearance which makes using a closed model relevant, while at other perhaps more turbulent times to do so would falsify the assumptions upon which the closed model is based. In the same way, differences in the subject of analysis justify the use of a closed model.

The closed system should, as will be explained below, be understood as a special analytical form within a wide range of macroeconomic systems.[3] When the closed form of analysis is chosen, it is often because of practical concerns, as a closed model is easier to formulate mathematically, which alleviates the practical calculations and gives what looks like more precise results.

Let me begin with specifying what is meant, according to an encyclopae-dia, by a system: 'a group of related parts that work together as a whole for a particular purpose' (Longman, 1995: 1465). The metaphor of the macroeconomic landscape appears to be contained in the definition and can thus be understood as a system.

Dow (1996) characterizes a macroeconomic analysis as a thought experiment within the framework of a macroeconomic landscape. Macroeconomic theory should justify the causal relations of the landscape. Whether the mental experiment can be completed within the framework of either a closed or an open system will be primarily justified inductively or empirically. These thought experiments can be conducted in either open or closed systems. She actually uses the heading 'closed and open systems of thought' (Dow, 1996: 13).

Distinguishing between closed and open systems, she describes a closed system as one whose bounds are known and whose constituent variables and relations are known, or at least knowable; as opposed to the open system, where not all constituent variables and relations are known or knowable, and thus the boundaries of the system are not known or knowable (Dow, 1996: 14). Dow is stating directly that a characteristic of an open system is that not all variables are known or knowable. This reflects the situation when uncertainty is dominant. On the other hand she is opening up the possibility to create subsystems, where uncertainty is reduced to risk. In that case, the range of possibilities is limited, and the relevant variables are assumed to be stochastically stable, so it is legitimate to complete what Dow calls a 'semi-closed-system analysis'[4] within such parts of the macroeconomic landscape.

I will return to this epistemological concern, for example with the choice between a partially closed and an open analytical model. Open and closed models are not necessarily analytical opposites. A model is only perfectly closed when the whole macroeconomy is analysed as a laboratory experiment, where the borders to the surrounding world are closed and the experiment in principle can be repeated indefinitely. If that is the case, an open model becomes irrelevant, because exogenous variables can be changed at discretion, and not only can the economic processes be repeated, but they are also reversible or ergodic, which makes it reasonable to assume that the individual agent knows the future with certainty.

A CLOSED SYSTEM: A LABORATORY-SHAPED REALITY WITHOUT UNCERTAINTY

> [A] closed system [is] a complete and essentially unalterable system (of ideas, doctrines, things etc.); a material system in which the total mass or energy remains constant; a self-contained realm, unaffected by external forces. (Oxford English Dictionary, online, quoted in Chick (2003))

A closed system analysis has many traits in common with a laboratory experiment, where the complete apparatus or model is isolated from its surroundings, or where the interaction with its surroundings is controlled by the scientist. A general equilibrium model has the same characteristics as a closed model, and that is why Andersen (2000) uses the laboratory analogy when describing the macroeconomic method (see Chapter 1).

The simple equilibrium model, as described in the Introduction, is built upon the principles of maximum reductionism:

- For a start the model is isolated from the surrounding world. It is only the scientist in the controlled laboratory environment who allows external shocks and structural change to occur.
- The smallest analytical particle is the individual economic decision-maker, who is assumed to display behavioural stability, because the preference structure is exogenously given. Therefore rationally behaving individuals with exogenously determined preferences are used in the laboratory model, as elementary particles, the smallest building blocks. The representative agents have rational expectations. That is to say, they are assumed to know the model's equilibrium solution, which can only be fulfilled in a closed model.

- The expectations consistent with the model are based upon externally determined prices; these prices cannot be changed by the
  agents.
- The model's assumptions are only internally consistent in general
  equilibrium.

A Macroeconomic Laboratory

The development of this idealized laboratory model has led to a displacement of the analytical focus point for neoclassical macroeconomic
research. As described in the Introduction it is the characteristics of the
closed ideal model, not reality, that has become the subject matter of the
macroeconomic analysis using the general equilibrium model. Because
of this change of focus the laboratory results will only yield statements
relating to the characteristics of the ideal models which do not necessarily
result in a better understanding of reality.

It is of course a legitimate research project to analyse the characteristics
of an ideal model. But this project has displaced the focus of the analysis from an attempt to uncover aspects of the real world, to become an
analysis of a closed and often normatively organized economic system.
The normative aspects will be built into the model's axiomatic base. These
characteristics remain normative unless they can be empirically justified.
The analysis of the characteristics of the ideal model does not focus on
understanding factual and recognizable reality; on the contrary the focus is
on understanding the ideal, and suggesting how specific results in the ideal
model can be achieved based upon assumptions of the closed model.

This type of laboratory experiment can also be strategically formulated.
Analyses can be done on what form of increased economic efficiency can
be achieved within the framework of the laboratory model. Such analyses
can proceed by incorporating a regulation which exists in reality and then
calculating consequences related to removing or changing the observable
regulation. Eventually it is demonstrated that within the ideal (closed)
market model the removal of the regulation and/or the imperfection will
have beneficial effects on market efficiency and hence on 'welfare'. The
implication of this kind of laboratory experiment, which rests exclusively
on the World 2 level of analysis, is deductively determined by the model's
axiomatic base in combination with the chosen analytical method.

When World 2 is considered independently of World 1, it is the laboratory model which becomes the subject matter. This is the case in 'pure'
laboratory experiments. First the ideal is defined, whereas the validity
area, where the result of the analysis is the result of mathematical calculation, is hardly discussed. The outcome of the laboratory experiment is

heavily dependent on the choice of analytical method. This question will be studied in depth in Chapter 6.

Within the laboratory the ideal market model is the 'looking glass' through which aberrations from market-clearing equilibrium can be studied as so-called imperfections. In neoclassical mainstream literature the aberrations are studied as consequences of rational individual behaviour in a closed system of imperfectly functioning markets, for instance due to menu costs, efficiency wage, union power, asymmetric information and credit rationing. These imperfections change the incentive structure of the representative agents away from that of the ideal economic agent with rational expectations. Laboratory experiments can then indicate the 'cost of imperfections' by calculating the greatest deviations from the ideal outcome.

In the laboratory the results of the analysis, as mentioned, are considered as compatible with reality. The interpretation of the laboratory results is the best knowledge we can get about reality, because the model is the analytical reality. The real reality, the one outside of the laboratory, is not relevant for the analysis, because we have no systematic knowledge of matters left out. If the master of the laboratory had such knowledge, he would, of course, have incorporated it into the laboratory model. What is omitted are unsystematic, random or irrational aberrations. These aberrations are considered as unimportant because they are assumed to disappear, if the market processes are left to themselves. Random events will cancel out due to the law of large numbers, and people behaving irrationally will either learn to be rational or be washed out of a competitive market. Hence, the ideal market model is the only one which can generate a purely deductive presentation of reality based on the axioms of rationality.

Based upon these assumptions the ideal model is an analytically relevant description of the macroeconomic landscape. Therefore, it is claimed, the model is relevant for analysis of the long-run consequences of shifts in structures and price regulations. The longer the time horizon of the analysis, the greater the concurrence between the abstract, ideal model and the picture of reality created within the laboratory, because in the long run the laboratory model will be cleansed of the many random events; then the rational expectations hypothesis will demonstrate its analytical superiority.[5]

OPEN MACROECONOMIC SYSTEMS

Laboratory models are well-defined special cases within the corpus of macro-models. These are clockwork models, which give precise answers and which only to a limited extent are empirically based. In Keynes's own words, this is not a relevant procedure to use when the object of our analysis is the genuine macroeconomic reality:

> The object of our analysis is, not to provide a machine, or method of blind manipulation, which will furnish an infallible answer, but to provide ourselves with an organised and orderly method of thinking out particular problems; and, after we have reached a provisional conclusion by isolating the complicating factors one by one, we then have to go back on ourselves and allow, as well as we can, for the probable interactions of the factors amongst themselves. This is the nature of economic thinking. Any other way of applying our formal principles of thought (without which, however, we shall be lost in the wood) will lead us into error. (Keynes, 1936: 297)

The ontological reflection suggests that the macroeconomic landscape appears as an open system. The *Oxford Economic Dictionary's* definition of an open system: '[is one] in which the total mass or energy fluctuates; an incomplete or alterable system (of ideas, doctrines, things, etc.)'. This definition highlights the central conditions characterizing the macroeconomic landscape.

The analysis of the economic landscape is in focus in another of Keynes's aphoristic definitions: 'Economics is a science of thinking in terms of models joined to the art of choosing models which are relevant to the contemporary world' (from a letter to Roy Harrod, July 1938; (*CWK*, XIV: 296). It is an impressive statement, although I could have wished that Keynes had written '(macro)economic methodology' instead of just 'economics'. But let that stand as my interpretation. For Keynes, economics was concerned with methodology, but not exclusively. The trick is in developing a model that epistemologically fits the specific focus of World 1 which is under investigation. It is not a model for 'all seasons': quite the opposite. We must always, to begin with, consider how the macroeconomic landscape is organized, where the relevant limitations are drawn, which markets can legitimately be aggregated or maybe even left out of the first round of analysis.

A relevant macroeconomic model will be characterized by being an incomplete and alterable system: incomplete, because we do not have a thorough picture of the deep stratum (see Chapter 2); alterable, because the model needs to be contextually relevant to conditions in reality that are continually changing. On the other hand it is also true that if all parts of the landscape are modelled as unstructured open sub-systems, it becomes impossible to complete a macroeconomic analysis.

An open system is also characterized by not giving, or not necessarily wanting to give, a mathematical formulation of all the factors included in the model. We know expectations play an important role in macro-economic development; but in the open model we do not have sufficient knowledge to give a formulaic representation. Expectations-formation must remain partially unspecified if the model is going to be used to describe reality. It is exceedingly difficult to formulate an expectations hypothesis which at one and the same time has a form that can be included in a mathematical system and does not unrealistically idealize reality. Along with this it must be taken into account that expectations-formation is constantly changing, influenced by new information.

The ephemeral nature of expectations is an important reason why post-Keynesian models must remain open in their fundamental structure. For that reason alone they cannot deliver precise predictions. They can however supply conditional statements about the future, not least depending on the character of expectations-formation. The relevance and quality of the predictions depend also upon the realism of the assumptions being used.

A fundamentally open structure does not exclude short-term analytic semi-closures, where specific parts of the macroeconomic system are made objects for a formalized presentation. The important analytical concept developed by Keynes is effective demand. This concept was presented by a temporarily detachment of changing and uncertain expectations from the analytical model, see Box 5.1. By doing this he was better able to streamline his analytical tools. This method is an example of the unavoid-able balancing of, on the one hand, formulating the theory of effective demand as simply as possible by the use of semi-closures, without on the other hand losing analytical relevance by detachment from reality through mechanical quantification. The researcher should always be conscious of this balancing process between analytical convenience and social ontol-ogy (complexity). Simplification is necessary because effective demand is so influenced by expectations. As long as expectations are assumed to be constant within the semi-closure, we are at the best only halfway through the analysis. The more unrealistic assumptions behind the semi-closure can afterwards be loosened before the direction and strength of the impact of changes of effective demand can be concluded.

The trick is to find an analytical model that catches the important traits of the macroeconomic reality that is usually characterized by an open and stratified ontology. A mechanical habit of model-building will con-tradict the assumption that the macroeconomic landscape is open. As we shall see in Chapter 6, Keynes remained rather sceptical of Tinbergen's econometric investigation of investment demand in the interwar period. According to Keynes's judgement, Tinbergen's fundamental assumption that the macro-investment function should remain stable throughout the period was not fulfilled. In this case Tinbergen, according to Keynes, had

BOX 5.1   EFFECTIVE DEMAND: AN EXAMPLE OF A SEMI-CLOSURE ANALYSIS

'Effective demand' is a central theoretic concept in *The General Theory*. It is defined by Keynes as that 'amount of employment which [the entrepreneurs] expect to maximise the excess of the proceeds over the factor cost' (Keynes, 1936: 25). To simplify the analytical content of the concept, Keynes enacts a semi-closure, by assuming that firms' expectations are correct: that is to say the willingness to supply equals realized demand. This semi-closure allows Keynes analytically to equate *supply* and *expected demand* and is followed by the chapters in *The General Theory* about consumption and investment decisions and the multiplier.

A part of the methodological practice of making use of a semi-closure is to evaluate the realism of the applied assumptions. The analytical relevance of effective demand depends upon it. This evaluation will not be carried out here. It is sufficient to mention that the closer the macroeconomic landscape approaches to full employment, the more unrealistic this assumption of making expected demand and realizable production equal.

Keynes used the term equilibrium as a characterization of the analytical outcome achieved by using a semi-closed model and knowing that he had left out a number of factors, which in other connections and in a total analysis would be important. This he did to purify initially the main analytical outcome of the principle of effective demand and of the multiplier process. Keynes did not use the analytical term equilibrium in the sense of market clearing, but in the sense of 'no further changes'. That is to say, that equilibrium refers to a condition where the extrapolated effects of an exogenous shock, within the model framework, are exhausted without necessarily clearing the labour market. Taking into account the assumptions upon which the semi-closure is based, the new equilibrium will, when compared to the starting point, give an indication of some economic tendencies which the exogenous shock has caused (see Chapter 6 on equilibrium).

gone too far when he assumed a semi-closure within which the investment behaviour could be statistically investigated in a meaningful way. The interwar period was characterized by expectations of the future that changed dramatically and unpredictably.

Parts and Wholes

> The atomic hypothesis which has worked so splendidly in physics breaks down in psychics. We are faced at every turn with the problems of organic unity, of discreteness, of discontinuity – the whole is not equal to the sum of the parts, comparisons of quantity fail us, small changes produce large effects, the assumptions of a uniform and homogeneous continuum are not satisfied. (*CWK*, X: 262)

Models attempting to explain the macroeconomic landscape should be based upon the economy as a whole. This matter of fact raises a number of methodological questions:

- Firstly, 'the whole' is difficult to analyse all at once, which in all fairness is part of the practical reason to use a general equilibrium model, where in principle all markets are included, but at the price of a closed laboratory model.
- Secondly, practical experience shows that the way to make the most relevant semi-closures within the macroeconomic landscape depends upon the purpose of the study and the nature of the object of the study.

From Micro- to Macro-Theory

The macroeconomic result, in principle, is merely the outcome of all microeconomic actions. Hence, it is persuasive to suggest that the starting point for the macroeconomic analysis is individual actions that are subsequently aggregated. This line of thought is the basis for realizing the call by neoclassical economists for an explicit microeconomic foundation for macroeconomic theory when developing models. This requirement is fulfilled with regard to the behavioural relations by the introduction of the so-called representative agents who behave in accordance with the axioms of individual rationality.

As I discussed in Chapter 4, this analytical method requires homogeneity of the microeconomic base, if one typical agent's behaviour can represent the behaviour of all agents in the economy. Every single agent's excess demand function must in that case be linear, and the distribution among the agents of all the other explaining variables – among others, income – must remain unchanged if there is going to be in a mathematical sense concurrence between individual agents' microeconomic behaviour and the macroeconomic behaviour. Furthermore, traditional microeconomic theory built upon the assumption of given and constant preferences and the process of optimization is undertaken under the constraint of everything else remaining unchanged, especially concerning expected prices and income. These assumptions are very restrictive when one takes into consideration that the purpose of macroeconomic analysis will often be to illuminate possible but unknown trends in the gross national product, employment and relative prices, including real wages, which cannot be assumed to be parametrically given unless the economy is in a general market-clearing equilibrium, that is, that individual agents have rational expectations. If these expectations are not fulfilled, then actual microeconomic behaviour will deviate from intended behaviour and the representative agent's behaviour cannot give a correct representation of the complex macroeconomic behaviour. Aggregating the intended microeconomic behaviour will therefore, even in cases where agents are similar, not be an adequate description of likely macroeconomic behaviour.

If the microeconomic theory's *ceteris paribus* assumptions are not fulfilled, then the microeconomic-based macroeconomic conclusions cannot be assumed to take place. Any unexpected change will by definition imply that the initial expectation is no longer fulfilled, thereby making the actual transactions deviate from the sum of the intended actions. Within a money-based market economy, individual transactions are connected. A large number of different transactions will break the *ceteris paribus* clause; the macro-result cannot be calculated as the sum of microeconomic intentions and the construct of one representative microeconomic agent is a mirage. There is an inbuilt methodological contradiction in macro-models that are based on traditional microeconomic theory with individual agents, optimizing based upon the assumption of, among other things, parametrically given prices (Hartley, 1997). This is a well-known problem within post-Keynesian macroeconomic theory and discussed under the label of 'the fallacy of composition'; see Chapter 7.

Briefly about the Fallacy of Composition

The fallacy of composition occurs when incorrect macroeconomic conclusions are drawn from a misplaced analogy between macro-behaviour and microeconomic behaviour. The classical mistake of this type is found when an analogy based upon individual households' behaviour is applied to the macroeconomic result; for example, that an increase in individual saving will result in increased saving for society as a whole, or that an individual wage reduction will result in increased total employment. There is a great difference between reasoning inside of or outside the general equilibrium model.

General Equilibrium

When a general equilibrium model apparently avoids the prevalent conflict between micro-founded behaviour relations and macroeconomic conclusions, the explanation is that in this case the argument is confined within the framework of a closed model, where the analysis describes a general equilibrium and the equilibrium values are known beforehand, that is to say that the macroeconomic outcome is given. The starting point of the analysis is a general equilibrium, where all the agents' intentions are satisfied. That is the definition of general equilibrium; all agents have optimized their individual economic preferences given the structural character and the relative prices. As a main rule it is assumed that general equilibrium is characterized by perfect competition on all markets, but it is not a necessary assumption to achieve this result of concurrence between individual optimization and macroeconomic equilibrium. A similar analytical result is achievable in cases of, for instance, trade union power; see for instance the DREAM (Danish Rational Economic Agent Model), where trade unions are assumed to determine real wages. If the trade union monopoly is lifted in this laboratory model, then wage-earners and firms are assumed to optimize on an individualistic basis where a perfectly competitive market-clearing real wage rules.

This potential fallacy of composition is not a matter of whether the actors are assumed to behave rationally on an individual basis, but whether the macroeconomic model *a priori* has been restricted in such a way that implies a concurrence between individual expectations and the analytical outcome of the model:

1. the individual expectations always concur with the result of the system: 'rational expectations';
2. the representative agent is equal to the average of the individual agents;
3. there is permanent market clearing;
4. individual preferences and production functions are 'well behaved' (see Chapter 7).

If these conditions are fulfilled, the mathematical solution will express concurrence between the summation of the microeconomic behaviour and the result at the macro-level, which by construction prevents the fallacy of composition being committed within the model.[6]

On the other hand, if just one of the above-mentioned four assumptions does not hold in the analytical model, then the microeconomic expectations and the macroeconomic results will not be identical. When that is the case and one tries to draw macroeconomic conclusions based only upon micro-economic behaviour and/or single market analysis, then the *ceteris paribus* assumptions are not fulfilled, which is the main reason for committing the fallacy of composition. This problem is examined in depth in Chapter 7.

In general, the risk of committing the fallacy of composition can be reduced by employing a methodology that emphasizes the importance of an empirical foundation. The crucial methodological point is the process of aggregation: how millions of microeconomic activities can be represented in a few macroeconomic causal relationships. Via the interlinked market processes, a large number of individual (and somewhat different) microeconomic decisions are analytically transformed into aggregate units, which I have chosen to call macro-actors (see Chapter 3). Hence, the macro-actor should in an analytical sense be understood as a contrast to the representative microeconomic agent. The latter is just a microeconomic average which is assumed to mimic the individual rational behaviour with full foresight. The macro-actors' analytical behaviour (in the macro-markets) cannot, as previously discussed, due to the presence of uncertainty be deduced only from traditional microeconomic theory. One important analytical difference between the expectations-formation of the representative agent and the macro-actor is that the representative agent can be assumed to behave as though he knows the future, whereas the macro-actor behaves in accordance with the fact that the future is uncertain. Hence, macro-behavioural relations have to be contextual and cannot be deduced independently of the macroeconomic landscape, that is, the economy as a whole.

This leads to an important conclusion, that the macroeconomic behavioural relations which make up the dynamic element in the post-Keynesian macro-model cannot be determined independently of the macroeconomic landscape. They are an integrated part of the landscape and contribute to the analytical openness and by that to the macroeconomic uncertainty.

> Important mistakes had resulted, he [Keynes] believed, from 'extending to the system as a whole conclusions which have been correctly arrived at in respect of a part of it taken in isolation'. (O'Donnell, 1989: 178, quoting *CWK*, VII: xxxii)[7]

Macro-Analysis: One Market or Several Markets?

In most of the modern neoclassic textbooks the labour market is depicted as in Figure 5.1, in that the new-Keynesian variant to a large degree is seen as mainstream in neoclassical macro-theory, as it was portrayed in Chapter 1 with the affirming Figure 1.2.

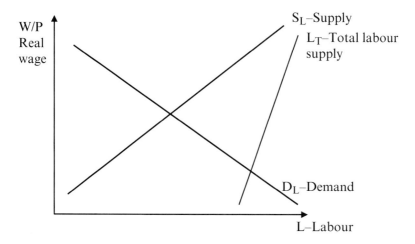

Figure 5.1   New-Keynesian labour market model

The demand and supply functions in Figure 5.1 are derived from the theory of a representative micro-agent, which assumes the validity of the *ceteris paribus* assumption. The functions are derived independently of one another and not affected by changes in other parts of the model. It is a single-market laboratory model, isolated from the rest of the general equilibrium model. In this laboratory a thought experiment is carried out. Here it is assumed that all the other parameters are under control and express their equilibrium values.

The neoclassical employment model described here is derived from a labour market theory based upon methodological individualism. Using methodological individualism as the foundation for macro-theory assumes that each individual acts independently and that behaviour is independent of context. If these assumptions are fulfilled, and the *ceteris paribus* assumptions are considered legitimate, the model establishes a clear causal relation between real wages and employment.

In a general equilibrium model that satisfies the aforementioned conditions for using methodological individualism, the researchers have assumed beforehand that all output will always be sold, either as consumption for wage-earners or as investment goods to firms. Part of the axiomatic base for the analysis is that supply creates its own demand, thereby rendering unemployment the result only of lack of real wage adjustment. This is not a new insight, but the implication of the assumptions made.

However, in new-Keynesian models involuntary unemployment can be present during the adjustment phase following an exogenous fall in demand for labour. The 'automatic' increase in private sector employment

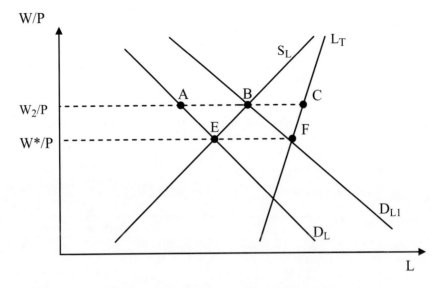

Figure 5.2   Unemployment in the new-Keynesian labour market

will, according to the model, require a real wage reduction. If this is not the case, real wage inflexibility is given the blame. Wage inflexibility is seen as caused either by institutional market power, or due to a rational delay in adjustment because of, for example, efficiency wage, transaction costs, minimum wage, labour market law or other structurally determined factors; see for example Begg *et al.* (2001). As is also seen from Figure 5.2, then a lower real wage apparently should eliminate involuntary unemployment – the part of unemployment that is not a result of individual optimization in a completely competitive equilibrium.

The adjustment process in an isolated labour market is described as follows, taken from a conventional textbook:

> Now labour demand falls to D_L. Until wages adjust, BC [voluntary unemployment] remains unchanged, but a number of people represented by AB has become involuntarily unemployed, pure excess capacity in the labour market. Boosting labour demand again could move the economy from A back to B. However, in the absence of an increase in demand, involuntarily unemployed workers are assumed slowly to bid wages down, moving employment from A to E. (Begg *et al.*, 2001: 203–4)

Assumptions about methodological individualism and nice model characteristics steer employment within the model clear of the fallacy of composition, but cannot guarantee that macroeconomically incorrect

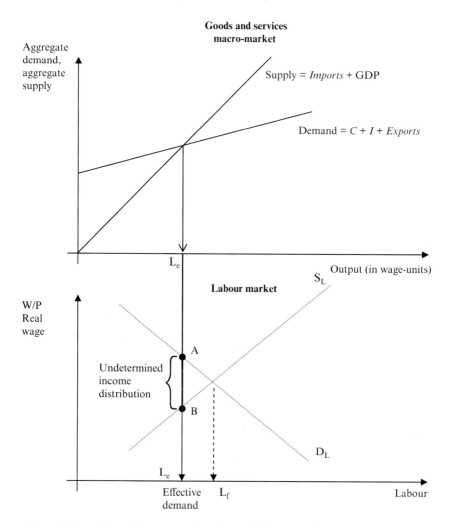

Figure 5.3   A simple integrated goods and labour markets model

conclusions are avoided outside equilibrium, where *ceteris* is not *paribus* and expectations are not fulfilled, which is illustrated in Figure 5.3. Here the point is that the market-clearing equilibria in the goods and labour markets are obtained at different levels of employment. This discrepancy causes tension and calls for further adjustment, which is unexplained in Figure 5.2, where demand and supply are assumed to be independent.

To the extent that the assumptions of the model are not fulfilled outside of general equilibrium, it is inconsistent from a modelling point of view to isolate the labour market from the macroeconomic system as a whole. In such cases of misplaced isolation macroeconomic conclusions cannot be drawn about any situation outside full equilibrium. Hence, the isolated labour market cannot give a coherent picture of how the adjustment to a new equilibrium may be established. Misplaced isolation of, for instance, the labour market might lead to analytical mistakes when other markets are discarded, as illustrated in Figure 5.3. Here a simple diagram is shown connecting real wages and aggregate demand outside of general equilibrium. The effects of a fall in demand for labour cannot be explained in the labour market alone. This expansion of the analytical perspective to include the markets for output demonstrates the link between effective demand and (un)employment. The necessity of including all relevant markets is not caused by the openness of the macroeconomic landscape, but by the fact that even within the framework of a closed model misplaced isolation risks that relevant factors are excluded.

This absence of analytical singularity obviously becomes more apparent when in addition the mathematically specified analytical model is not 'well behaved'. In that case the relevant model might have a multiple set of solutions, perhaps as a consequence of the adjustment process being dynamic, perhaps because of nonlinearities within the mathematical model. The consequences of these closed-model complications will be studied in the following chapter.

Since Keynes was willing to accept the first classical labour market postulate, that the aggregate of firms' demand for labour can be depicted as a declining function of real wages,[8] it was possible for him to demonstrate the theoretical possibility of a macroeconomic unemployment equilibrium without having to ignore the whole of neoclassical micro-theory. Keynes accepted for the sake of argument that the private sector's rational macroeconomic behaviour could be described by the curve D_L. This assumption did not hinder Keynes from demonstrating one of his key points, that outside of general equilibrium any realistic macroeconomic analysis does not support the hypotheses of an automatic return to full employment. This conclusion is illustrated in the simple and closed model in Figure 5.3, where the goods and labour markets are both represented. This partial equilibrium model containing the goods and labour markets is drawn in two separate diagrams: one for the goods market (the simple 45° income–expenditure model) and one for the labour market (where the first neoclassical postulate is accepted and represented by the D_L curve: it is just a repetition of Figure 5.1). Here it is assumed that output and employment are tied together by a traditional short-period production function with a decreasing labour productivity (see below in Appendix 8.1, Chapter 8): the assumption that lies behind the downward sloping demand curve for labour. The limited usefulness of the figure of an isolated labour market *à la* Figure 5.2 is to demonstrate that any reasoning within the diagram is only valid when the entire macroeconomic system is in a state of general equilibrium. Outside general equilibrium this diagram cannot tell a coherent macroeconomic story. This should be read as a wake-up call to readers of a rather large number of textbooks, where Figure 5.2 is reproduced uncritically as a macroeconomic analysis of labour market adjustment.

An Integrated Goods and Labour Markets Analysis

Figure 5.3 illustrates the point that even within a closed-model analysis it is necessary to include causal relations which interlink relevant macro-markets. In the upper part of the figure planned effective demand for labour is determined by the intersection point between aggregate demand for and supply of goods (and services). The competitive structures in the goods and labour markets determine how the total factor income is shared between labour and capital. If there is perfect competition in both markets the point A in the labour market could be realized by goods prices adjusted to marginal cost determined by the given money wage and production function. If on the other hand firms compete only to a limited extent in goods and/or labour markets, they will be able to increase their share of factor income by reducing the real wage below point A. This is a labour market causal relationship which depends on the structures of the labour market and the size of effective unemployment.

In this closed-model analysis of two interdependent markets there is no mechanism that automatically secures that planned output and effective demand for labour (L_e) coincide with full employment (L_f).

If we move outside the framework of the above closed-model analysis and into the real macroeconomic landscape, then uncertainty prevails and has to be analytically integrated, which is one more argument against studying any macro-markets in isolation. We will not here examine which semi-closures within the open model could be relevant for analysing employment. These closures will in all cases be context-specific and temporary, a point which I shall return to in Chapter 8.

In *The General Theory* Keynes showed that demand for labour is derived from the effective demand for goods and services, which among other things is a function of the expected income. This means that the goods and labour markets cannot be analysed independently of each other. In *The General Theory* Keynes identifies the analytical essence. This consists of developing a macroeconomic theory which ensures that fundamental uncertainty is not forgotten. This happens because the unique role of expectations is recognized as being decisive for the understanding of effective demand (see Chapter 8). After having explained this to the reader he focuses on the components of aggregate demand and their determinants: the propensity to consume, the marginal efficiency of capital, and liquidity preference. While focusing on each single component, the others must be ignored. In this fashion the single demand components appear separated. A few chapters later he adds on the financial sector, and in this way he develops an integrated monetary production theory.[9] The model is then expanded with an analysis of flexible wages and at the end with a theory of price determination. In this manner Keynes demonstrates how more and more of the *ceteris paribus* assumptions can be lifted, thereby generalizing the theory.

This approach is probably chosen from the insight that one cannot analyse the whole landscape at once, which leads to the question of where the demarcation of the semi-closures can be drawn, because there is a trade-off between understanding parts of an integrated system and understanding the whole: '[T]here might well be quite different laws for wholes of different degrees of complexity ...' (*CWK*, VIII: 277).

The more complex the field of study appears, the greater inclination to reduce to smaller and thereby more homogeneous units; but there is a risk that this procedure will obscure important interactions. It is no easy matter placing the correct analytical demarcation lines in an uncertain structure.

The Sector Balances are an Integrated Part of the Whole and Cannot be Seen in Isolation

> Look after the unemployment, and the Budget will look after itself. (1933, *CWK*, XXI: 150)

In this chapter about the interrelationship between parts and the whole the question arises: how is a relevant sector balance analysis carried out? It is well known that a specific goal for the development in, for instance, the public sector balance is often set.[10] This goal is specified without considering the causes behind an emerging imbalance or the development in other sector balances. Each sector is analysed separately. The argument in favour of a balanced budget (or balance of external payments) is taken from microeconomic theory that in the longer run a household or a firm cannot spend more than it earns. Public debt is considered as a 'burden on future generations'. A balance-of-payments deficit is said to be a burden on international capital markets, because the deficit country has to borrow internationally.

But these comparisons between micro-agents and macro-sectors are not valid. The activities of one agent can be analysed as if the external conditions are exogenously determined. This is not the case with regard to sector balances. According to the conventions of national accounting it will always be the case that the sum of sectoral deficits and surpluses adds up to zero. This is the accounting equivalent to Walras's Law. It states that a deficit on the public sector budget must be identical to the savings surplus in the private sector (and the balance of payments) as shown below:

$$OS + PS + BB = O$$

where:
   OS = surplus on public sector consumption and investment budget
   PS = excess private sector savings (S_p-I_p)
   BB = the balance of payments current account (note: a domestic deficit
         is registered with a plus sign)

The national accounting system is equivalent to a closed system. One sector cannot have a surplus without at least one other sector having a deficit. A specific goal relating to the surplus in the public sector will, if the balance of payments is in equilibrium, be the same as stating the goal of aiming for a savings deficit in the private sector. This is a statement about identities and is not open for debate. But one may ask whether it is wise to recommend all member countries of the EU to aim for a surplus in the public sector budget, which is equivalent to asking for a policy that creates a savings deficit in the private sector in the member countries. This question cannot, of course, be answered independently of the general development in the private sector concerning employment, investment and inflation.

The appropriate development in the private sector savings balance will depend on the choice of the analytical model. In the general equilibrium model it is assumed that the individual private agent is in budgetary balance during his lifespan. This means that a stationary population with a homogenous age spread must be assumed to have a balance between income and expenditure, since the macroeconomic development is assumed to be equal to the sum of the individual agents' decisions. If the population is stagnating then rational agents will on average balance their private budget, because there is no involuntary unemployment. In that case the private sector is assumed to be in equilibrium. On this analytical background it is straightforward to recommend that the public sector also ought to be balanced. If the politicians try to expand public expenditure then the private sector equilibrium is disturbed. If on the other hand the population is growing, reflecting more young people than elders, then the private sector will have need of large investments, causing a deficit in the private sector, which will be mirrored by a public surplus.

Even in the laboratory model the sector balances cannot be viewed independently of one another. The public sector and the balance of payments must reflect the private sector's behaviour and it is pointless to state independent goals for these sectors.

When we move outside of the laboratory the mutual interdependence between the economic sectors is even more pronounced. The private sector balance is determined not only by the demographic mix but also by the effective demand for goods and services and the level of unemployment. High unemployment can be caused by excess savings in the private sector, which has to be mirrored by a deficit in the public sector (and/or a surplus in the balance of payments). A fiscal policy intended to reduce the public deficit will, at least initially, increase unemployment further while reducing private savings and real investment. In a post-Keynesian approach it will often be indeterminate whether savings or private investment is reduced the most, when fiscal policy becomes more restrictive. In that case the question whether a restrictive fiscal policy increases or decreases the public sector deficit remains open, which makes a specific goal for the public sector budget less sensible without a solid knowledge of the actual macroeconomic context.

Again one of Keynes's aphorisms, stated at the start of this section, seems to catch an important part of the answer to the question of how to improve the public sector budget: that it is employment that plays a pivotal role in private savings and investment, and accordingly in the public sector budget. Hence, a specific goal concerning the public sector budget should not be specified independently of employment in the private sector and the balance of payments.

SUMMARY

Neoclassical theory uses a general equilibrium model, the so-called laboratory model, as the main macroeconomic analytical tool for putting parts together as a whole. This ensures that all (specified) markets are included in the mathematical analysis based on rational representative agents optimizing individual welfare. This procedure is based on the understanding that the whole equals the sum of the parts.

In spite of Keynes's emphasis that macroeconomics concerns 'the economy as a whole', post-Keynesian analysis is not tied to a predesignated total model: quite the opposite, I am tempted to say. Outside the general market-clearing equilibrium a specific, context-independent analytical model cannot be named as the right one, because the following three conditions must always be respected:

1. Macro-behavioural relations differ from the sum of micro-behaviour.
2. The macro-markets are internally connected, which necessitates an integrated analysis.
3. The sector balances cannot be analysed separately.

Instead of aiming for one simultaneous analysis of the complete model, post-Keynesians recommend an iterative analytical process, which will be explained in the next chapter. The semi-closed macro-markets will be included in order of importance, organized the way that realistic macro-economic theory[11] suggests, which might result in a recommendation of a temporary use of a *ceteris paribus* clause. Then, as in the quotation from Keynes given above: 'we then have to go back on ourselves and allow, as well as we can, for the probable interactions of the factors amongst themselves' (Keynes, 1936: 297).

As a tool for this iterative analytical procedure the mapping of the macroeconomic landscape can be a useful initial guide.

NOTES

1. 'Model' in the sense of a structure of causality, not necessarily mathematically formulated.
2. I think that the terms 'system' and 'model' are far too often used as synonyms.
3. The inspiration from Keynes is apparent. He considered in *The General Theory* the classical full employment model as a special case, which was his reason for calling his book *The General Theory*.
4. I (Jespersen, 2005) have used the term 'tying shut' for that type of semi-closed subsystem.
5. It is illustrative that Keynes wrote in 1923, 'but this long run is a misleading guide to current affairs. In the long run we are all dead. Economists set themselves too easy, too useless a task if in tempestuous seasons they can only tell us that when the storm is long past the ocean is flat again' (*CWK*, IV: 65). Here Keynes does not deny the possibility that general equilibrium can occur, but rather challenges the relevance of this long-run phenomenon instead of focusing on the adjustment process.
6. Which possibly explains why Andersen and Haagen Pedersen (2005), creators of the DREAM, do not understand the relevance of discussing the possibility of committing the fallacy of composition to a realistic macroeconomic analysis when it is undertaken within a general equilibrium model.
7. When I cite *The General Theory* as (*CWK*, VII) rather than Keynes (1936) it is because the edition of *The General Theory* which is printed in the *Collected Writings* also includes the forewords to the German and French editions, where the above quotation originates.
8. Keynes's argumentation in *The General Theory* will be expanded below in Chapter 8.

9. This is also reflected in the book's title, *The General Theory of Employment, Interest and Money*. In this case it is thought-provoking that the laboratory model quite seldom, if ever, contains a financial sector with interest rates and private credit.
10. Within the EU Stability and Growth pact it is said that all member countries should aim at having balance or a minor surplus in the public sector budget.
11. Of course, depending on how the term 'macroeconomic theory' is interpreted.

6.   Equilibrium and path-dependence from a perspective of uncertainty

> I should, I think, be prepared to argue that, in a world ruled by uncertainty with an uncertain future linked to an actual present, a final position of equilibrium, such as one deals with in static economics, does not properly exist. (*CWK*, XXIX: 222, in a letter to H.D. Henderson, May 1936)

PROLOGUE: 'A LONG STRUGGLE OF ESCAPE'

This chapter covers an important methodological aspect of the macroeconomic discussion that began in 1936. As mentioned in the introductory chapter, there is a crucial, methodologically-based dividing line that runs through the history of macroeconomic theory and which defines the various schools of macroeconomic theory. It is the evaluation of whether an empirically anchored macroeconomic system can be analysed by using the general equilibrium method. This is an important dividing line on the analytical level (World 2). There are many reasons for this, reasons that have been explored in a vast quantity of macroeconomic literature since 1936. Not all the authors of these numerous books and articles have explicitly made clear that this fundamental question has been and still is a very crucial undercurrent in the debate between the orthodox and the heterodox macroeconomists. If they had, fewer bookshelves might have been needed (and much shadow boxing could have been avoided). In all fairness, it should be mentioned that it is only within the past 20–30 years that it has become clearer that there is such a methodological gulf separating the two positions. This is a comprehension process for which the numerous books have acted as a catalyst. Not until we focus closely on the analytical method does the importance of this dividing line stand out clearly.

Therefore, the chapter will also contain a description of why this critical dividing line is not always present in the macroeconomic discussion today, as we might wish. As pointed out by Keynes in 1934 (*CWK*, XIII: 485–92), this lack of clarity is due to the fact that generation after generation of economists within the Anglo-Saxon tradition have been taught economics within the framework of a market-clearing equilibrium model, regardless of whether it is a strawberry market, the labour market or the economy as a whole that is being analysed. When a macro-theory covering several markets was to be established, it was regarded as perfectly natural to keep it within the framework of market-clearing equilibrium models. The reason that this use of an equilibrium method could continue for so long was particularly due to a number of economists having natural-science aspirations that reinforced the ambition to describe macroeconomics in mathematical terms. In this way, the macroeconomic equilibrium came to be represented by the mathematical solution to a number of formalized partial market models (whether algebraic or geometric).

The choice of analytical method is important because it is decisive for the design of the macroeconomic model. In the interwar period this equilibrium model was increasingly perceived as a straitjacket on macroeconomic analysis, not only by Keynes. Understanding his 1936 book has involved a methodological discussion that little by little has made clear that the choice of analytical method is crucial. The difference of analytical methods which Keynes pointed at has led to two separate worlds of macroeconomics that still divide the profession this very day.

For Keynes, it had been 'a long struggle of escape from habitual modes of thought and expression' (Keynes, 1936: viii). In fact, the real novelty which came to him during the early 1930s was the comprehension that the neoclassical analytical framework of a long-run general equilibrium was irrelevant. He had himself used this framework when he wrote *A Treatise on Money* (1930), which caused him to write the following in the preface to *The General Theory:*

> When I finished it [*A Treatise on Money*], I had made some progress towards pushing monetary theory back to becoming a theory of the output as a whole.[1] But my lack of emancipation from preconceived ideas showed itself in what now seems to me to be the outstanding fault of the theoretical parts of that work ... (Keynes, 1936: vi)

Keynes had crossed the methodological Rubicon when he broke away from the general equilibrium method in macroeconomics, which prepared him to integrate uncertainty in a significant way. Then the use of money can more easily be given a rational, behavioural explanation when the axiom of general equilibrium is removed from the analytical model. This opened a whole new world for macroeconomic analysis that is much better fitted to the macroeconomics of the real world (World 1).

INTRODUCTION: TWO SEPARATE POSITIONS

In the neoclassical laboratory model, equilibrium is a well-defined mathematical concept. Equilibrium is equivalent to the solution of the mathematically formulated model. In the neoclassical basic model, general equilibrium means a simultaneous alignment of supply and demand (clearing) in all markets. Within the framework of the equilibrium model, markets with imperfect competition can also be specified, as long as this does not produce technical difficulties for finding a mathematical solution to the model. In cases of imperfect competition the equilibrium will continue to be determined by the solution to a mathematical system that describes supply and demand in all markets as a function of relative prices. Notably, an important part of the neoclassical research programme has aimed to prove the existence of such a mathematical solution, that is, a price vector for models with several markets, and to uncover what restrictions are needed on the design of the models in order to ensure that the price vector 'exists'; see the introductory chapter.

Post-Keynesians, on the other hand, have had some difficulties in giving the analytical concept 'equilibrium' a relevant interpretation with reference to the real level (World 1).[2] They did not see any immediate tendency to general equilibrium in the macroeconomic reality. On the contrary: even over longer historical periods, there is no sign of macroeconomic equilibrium in the form of full employment and stable prices. Similarly, the public sector budget and the balance of payments with other countries have demonstrated major fluctuations.

At first glance, therefore, it may seem rather contradictory even to use the term 'equilibrium' within the framework of realistic analytical macrotheory, where the objective is to perform analyses of a macroeconomic reality characterized by uncertainty and imbalances. The microeconomic decisions are undertaken on the basis of uncertain expectations, because in reality, there is a widespread and fundamental lack of knowledge about the future. Keynes was not using the market clearing definition of 'equilibrium' in *The General Theory*. 'Equilibrium' means something fundamentally different from the meaning employed by his neoclassical colleagues. To Keynes, equilibrium rather means 'no further change', a kind of analytical standstill.[3] I will return to this very important divide between market clearing and standstill as useful definitions when the use of open, semi-closed and closed system analyses is discussed.

When Keynes changed his use of the term 'equilibrium', he was aiming at a theoretically-based semi-closure with an analytical standstill, which corresponded with empirical observations and therefore did not necessarily imply market clearing. Standstill can have many other causes than market clearing, which can be explained by conditions in the deep stratum. For example, Keynes used the term 'equilibrium' for the situation with permanently high unemployment that characterized the British labour market in the period between the wars. In Keynes's terminology, equilibrium could best be understood as a locked macroeconomic condition caused by, among other things, uncertainty regarding the future, which in turn might cause a deficiency of effective demand (see Chapter 8).

It was only when this difference in the analytical use of the term 'equilibrium' was gradually made clearer (see for instance Chick, 1978, 1983; Chick and Caserta, 1997; King, 2002), that renewed intellectual energy led the post-Keynesians to make macroeconomic theory more realistic.[4] The analytical importance of the concept of equilibrium was subsequently toned down and has increasingly been replaced by the path-dependent form of analysis; see for example Setterfield (1997) and Cornwall and Cornwall (2001).

Before we take a closer look at the equilibrium concept in the two major macroeconomic schools, a semantic clarification may be useful. It is my intention to give the concept of equilibrium a 'value-free' interpretation. Equilibrium is not intrinsically good or bad from a socio-economic perception. Equilibrium is not a desirable quality in itself in a macroeconomic sense. Here the use of language is different from the more mundane, everyday language in domestic and business economics, where equilibrium is usually considered to have a positive meaning. When there is 'equilibrium in the budget', then the board of directors nod appreciatively: the income matches the costs; whereas a deficit would immediately raise eyebrows and demand a good explanation. 'Equilibrium' and 'balance' go hand in hand linguistically, and the second meaning is often transferred a little too uncritically to macroeconomic problems. This occurs especially within neoclassical macro-theory when it is presented as aggregated microtheory. What is right for the individual household is easily perceived as right for the entire household sector, and what is right for the household sector is applied also to the public sector economy (the inheritance from Smith); see also Chapter 5 on sector balances. When macro-economists argue that fiscal policy should be 'sustainable', that is, there ought to be equilibrium in the public budgets, then it is a normative statement, but justified by a particular choice of method. The argument that unemployment below the 'natural rate of unemployment' is not sustainable is also motivated by the use of the general equilibrium method, where a given 'structural equilibrium' (market clearing) is analytically defined. In the examples above the concept of equilibrium is clearly given a normative content determined by the condition of general market clearing.

I will argue that the concept of equilibrium should only be used when and if it can contribute to a better understanding of how macroeconomic reality really works and how actual macroeconomic tendencies can be affected.

THE EQUILIBRIUM CONCEPT IN THE LABORATORY MODEL

To begin this chapter I have just discussed the equilibrium concept in general. Now I will concentrate the argumentation on the more specific use of general equilibrium method within a closed macroeconomic model.

Within neoclassical theory there is a distinction between three different meanings of the word 'equilibrium', as listed in Figure 6.1. In the following section I will concentrate the discussion solely on the use of the concept of general equilibrium in macro-theory. Arrow and Hahn (1971) have the following introductory paragraph in their authoritative work *General Competitive Analysis*:

> There are two basic, incompletely separable, aspects of the notion of general equilibrium: the simple notion of determinateness, that the relations describing the economic system must be sufficiently complete to determine the values of its variables, and the more specific notion that each relation represents a balance of forces. (Arrow and Hahn, 1971: 1)

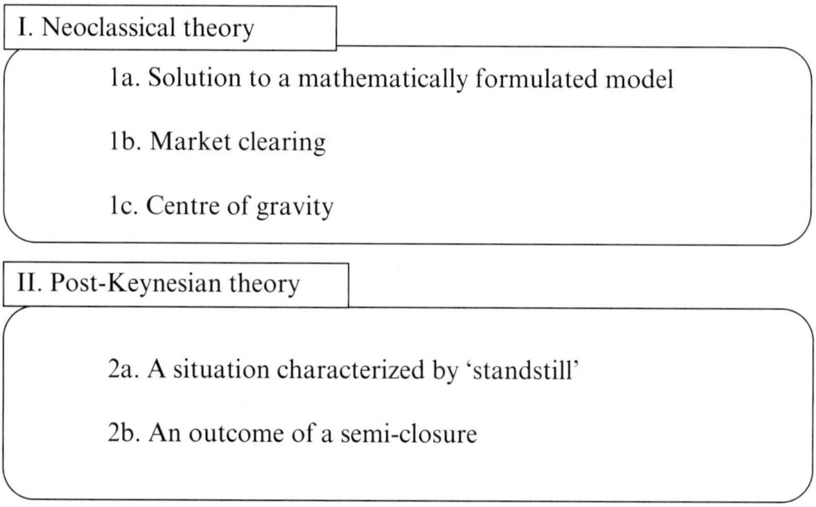

I. Neoclassical theory

    1a. Solution to a mathematically formulated model

    1b. Market clearing

    1c. Centre of gravity

II. Post-Keynesian theory

    2a. A situation characterized by 'standstill'

    2b. An outcome of a semi-closure

Figure 6.1   Use of the concept of equilibrium: an overview

Arrow and Hahn state here how the equilibrium concept is used in general equilibrium theory to ensure: (1) that the model has a solution; and (2) that the solution can be given a specific economic interpretation, characterized by a balance of market forces. To a large extent, these two attributes of the equilibrium concept contribute to determining the analytical content of the general equilibrium theory.

Furthermore, there is also a third use of the equilibrium concept in neo-classical macro-theory, which however lies outside the stationary general equilibrium model. This is the macroeconomic form of analysis, especially popular among new-Keynesians, where the general equilibrium solution is interpreted as a form of gravitation centre. See also the discussion in relation to Figure 5.2. If the macro-economy is out of general equilibrium as the result of a shock, then the general equilibrium solution of the model still stipulates the point to which the macroeconomic variables will subsequently move. The specific course will depend on the model's dynamic structure, which is stated as rationally caused inertia in the adjustment process of prices and wages to their general equilibrium values.

The closed, laboratory model is *a priori* designed in such a way that if there is full price and wage flexibility and perfect competition, then the model will always be in general equilibrium. But due to frictions in the market adjustment processes, which might have some empirical inspiration, it will take a sequence of periods before the general equilibrium is achieved. These adjustment processes can be interpreted as business cycles approaching the general equilibrium solution and are identified with market fluctuations, which by their analytical design are of a temporary nature; see for instance the textbook by Birch Sørensen and Whitta-Jakobsen (2005). Here, the structure of the analytical model is predesigned in such a way that the macroeconomic process sooner or later will reach the terminal position of general equilibrium. This is an example of how the new-Keynesians' attempt to bridge the gap between short-term cyclical unemployment and the long-term general (growth) equilibrium (with structural unemployment).

But even the short-term unemployment appears in new-Keynesian models as a solution to a mathematically formulated model, where market clearing is (partly) suspended due to price and wage rigidities caused by rational agents acting in an environment characterized by institutional frictions, such as transaction costs, clubs or misinterpreted information. Depending on the specific 'friction' the interpretation of the equilibrium with unemployment can be characterized as either a temporary, non-optimal market-clearing equilibrium (a mathematical solution) or a disequilibrium (non-market-clearing and temporary solution).[5]

The variables that are included in the closed laboratory model can, of course, be specified in growth rates. In such cases, the meaning of equilibrium will be expanded from flow equilibrium to a combined stock and flow equilibrium. The neoclassical growth model is assumed by design to be in permanent flow equilibrium period by period, where there is clearing in all markets.[6] Here the cyclical movements are skipped. The analytical point of departure is the long-term, general flow equilibrium described above. The dynamic growth features are added to the static model, partly through changes in the size and composition of the population, partly through increases in the physical capital apparatus, and partly through improved technology. The long-term growth equilibrium is determined by a constant ratio between physical capital and the labour force and is called a stock equilibrium. Obtaining such stock equilibrium as a solution to a dynamically formulated mathematical model places particularly restrictive requirements on the design of the mathematical relationships; these subsequently restrict the economic interpretation of the analytical results.

Equilibrium as a Solution to a Model

Let us start by examining the interpretation of equilibrium determined as a solution to a simple market model for supply and demand. If the relationship between supply and demand is formulated without indicating a time dimension, then they can routinely be drawn in a price–quantity diagram. Here, as a reflex, the focus is on the point of intersection of demand and supply as the only solution to the equation system. But the model will at least in principle have an infinite number of solutions depending on how 'equilibrium condition' is defined, which of course should be determined by economic reason. It is this equilibrium condition that closes the model in the mathematical sense. Each solution of the market model depends on how the equilibrium condition is designed. It is this extra equation, for instance 'demand equals supply', that gives the mathematical market model a specific closure. The condition of flow equilibrium could, depending on the institutional settings, take other more realistic forms than the abstract requirement of equalizing marginal cost and marginal utility. One could easily formulate an equilibrium condition where mark-up prices were normal business behaviour and/or wages were set by trade unions, making the mathematical solution deviate from the neoclassical ideal, but representing a higher degree of realism. In a model of a market where price and quantity are in constant fluctuation there is no reason to formulate an equilibrium condition. Accordingly, if there is no standstill in the market, then we are not dealing with a repetitive state.[7] In that case the solution to the mathematical model cannot be interpreted as equilibrium in economic terms and, therefore, is not analytically helpful.

The existence of equilibrium is of pivotal importance in the closed, laboratory model. Without an equilibrium condition the model will be underdetermined.[8] An important part of the scientific work in the laboratory, therefore, is the analysis of what is needed in the mathematical design of the macroeconomic behaviour relationships and of equilibrium conditions in order to guarantee general equilibrium. Proof of existence of general equilibrium has constituted a considerable part of the neoclassical researchers' work. Arrow and Debreu (1954) concluded that equilibrium is only guaranteed if the model contains a complete set of markets with perfect competition characteristics, so that in principle it is possible to trade in actual and (all) future markets at the very same time. Arrow and Debreu's merits lie in carrying out a proof that a solution exists for a laboratory model with such characteristics This is a strict analytical examination of a mathematical model's characteristics that only has the one thing in common with real-level economics (World 1): that within the Arrow–Debreu model the same words for variables as in the open macro-model are used, like markets, prices, competition, employment, and so on, which have only a linguistic affinity with reality.

Much neoclassical research has subsequently centred on extending the proof of existence to models which include markets for money, imperfect competition, economies of scale in production and so on. Arrow and Hahn (1971), among others, have proved that the existence of a general equilibrium is not limited to equilibrium conditions solely based on perfect competition. Since then, the proof of existence has also been carried out under the assumption of other 'imperfections', characterized by, among other things, asymmetric information and the absence of markets. These results have had the consequence that general equilibrium theory is no longer synonymous with the assumption of perfect competition.

However, there is a risk that the results of this equilibrium exercise will take on a prescriptive characteristic, which leads directly to the analytical trap which Lawson (1997) referred to as an 'epistemic fallacy'. This fallacy is committed when analytically achieved conclusions are assumed to be coincident with what we can know about reality. Hahn (1984) also warns against confusing the equilibrium solution with reality:

> To many economists Keynesian economics deals with important relevant problems and general equilibrium theory deals with no relevant problems at all. ... This view ... has, alas, an element of truth. This [is] quite simply that general equilibrium theorists have been unable to deliver one half at least of the required story: how does general equilibrium come to be established? (Hahn, 1984: 175)

Market Clearing

Market clearing based on the assumptions of perfect competition and atomistic market behaviour is a mathematically convenient model design. 'Voluntary' transactions are assumed to be carried out when the externally determined price has adjusted itself in such a way that supply equals demand. Within this framework of auction-like 'trade structures', market clearing is the normal condition. The entire point of these auction systems is to make the price so flexible that any *ex ante* excess demand or supply is eliminated through price adjustments. Hence, in these flex-price markets (to use Hicks's, 1989, terminology) quantities can always be traded, but at the expense of an uncertain price. This 'market clearing' procedure therefore more resembles a practical solution to a structural problem on the supply side (of storage capacity or a need for cash). Flex-price markets are empirically characterized by rather large fluctuations from day to day, which could hardly be interpreted as a state of tranquillity. Hence, market clearing might take place, but to call this situation 'equilibrium' is a misnomer. Price fluctuations create uncertainty with regard to the future. Flex-price markets are well suited for speculation driven by 'the activity of forecasting the psychology of the market' (Keynes, 1936: 158). These flex-price changes are seldom caused by changes in the underlying macroeconomic landscape, but rather are a reflection of partly self-fulfilling expectations mainly in the financial markets. If unanchored expectations are unfolding within a flex-price trade structure, where demand and supply is unlimited then substantial price waves can be set in motion. In a functional sense the market might clear continuously, but the price changes may not necessarily contribute to macroeconomic stability. Hence, market clearing in tradeable terms is not a guarantee of macroeconomic balance, let alone tranquillity.

The existence of general equilibrium is a theoretical possibility. But the microeconomic-based general equilibrium theory has an inherent consistency problem when efforts are made to apply equilibrium to World 1. Representative microeconomic agents are assumed to know the price vector that is relevant for them. It is externally given and exogenous in relation to the agents. But, outside general equilibrium, the agents cannot know this price vector, unless clairvoyant abilities are attributed to them. If agents do not have full knowledge of the market-clearing prices, then they lack the necessary information to establish a general equilibrium.

On a strictly analytical level, the thought experiment can be performed that the agents woke up in a general equilibrium. But general equilibrium cannot be established through a realistic adjustment process, since this would require knowledge by the agents of equilibrium prices which is only available *in* general equilibrium. On the contrary, it is a necessary condition for the existence of a price vector in general equilibrium that agents have prior knowledge of this price vector. In other words, the actors are assumed *a priori* to have a knowledge which is unknowable. This causes internal contradiction in the model; see Robinson (1974) and Hahn (1984).

Following this argument it is not unfair to conclude that the original Arrow–Debreu equilibrium model was underdetermined with regard to information, unless all transactions occurred at exactly the same time. A model-specific solution to this deficit of information is the assumption of 'rational expectations': that the agents know in advance the price vector that creates general equilibrium. The assumption of rational expectations ensures that market clearing can take place at equilibrium prices. On the other hand, the assumption about complete knowledge of the future definitively separates the laboratory model's analytical results from the real level.

Proof of the existence of general equilibrium is thus in the present form only relevant on the analytical level (World 2).

A Gravitation Centre

The above discussion on the use of the equilibrium concept has primarily been connected to the market-clearing condition where the agents had their price expectations satisfied when carrying out voluntary transactions. Now the question is which equilibrium concept can be used on a consistent analytical basis, when there is no continuous coincidence between supply and demand on all markets (lack of market clearing). This is a difficult question to answer within equilibrium economics.[9] It depends on the laboratory model's dynamic characteristics. The mathematical specification of behavioural functions that do not violate the long-period general equilibrium seems to be an important criterion in new-Keynesian macroeconomics. Behavioural relations and production functions have to be well behaved. The model is designed in such a way that if the macroeconomic system is struck by an external shock, even an unforeseen one, it will adjust to a new general equilibrium – otherwise it is considered misspecified and not suitable for analytical purposes.[10] The solution to this dynamic problem lies partly in selecting the right set of *a priori* assumptions about economic behaviour, market integration and dynamics (general gross substitution; Davidson, 2003). What assumptions should be fulfilled in order to ensure that the adjustment will draw prices and quantities in the direction of the general equilibrium solution? There are still no unequivocal research results which can precisely state the demands on the construction of the dynamic structure that would 'guarantee' convergence (Ingrao and Israel, 1990). In small macroeconomic models where economic behaviour is made very restrictive and/or the number of agents is reduced drastically (which among other things are the hallmarks of real business cycle models) and full predictability is assumed, it is rather easy technically to ensure convergence to the long-run gravitation centre in any model. Small dynamic equilibrium models with few agents that are assumed to have limited information are also included in 'game theory', which lies outside my actual macroeconomic focus.

Simulation models can also be used to uncover the micro-based equilibrium model's dynamic characteristics. Hahn and Solow (1996) show that the simulation results that can be achieved with completely traditional neoclassical models often have multiple long-term solutions that are dependent on the design of behavioural relations, equilibrium conditions and the initial situation. If the dynamic characteristics are given the form of non-linear, differential equations, the simulation results' dependency on the initial values will be enhanced (the so-called 'butterfly effect'; see for example Ormerod, 1998). In the case of multiple solutions, it is not sufficient to assume that the agents are equipped with rational expectation, since agents cannot know *a priori* which solution the model will converge towards. Hence Ingrao and Israel (1990: 361) drew the following negative conclusion:

> While no agreement has yet been reached as to the implications of the results concerning uniqueness, those concerning global stability (i.e., the market's ability to attain equilibrium) are unquestionably negative.

This result, that there is no guarantee of convergence to general equilibrium within neoclassical macro-theory with a conventional microeconomic foundation, is clearly an extension of the critique that Keynes already asserted in his 1934 paper, though he did it on an intuitive basis. Joan Robinson made this point more explicit during and after the capital controversy with, among others, Samuelson and Solow in the 1950s. See for example Keen (2003). The analytical implications of working with an open system started to be a more explicitly integrated part of the post-Keynesian approach to macroeconomics during the 1980s. When the methodological consequence was digested it became apparent that the neoclassical synthesis and later on the new-Keynesian general equilibrium macroeconomics had very little to do with Keynes's methodological approach to macroeconomics.

Hence, Keynes's analytical use of the concept of equilibrium had to be reconsidered, especially with regard to analytical methods which made World 3 deviate from World 2. This had to be discussed thoroughly so that the epistemic fallacy could be avoided.

EQUILIBRIUM AND UNCERTAINTY IN POST-KEYNESIAN THEORY

When the equilibrium concept is used within neoclassical theory it seems to be unproblematic. On the other hand it is inevitable that the very same concept has given rise to considerable discussion in post-Keynesian theory. As described above, neoclassical macroeconomic theory has a long methodological tradition of using the concept of 'equilibrium' in the meaning of the solution to a formalized model.

This use of the equilibrium concept is in clear conflict with the macroeconomic methodology inspired by critical realism and described in Chapter 2. The main concern here was to ensure correspondence between the real and the analytical levels in order thereby to ensure a certain degree of realism. When the macroeconomic ontology is characterized by uncertainty and often also by the absence of market-clearing mechanisms, then the use of the neoclassical concept of equilibrium, not to mention general equilibrium, hardly makes any sense. A useful point is made by Lawson's (2005) emphasis on the fact that in order for the equilibrium concept to be relevant, it must be useable at both the ontological (real) and the theoretical (analytical) level.

Equilibrium Means 'No Change'

To the extent that the equilibrium concept is analytically relevant at all, then the post-Keynesians, with inspiration from Keynes, have used it as a characteristic of a macroeconomic condition characterized by 'no change'. So Keynes developed an analytical method that could explain the consistently high unemployment in Great Britain during the interwar period. This was an empirical condition that hardly changed at all over a long period of time and could not be described as a condition with market clearing. He nevertheless called this condition an 'equilibrium' since there did not appear to be any inherent forces in the macroeconomy that could lift Great Britain out of this stable 'unemployment equilibrium'. The same condition in the labour market has also been familiar to a number of continental European countries. From the early 1990s Germany, France, Italy and Belgium have all had unemployment rates of about 10 per cent, and there is not yet any prospect of a substantial change in the direction of full employment. On the other hand this specific level of unemployment seems not to represent a market-determined gravitation centre which could be given a neoclassical interpretation of a constant level of structural unemployment.[11] In fact, there is little in the macroeconomic structures that explains why the macroeconomic system should lock itself into a position of high, but for quite some time stable, unemployment. As long as macroeconomic policy is stuck, the unemployment condition seems to go on without any inherent pulling power that could change the situation automatically, either for better or for worse. It should also be taken into account that a situation like this that has lasted for a number of years has a tendency to become embedded, because unemployment is considered as a normal condition. In such cases wage-earners and trade union leaders might reduce their aspirations. Unemployment is a macroeconomic phenomenon, but the distribution of unemployment is partly an individual problem. In countries with persistently high unemployment, social behaviour changes, because of increased uncertainty related to obtaining wage income. One is simply fooled if full employment is expected to be the most likely outcome. At the same time, firms change their hiring procedures when labour is always available. Trade unions take into account that wage demands must be adapted to the power structure in the labour market. No society will remain structurally unaffected by long periods of high unemployment. Similarly, the very low level of unemployment in the first three decades after the end of the Second World War left its mark on the mood in the labour market and on the power of the unions back in the 1960s.

In the light of constantly changing socio-economic structures, the term 'equilibrium' seems linguistically misleading. The entire socio-economy is never in a state of no change. The foundation is constantly moving and changing, even when a few central macroeconomic indicators on the surface display surprising stability over a longer period of time. It would therefore be more suitable to refer to the socio-economic development process as path-dependent, since the past always exerts an influence, just as the future is uncertain. No macroeconomic development can remain unaffected by previous events, irrespective of whether the unemployment figures have been at 5 per cent, 10 per cent – or even 20 per cent in parts of Eastern Europe – over a longer period of time. In any case all market economies have an underlying dynamics in the production structures that results in shifts among sectors, even under a surface of unchanged macroeconomic data; farms become mechanized, old factories are dismantled, new industries pop up and public and private services develop, even if the overall unemployment rate remains by and large unchanged.

A Temporary Semi-Closure[12]

The continued use of the equilibrium concept, even in the post-Keynesian tradition, is often inspired by the desire to use a formalized model, whether algebraic or geometric (Setterfield, 1997). Formalized equilibrium models have some well-established, pedagogical characteristics. The presentation of aggregate demand within the traditional 45° income–expenditure model has been instrumental for the circulation of Keynesian macroeconomics and can hardly be overestimated. This model was an important first step back in the 1950s towards establishing an analytical understanding of the important point that the macroeconomic development is also influenced by demand factors, and that there is no autopilot to guide the macroeconomy towards full employment. However, to call the intersection point between aggregate demand and the 45° line an equilibrium would give the student with a neoclassical training a wrong connotation. It is just a pedagogical device to clear up a theoretical point about how aggregate demand can be transformed to effective demand for labour: it is a point of standstill with given expectations. In that sense equilibrium means no further changes, given the assumptions behind this semi-closure within an open model.

Such a standstill with persistent unemployment might go on for years, if expectations are given. This is not to say that unemployed people feel themselves in a voluntary optimum with no job, but they do not have, individually (or even collectively), the power to change this employment situation, because they cannot by themselves change the effective demand for labour (see Chapter 8). This analytical semi-closure should only be used to illustrate the causal relation between aggregate demand and employment as discussed in Chapter 5 and illustrated in Figure 5.3. The analytical content of the simplistic 45° income–expenditure model was not that employment, given the assumptions, will remain at a specific level for ever, nor is it an indication of an unavoidable gravitational centre of structural unemployment. On the contrary, an empirically observed, persistent high employment is a theoretical challenge, to explain why effective demand for labour seems to be rather invariant for a considerable period of time. The answer is not straightforward; but we should investigate how uncertainty influences people's behaviour. Here, we had better take a look into the deep stratum of the macroeconomic landscape, where we might look for conditions of stability. The pedagogical task is to uncover causal mechanisms which can explain the trend in effective demand for labour. Herein may lie a part of the explanation for the apparently constant level of unemployment.

The inclusion of power relations and market structures are also important as supplementary explanatory factors. They lie in the deep stratum and cannot readily be made the subject of an analytical semi-closure that can be modelled. A thought experiment is required here. For example: can unemployed workers increase total employment by lowering their reserve wage? They may by doing this be able to improve their own individual employment prospects; but that will happen at the expense of an employed colleague, as long as effective demand for labour remains unchanged at the macro-level. As we shall see in Chapter 8, effective demand depends on the firms' expectations of sales in the future. The firms have the power to change the level of employment, which would happen if they expect aggregate demand to change, whereas individual wage-earners are powerless in an atomized labour market. If jobs are too few, individual workers cannot force firms to increase employment. That will only happen if firms become more optimistic with regard to the future. Otherwise, there will still be too few jobs, and the situation with involuntary unemployment will remain unchanged which Keynes happened to call an equilibrium.

Keynes's pedagogical point was thus that he wished to demonstrate that this condition (of no change) and continued unemployment is not a short-run *dis*equilibrium phenomenon (Kregel, 1976: 213) but a condition determined by structures rooted in the deep stratum that could lead to a permanent 'no change' situation, if nothing external to the macroeconomic landscape happened. In that case, Keynes said, the 'economic system may find itself in stable equilibrium' (Keynes, 1936: 30); see also Chapter 8.

In such a 'stable macro-equilibrium' there are naturally a lot of underlying, microeconomic dynamics, since there are always firms that make mistakes in their production planning. But the condition of no change is characterized by mistakes not having any systematic direction. Some firms are too optimistic, others too pessimistic. These firms are, under normal circumstances, randomly distributed and therefore cancel each other out on the macro-level, as long as effective demand is unchanged. The microeconomic dynamic will also be influenced by the fact that part of the workforce is continuously replaced. People retire and new generations enter the labour market. The structure of a vital market economy causes a large number of appointments and dismissals, whereby there will also continuously be a certain replacement of individuals in the unemployment queue, without any necessary change in the overall macroeconomic employment and unemployment: a statistical macro-equilibrium. But the uncertainty on both the micro- and macro-level will contribute to the above-mentioned accidental process of expansion and contraction which in practice will rarely have a mean value of zero. So even if the overall effective demand in the theoretical model seems to be unchanged, in practice, deviations will occur that will help to explain smaller cyclical fluctuations, to which Keynes only allocates a single chapter, 'Notes on the trade cycle' in *The General Theory*. This comparative neglect can be seen as an expression of the fact that his focus is on the structural conditions that may lock the economy into a position of 'no change' or of less than full employment for quite a while.

Keynes's pedagogical point in using the term 'equilibrium' is to show that persistent unemployment does not have to be explained by wage and price inflexibility. On the contrary, Keynes carried out the thought experiment in Chapter 19 of *The General Theory*, with the title 'Changes in money-wages', of letting prices and wages be fully flexible and then showing – in the analytical model – that this flexibility does not necessarily lead to changes in the level of employment. Critical to Keynes's conclusion is, of course, how such flexibility would influence effective demand which, among other things, is influenced by the state of confidence and long-term expectations.

It seems to me that the most important reason to give special attention to the term 'equilibrium' in the meaning of 'no change' is that it provides a pedagogical insight into the function of the macroeconomic system that might otherwise be difficult to explain if everything in an analytical sense was fluid. By setting up initially a macroeconomic landscape the researcher might get inspiration to establish some (temporary) analytical semi-closures. Here the macroeconomic mechanisms can be analysed under the assumption of unaltered expectations, with no guarantee of perfect certainty or full information. In this way, Keynes avoids the epistemological dilemma that had so far characterized the neoclassical unemployment analyses (not least Pigou, 1933), that their unrealistic assumptions with regard to economic behaviour, level of information and structures of markets had no reference to reality and therefore could not contribute either to an understanding of the persistent unemployment or to how to cure it.

Equilibrium in Relation to the Deep Stratum

In *The General Theory* the concept of equilibrium is used rather sparingly. Keynes is primarily occupied in describing causal mechanisms in a world characterized by uncertain expectations. In situations where it cannot be misunderstood, including a couple of the summarizing chapters, he does however use the term 'equilibrium' to describe a condition of immutability that can occur when the decision-makers (on average) experience a convergence of what they expect and what they realize.

As one of the first who labelled himself a post-Keynesian, Jan Kregel used such an expectations-defined equilibrium concept to illustrate some important analytical points in *The General Theory*. For Keynes, 'the principle of effective demand' was the analytically new concept that could be used to gain insight into the causal mechanisms that generate macroeconomic trends. Kregel wanted to give a methodological exposition that could provide a more nuanced understanding of 'effective demand'. Analytically it does not bring us far only to acknowledge that the future is uncertain and that 'we simply do not know'.

Kregel (1976), taking his point of departure in the summarizing Chapter 18 of *The General Theory*, asked the following question: what if all expectations are met? In this case, the actors would find themselves in a permanent state of 'no change' since no actor would have any incentive to change his situation as long as everything else is expected to remain unchanged. Firms are assumed to be profit-maximizing and households are assumed to optimize on the basis of the income budget available to them. (There is no reason not to assume wages and prices to be parametrically given to the individuals – in fact this is the standard assumption in microeconomic theory.)

> It was this purely static model, divorced from disappointment and shifts in expectations, that Keynes finally preferred to use for demonstrating that unemployment was not a short-run disequilibrium phenomenon, ... that *in theory* the system could settle *in equilibrium* at almost any level of employment ... (Kregel, 1976: 213–14, emphasis added)

This is an important analytical insight. However, it should not be confused with reality. But we see that it may be shifts in expectations that explain changes, not only in the model, but also in the real world.

Kregel (1976: 214–17) then analysed the consequences of shifts in two different types of expectation in the analytical model: short-term and long-term expectations respectively.

Reading *The General Theory*, however, gives the impression that Keynes had focused on a broader spectrum of 'macro-actors' than just firms and households or employees, and therefore also had a more nuanced expectations structure. This can be seen from the fact that Keynes, before he carries out his thought experiments, is very careful to undertake an ontological reflection on the actual conditions. A number of chapters in *The General Theory* are therefore dedicated to a description of how the behaviour and formation of expectations by different categories of actors can be observed in the real world: the firms (Chapter 3), the households (Chapters 8 and 9), the real investors (Chapter 11) and the financial speculators (Chapter 12).[13]

Starting with stationary equilibrium, where it is assumed (completely unrealistically) that all actors' expectations are fulfilled, the assumptions of constant expectations are dropped one by one. The consequences of the initially introduced assumption of given and fulfilled expectations can subsequently be analysed one by one:

- Firms can misjudge the aggregate demand.
- The households can misjudge their real wages (and house prices can develop differently from expected).

- The firms' long-term expectations and/or the interest rate can change.
- The behaviour of financial investors and speculators is guided by very short-term expectations and seldom based on real economic performance.[14]

In step with the assumptions being lifted, we are faced with an increasingly complicated analytical model structure, where changes in each of the expectation categories can also exert mutual influence. Kregel (1976: 217) concludes:

> If, however, realisation of error alters the state of expectations and shifts the independent behavioural functions, Keynes's model of shifting equilibrium will describe an actual path of an economy over time chasing an ever changing equilibrium – it need never catch it.

It is clear that Kregel is on the track of the method that later developed into an actual path-dependent analysis, where more and dynamic factors are put into play at the same time within a framework of a given historical context. In that respect Kregel made an important eye opener for the method implied in *The General Theory*. In Keynes's hands, short-period equilibrium is an analytical tool to understand tendencies, including persistent unemployment. When all of the restrictive assumptions related to the construction of semi-closures are lifted, post-Keynesian macroeconomists will be faced with an analytically open model that at best may indicate a historical-deductive path through the landscape.

As mentioned earlier, Keynes rejected as early as 1934 the idea that a general equilibrium model could be a relevant analytical tool for understanding long-period macroeconomic development. Kregel makes an important contribution to operationalizing the model-related understanding, but Kregel does not really discuss whether a shifting equilibrium model is analytically relevant for long-period macroeconomic analysis. Within an open system analysis there is no well-described goal to chase. This is why full employment in Keynes's analytical framework cannot be a precondition for undertaking long-period analysis. Furthermore, full employment is not necessarily a point of rest. Had Keynes lived long enough, the development throughout the 1960s would have been an example of a state of macroeconomic 'overshooting'.

Kregel's analytical use of a shifting equilibrium method was a pioneering contribution to an understanding of the interpretation of Keynes's methodology in the direction of the so-called 'open-system *ceteris paribus*' method (OSCP method),[15] see especially Chick and Caserta (1997), Chick and Dow (2001), Setterfield (2001) and Chick (2003). It is understandable therefore that at the time, Kregel hesitated to draw the full consequence of his proposed method of shifting expectations: that in the long period there is no equilibrium to 'chase', since the macroeconomic landscape is open. In any case, Kregel laid the foundation for a new, method-based understanding of Keynes's macroeconomic analysis, which describes the macroeconomic development as tendencies rather than equilibrium.

In this post-Keynesian perspective it is preferred that tendencies, as a rule, will be the operative result of our analytical efforts. Here, Kregel showed a methodological way to understand and analytically pursue an empirically observed trend, as being determined by changes in expectations of an uncertain future, drawn through a historically established landscape.

When all expectation variables are brought into play at the same time, it becomes increasingly difficult to follow the analytical path in World 2, not to mention transferring it to World 3; see below on the path-dependency method. In this situation the firms will, with changing expectations, find it very difficult to distinguish between actual (realized) and aggregate (expected) demand. Even the analytical model will be difficult to interpret when the expectations-formation is 'set free'.

Path-Dependent Tendencies rather than Equilibrium

In light of the conclusion above, the possibility of using an analytical middle form seems appealing. Here, we suggest that realistic macroeconomic analyses should use a method of semi-closure in the short period (Lawson, 1997), which in the long-period analysis is replaced by an indication of a likely tendency or a path. This method is based on the assumption, as described in the previous section, that it may be possible to establish relevant semi-closure(s) within the macroeconomic landscape.

How can this analytical method be used in practice, and how can a sufficient congruence between model and reality be ensured? Here Keynes provides us with an illustrative example in his analysis of public investments and the multiplier effect. He takes as his point of departure a relevant segment of the macroeconomic landscape, a semi-closure, then he releases an exogenous force – in this case public investment – and makes it work its way through that part of the landscape. When this force has exhausted its effect, the researcher can trace tendencies with regard to output and employment, the 'multiplier effects'. This is just step one. Now the researcher might ask about the financial implications of public investment. An extended semi-closure has to be established. Quite quickly it will be demonstrated that tendencies within the financial sector are crucially dependent on how expectations are formed, about which we have very little empirically-based knowledge.

In other words, the best we might expect to get as results from long-period macroeconomic analyses using the OSCP method is some path-dependent tendencies. This analytical method using semi-closures is not a pathway to finding a general macroeconomic development, but rather an attempt to give an indication of the direction and perhaps the speed of the development over time in the main macroeconomic variables.

The concept of long-period equilibrium within post-Keynesian macro-theory seems therefore no longer to have an important role as a relevant analytical concept, whether in terms of market clearing, gravitation centre or even as a description of a 'condition of no change'. The equilibrium term has been taken over by analytical tendencies that can be described within the framework of a path-dependent analysis, where it is the 'causal mechanisms', structures and power relations in the deep stratum of the macroeconomic landscape that shape our understanding of the development of macroeconomic variables.

The General Theory has many passages that support the interpretation of Keynes's method as a path-dependent analysis of empirically observed tendencies. For example, this is how Keynes describes a process where wage formation is made fully flexible:

> Let us, then, apply our method of analysis to answering the problem [of changes in money-wages]. ... (1) Does a reduction in money-wages have a direct tendency, *cet. par.*, to increase employment, '*cet. par.*' being taken to mean that [the other independent factors] the propensity to consume, the schedule of marginal efficiency of capital and the rate of interest are the same as before for the community as a whole? And (2) does a reduction in money-wages have a certain or probable tendency to affect employment in a particular direction through its certain or probable repercussions on these three factors? (Keynes, 1936: 260)

It should also be kept in mind that Keynes had at this stage frozen a number of 'given factors', most of which can be labelled structural variables. He did so in order to concentrate on the cultivation of the important new analytical concept of 'effective demand'. In the long-term perspective these factors would necessarily also have an influence on the macroeconomic tendencies. Keynes explicitly mentioned the following:

- 'The existing skills' and quantity of available labour.
- The existing quality and quantity of available equipment.
- The existing technique.
- The degree of competition.
- The tastes and habits of the consumer.
- The disutility of different intensities of labour.

- The activities of supervision and organization.
- The social structure.

He continues: 'This does not mean that we assume these factors to be constant; but merely that, in this place and context, we are not considering or taking into account the effects and consequences of changes in them' (Keynes, 1936: 245).

The more long term the perspective one wishes to illustrate, the more important it is to include these structural factors, although uncertainty will be even more prevailing. The longer the time horizon is expanded into the future, the less useful the OSCP method becomes, because uncertainty will increasingly prevail over any analytical result.[16] However, a number of these given factors are determined by the historic process and over time become to a certain degree endogenous. This applies especially to the development in 'available equipment' and technology, just as 'available labour' is partly a consequence of the birth rate 15–20 years earlier.

'Equilibrium' and 'Tendency' could Go Together

In his summarizing Chapter 18, Keynes used the term *quaesitum* for the development in the macroeconomic variables which he had special focus on. In *The General Theory* these were employment and output. As already mentioned, these two variables exhibited a surprising stability in the period between the wars. There was no tendency to 'boom or bust'. The use of the term 'equilibrium' for this underperforming macroeconomy upset his classical colleagues[17] – how could a situation with 10 per cent unemployment be considered an equilibrium? They did not understand Keynes's use of the concept of standstill rather than market clearing in his attempt to get his new theory to correspond better with the real world which showed persistent unemployment. Maybe it would have facilitated communication with his colleagues if he had more consequently used the term *quaesitum* for the focus of his macroeconomic analysis, which could then have included both 'equilibrium' and 'tendencies'.

In order to give the reader a slightly more practical demonstration of how his analytic model could be used, he gave a number of illustrative examples in his Chapter 18. If one had not read the previous 17 chapters, this rather heavy-handed use of the OSCP method could give the reader associations with the use of a closed model, which is why he repeatedly emphasizes that:

> The division of the determinants of the economic system into the two groups of given factors and independent variables is, of course, quite arbitrary from any

absolute standpoint. The division must be made entirely on the basis of experience, so as to correspond on the one hand to the factors in which the changes
seem to be so slow or so little relevant as to have only a small and comparatively
negligible short-term influence on our *quaesitum*; and on the other hand to
those factors in which the changes are found in practice to exercise a dominant
influence on our *quaesitum* ... (Keynes, 1936: 247)[18]

I find that this quotation gives the flavour of the OSCP method or the
method of temporary closures. It is a powerful tool to uncover theoretical understanding of observed tendencies of the macroeconomic variables
which are in focus in our analysis, which Keynes called our *quaesitum.*

These are the arguments why I believe that the equilibrium concept
should be abandoned within post-Keynesian macroeconomic analysis and
be replaced by tendencies detected by the use of the OSCP method with the
aim of providing a path-dependent understanding of our *quaesitum.*

SUMMARY

King (2002) is right when he says that the equilibrium discussion has
plagued post-Keynesian macroeconomic theory, at least until the use of
the equilibrium concept by Keynes (1936) was cleared up. Here, equilibrium is neither a solution to a mathematical model nor a market-clearing
condition. Furthermore, in his 1934 paper Keynes had already expressed
his doubts about whether the market system – regardless of how perfect
the competition might be assumed to be – actually had convergent
characteristics. But the decisive analytical breakthrough first came with
the dismissal of Say's Law and thereby with 'general equilibrium' as a
relevant concept for understanding the macroeconomic landscape. This
occurred in recognition of the fact that the macroeconomic landscape has
an open ontology especially in the long term. When this is acknowledged,
it becomes apparent that no meaningful gravitation centre can be specified for the long-run macroeconomic development. Equilibrium in the
sense of 'no change' therefore becomes less interesting and can advantageously be replaced in macroeconomic analysis by context-dependent
development tendencies. Thus the nightmare that was connected to the
discussion of and about equilibrium in connection to macroeconomic
analysis seems finally to have been brought to a methodological end:
general equilibrium can be relevant in the analysis of the characteristics
of the ideal model, whereas a path-dependent development process is
relevant for understanding an open macroeconomic system characterized
by uncertainty.

APPENDIX 6.1   ON THE FORMALIZATION OF ECONOMIC THEORY

I do not myself attach much value to [mathematical] manipulations of this kind ... . Perhaps the best purpose served by writing [the elasticities] down is to exhibit the extreme complexity of the relationship between prices and the quantity of money. (Keynes, 1936: 305)

I mentioned earlier that economists such as Varian (1999) delimit economic theory to include only analysis of subject fields where a formalized model can be brought into meaningful use. Here it is the method, the hypothetical-deductive and formalized method, which determines whether the research in question lies within the economic field. It seems unnecessarily restrictive to allow the method to determine the demarcation of the research subjects within a social science, which can only be explained by an overindulged natural science ambition. On the other hand the analytical precision that follows from formalization can seem seductively convincing where it is relevant.

Lawson (1997) is similarly close to going too far in the opposite direction with his view that any form of formalization within economics is misleading, because in his opinion the social ontology is an obstacle to meaningful formalization in all cases (see Lawson's four points of criticism of neoclassical economics referred to above in Appendix 2.2, Chapter 2). According to him, mathematics as an analytical tool is not suitable for understanding economics. In Lawson (2003), this view has mellowed slightly in that he is open to the possibility that semi-closures can be relevant, in which case a formalization would be acceptable, as long as the analysis result is not overinterpreted.

As already mentioned, Keynes was educated as a mathematician and had earned his first academic merits for a fellowship thesis on the subject of probability theory, so he must be assumed to have known his maths. Therefore it cannot have been a lack of insight that led him to adopt a rather reluctant stance on whether formalization is a conducive method within macroeconomics. For Keynes, there was no doubt that macroeconomics should be limited in relation to the subject field that lay on the real level, whereas it should be the ontology that determined which method of analysis could be used to the greatest advantage. It was the study of the causal factors that determined output and employment in the entire economy, which was in focus. Here, the method must be adapted to the ontology of the subject field, and not the reverse.

Does this mean that formalization was anathema to Keynes? Absolutely not. Keynes considered it to be particularly important to be able to quantify the theoretical concepts he was working with. For example, he made a calculation of what size the income multiplier might be. To carry out this calculation, it is necessary to formalize the multiplier. On the other hand, it is important for Keynes to emphasize that this is not a calculation of an economic regularity, but merely an indication of the size of a tendency (in this case the multiplier) in a given historical context and, as usual, marked by uncertainty.

It is important, therefore, to keep in mind that formalization is only methodologically legitimate when analysing some material that displays regularity and that is homogeneous over the time frame relevant for the analysis. If these assumptions are satisfied, then the analysis has the obvious strength that the results achieved have a high degree of precision. Mayer (1992) asks in his book, *Truth versus Precision in Economics*, whether an unconditional requirement for formalization does not come to entail an unnecessary delimitation of the subject field when precision is given a high priority. It is a matter, as Chick (1998) so aptly put it, of knowing the appropriate limits to the usefulness of formalism.[19]

It would also be a mistake to claim that mathematics can be used to prove an economic relation to be valid at the real level. A proof is used about a statement to ensure that it has universal validity, but since the macroeconomic basis is under constant change, circumstances concerning reality cannot be changed. It is impossible to prove the 'existence' of a general equilibrium in World 1. At best, it is possible to calculate the necessary conditions for the existence of a general equilibrium in World 2.

However, formalism can be used to create operational definitions that provide some logical connections for the use of connected, macroeconomic variables. On the other hand, no new insights can be gained when these definitions are applied to reality.

NOTES

1. Keynes is referring to the fact that neoclassical macro-theory, because of its assumption of general equilibrium, could not on a theoretically consistent basis integrate money (and the financial market) within the framework of a macroeconomic model. This is still the case; see Andersen (2000) as an example. Furthermore, money is not present in the Danish Rational Economic Agent Model – (DREAM).
2. King (2002: 189) refers to 'the incubus of equilibrium'. 'Incubus' status arose from the lack of understanding of the different use of the concept of equilibrium within neoclassical and post-Keynesian economics. It is a source of confusion that the word 'equilibrium' can be given so many different meanings.
3. One of the pioneers contributing to this different conceptual understanding of equilibrium is Chick (1978).
4. It is the continuous attempts to incorporate fundamental uncertainty into macroeconomic theory that is one of the main characteristics of post-Keynesians economics. A pioneer in that respect is Davidson (1972).

5. Skidelsky (1992: 572–610) describes how Keynes's rather specific use of the term 'unemployment equilibrium' upset his colleagues. For them, this use was a clear sign that Keynes had not understood that equilibrium entailed market clearing. In particular, the large group of economists who later developed the neoclassical synthesis could not accept Keynes's use of the equilibrium concept. 'If he had only called the condition with unemployment disequilibrium, then much of the subsequent interpretation would have been easier and the effective demand could have continued to play a prominent role', was often the view that was put forward by old-Keynesians.

6. See also the introductory chapter where the difference between flow equilibrium (Walras equilibrium) and stock equilibrium (stationary state) is presented.

7. One could in principle imagine stationary cycles (or fluctuations) of a repetitive kind, but hardly within a macroeconomics of the real world.

8. This was one of Keynes's accusations of the classical macro-model: that it was one equation short of being determinate (see Chapter 8).

9. New-classical economists abstain from this discussion. They have once and for all decided that any economic outcome is caused by voluntary market clearing; see Lucas (1981).

10. In Appendix 8.1, Chapter 8, I describe in more detail Keynes's critique of Pigou's model-analysis of exogenous demand-shock, which in Keynes's opinion, is inconsistent with respect to the employed model. This problem seems also to be present in several and more recent macroeconomic textbooks, for example Begg et al. (2001) described in Chapter 5.

11. When for instance Germany and Italy are considered, the labour market laws and social benefits are quite similar throughout the entire nation, but the size of unemployment differs substantially from region to region.

12. Keynes, however, did not use the term 'semi-closure'. It is taken from Lawson (1997).

13. Ontologically evaluated, this typology of actors and their motivations is a critical difference between Keynes and post-Keynesians on the one hand and micro-based macro-theory on the other.

14. The price of financial assets is in any case determined by contrasting expectations: existing shares and bonds are sold when buyer and seller both expect to gain from the transaction. In other words, the buyer expects the price to go up and the seller expects the price to fall.

15. I will not disguise the fact that I am somewhat hesitant about the reuse of the term of *ceteris paribus* that originates from Marshall and which was solely associated with microeconomic analysis.

16. This is a major difference from the new-Keynesian methodology. Here, the long-period general equilibrium is known with certainty, when expectations are fulfilled; whereas the adjustment process leading up to the terminal point might be disturbed by 'creaks and groans and jerks and interrupted by time lags, outside interference and mistakes' (*CWK*, XIII: 486); see Chapter 1, where Keynes's characterization of a self-adjusting system is presented.

17. Note that Keynes's use of the term 'classical' is quite consistent with the fact that they had all used the equilibrium method.

18. See also the passage from Keynes, 1936: 297: 'The object of our analysis is not to provide a machine …'.

19. A further clarification of the role that formalism can be allocated, depending on whether it is an open or closed system that is to be analysed, is found in Chick and Dow (2001).

7.   The fallacy of composition

The fallacy of composition occurs when one incorrectly attempts to generalize
from a relationship that is true for each individual, but is not true for the whole.
(Oswego, 2006: 3)

INTRODUCTION: FROM MICRO TO MACRO IN A HISTORICAL PERSPECTIVE[1]

It is the ambition of the neoclassical schools that the methodological point of departure should be methodological individualism. This is based on the assumption that the stable building blocks for the economic system are the individual preference structures that are assumed to be independent of the economic environment. The individual has integrity in relation to his or her own economic dispositions. Rational choices are made with the goal of optimizing the individual utility based on existing knowledge. With this methodological point of departure, the aim of neoclassical macroeconomics is to develop a theory that can detect important phenomena for the aggregated economy. Since individual behaviour is assumed to be the stable primary element, the neoclassical methodological demand is for macroeconomic models to have an explicit and consistent microeconomic foundation (see for example Andersen, 2000).

This demand for an explicit microeconomic foundation was formulated after the failed attempts to explain the economic development throughout the 1970s with the large, so-called Keynesian, macro-econometric models (Harcourt, 1977). This model tradition was internationally represented by, among others, Franco Modigliani and Lawrence Klein. In Denmark, this empirical and 'Keynesian' model tradition was from the early 1970s represented by the model in the Ministry of Finance (ADAM) and the model in the Danish Economic Council (SMEC) respectively (Andersen, 1975b). The history of the first macroeconomic models is told in detail in Andersen, 1975b. As described in Chapter 1, these models were based on the 'neoclassical synthesis' and did not contain an articulated microeconomic foundation.

The (new) neoclassical critique of this macroeconomic or macroeconometric tradition was expressed by Lucas and Sargent (1978) and others at the end of the 1970s. At that time it had become evident that the models were unable to describe, among other things, the 'stagflation' that had characterized the macroeconomic development throughout the 1970s.

The 'new' methodological requirements were formulated in such a way that consistent, macroeconomic theory should be built up 'from below' to avoid *ad hoc* assumptions about aggregated economic behaviour on the macroeconomic level. It is the individual's preferences which, as mentioned, are assumed to be invariant towards macroeconomic and political development. According to this argumentation, one important reason for the 'old' macro-econometric models breaking down was related to the accusation that macroeconomic behavioural relations were specified in an *ad hoc* way and that parameters were determined by statistical evidence derived from the historical past. The estimated parameters within the econometric models would therefore not be invariant towards changes in, among other things, the economic policy which the collapse of the models' explanatory power in the 1970s was attributed to.

The macroeconomic slate had to be washed clean, for which purpose a new neoclassical, macroeconomic model tradition was developed, where microeconomic-based behavioural relations formed the model structure, as described in the Introduction. The 1995 Nobel Prize winner, Robert Lucas, is one of the main architects behind this research strategy, which is widely accepted by neoclassical macroeconomists today and also forms the basis of for instance the Danish Rational Economic Agent Model (DREAM), among others. As already mentioned, in 1987 Lucas wrote a programme declaration for his continued research within economic theory:

> The most interesting recent developments in macroeconomic theory seem to me describable as the reincorporation of aggregative problems such as inflation and the business cycle within the general framework of 'microeconomic' theory. If these developments succeed, the term 'macroeconomics' will simply disappear from use and the modifier 'micro' will become superfluous. We will simply speak, as did Smith, Ricardo, Marshall and Walras, of *economic* theory. (Lucas, 1987: 107–8)[2]

The new-classical[3] macroeconomists have certainly selected an exclusive company as their role models. But it is still surprising that Lucas has to look back more than 100 years in economic thinking to find the icons for his (macro-) economic thinking.

Lucas disregards macroeconomic thinking in the tradition of Keynes and his contemporaries. He does this with reference to, among others, the Modigliani–Klein tradition, which he identifies with Keynesian economics. But here he makes a grave mistake by equating Keynes's macroeconomic theory with the neoclassical synthesis that lies behind the 'large macro-econometric models'. If Lucas had taken a sincere interest in, for instance, Keynes's critique of Tinbergen's early econometric work (the original contributions are printed in *CWK*, XIV), then it would have been apparent to him that it was not Keynes's macroeconomic theory that was under attack for methodological inconsistency, but rather the macroeconomic theory that had the 'neoclassical synthesis' as its point of departure (Togati, 1998).

The Microeconomic Basis for General Equilibrium Theory

Lucas's critique was directed at the 'neoclassical synthesis' rather than at Keynes's or post-Keynesian macroeconomics. He could, with considerable accuracy, claim that there was no congruence between individual optimizing behaviour and the applied macro-theoretical foundation. The individual agents' expectation formation can only reasonably be assumed to be stable if it is anchored in a structure that is invariant towards changing external conditions, including government policy. If it is possible to formulate successfully the agents' 'true' expectations-formation, then it would be cleansed of systematic errors, since the rational agents should be assumed to have learned from their previous mistakes. Formation of expectations should be a forward-looking process, not backward-looking. In the past there will always have been errors committed. Such forward-looking procedures are not the case, either in the Keynesian macroeconometric models or in the monetarist models, so they were both accused by new-classical economists of having either *ad hoc* expectations-formation or mistaken expectations included in their models. This critique was made regardless of the fact that the neoclassical synthesis and the monetarist models were all framed within the general equilibrium method.

Lucas presented an apparent methodological brainwave when in the 1970s he launched the hypothesis about rational expectations-formation. The hypothesis is based on the assumption that we basically know very little about the agents' expectations-formation, but if agents are rational, then they will learn from their systematic mistakes. Why not, then, take as the point of departure that the agents do not make any systematic mistakes and that they optimize their economic behaviour on this basis? For, as Lucas argued, if the agents actually had this knowledge and did not use it fully, then it would be a case of irrational behaviour. At this point in the theoretical presentation it is often added that it might be the case that the individual agents do not have full knowledge of the future, but stochastic errors will even out in great numbers, which gives the representative agent the knowledge that is required for him to behave in accordance with the assumed full information. Therefore, the only microeconomic behaviour that is invariant in relation to the macroeconomic development is the assumption that the representative agents have correct expectations, which is the same as assuming that he knows the (model-based) future.[4] This argument has the logical implication that the theoretically most relevant part of the analytical model will always be the position of general equilibrium, where agents will act in accordance with their rational expectations. On the other hand, there might be some institutional obstacles to a smooth learning and adjustment process of reaching general equilibrium, which may delay in analytical time the arrival at the position of general equilibrium. Agents might know that due to transaction costs, delayed information and so on there can be an element of rational inertia in the adjustment process which will take some time to overcome. But as long as the preference structures are invariant to this inertia, agents will learn and the general equilibrium is still a highly relevant analytical point (which applies especially to the new-Keynesian macroeconomics).

In modern neoclassical analytical practice, 'rational expectations-formation' is an indispensable, model-based precondition for ensuring consistency between the sum of the rational, individually decided actions of the representative agents and the general equilibrium solution. In such models there is a predesigned coincidence between the micro-level and the aggregated macro-level, which was also Lucas's research ambition.

This requirement of a firm microfoundation behind the behavioural relations of the representative agent on the macro-level is by construction made to look like a mirror picture of the behaviour of one optimizing micro-economic agent under the assumption of full knowledge about all equilibrium values. Furthermore, perfect market clearing is usually assumed on each market in the new-classical model. The equilibrium solution of one market becomes similar to the market solution within the general equilibrium. Hence, results obtained from a specific market experiment are also valid in the generalized market model. A well-known example is the labour-market model assuming rational expectations and market clearing; from such a model the researcher can deduce the general equilibrium implication from the labour market in isolation (see Figure 7.1). Within this stylized neoclassical labour market model it is concluded that:

1. An exogenous change in the preference structure of the representative agent, for example an increased propensity to supply labour at a given real wage, will make the representative agent work more hours and, due to the perfect market-clearing mechanism, the real wage will fall and the overall employment will go up.
2. A reduced social benefit will change the relative price between work and leisure, which will make the representative agent supply more

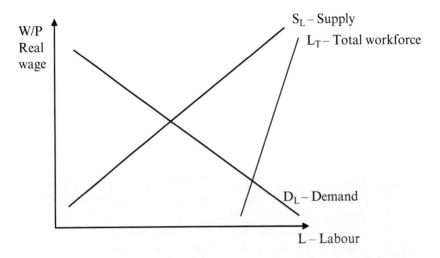

Figure 7.1   The new-Keynesian labour market with representative agents

labour, and employment is increased. But this is not the end of the story, because the representative agent with rational expectations knows that lower social benefit also means lower tax rates to balance the public sector budget. Lower taxes (depending on the initial tax structure) might change the relative price between work and leisure even further, but once again the composite analytical result is made up of what could be expected by aggregated microeconomic behaviour.

3. In case of involuntary unemployment due to rigid real wages the analytical result of a lower money wage is equally trivial as long as the demand curve for labour is downward sloping. There is no reason to bother oneself with a macroeconomic argument, because a lower wage means increased profitability at the micro-level and, therefore, also at the level of the representative (macro-) firm.

Hence, within this kind of neoclassical macroeconomic model with an explicit micro-foundation, where among other things uncertainty is abandoned and a general equilibrium solution is axiomatically imposed, it will hardly make any sense to discuss whether the fallacy of composition can happen.[5]

Keynes's Microeconomic Foundation Characterized by Uncertainty

Though an individual whose transactions are small in relation to the market can safely neglect the fact that demand is not a one-sided transaction, it makes nonsense to neglect it when we come to aggregate demand. This is the vital difference between the theory of the economic behaviour of the aggregate and the theory of the behaviour of the individual unit ... (Keynes, 1936: 85).

It is not the question of whether a microeconomic foundation is relevant for macroeconomic theory that divides neoclassical and post-Keynesian macroeconomic analysis. On the contrary, it is how a relevant microeconomic foundation can be formulated and whether it can be incorporated into an analytical macroeconomic model that describes an open and structured landscape.

On the basis of Chapter 1, it is obvious that Keynes considered the general equilibrium macroeconomic model as a very special case, since it is based on so many, and empirically very unrealistic, assumptions. For Keynes, the macroeconomic landscape was open, without a clearly defined gravitation centre and without any rigid expectations-formation. The normal condition of the macroeconomy was therefore characterized by constant change, which methodologically pointed towards a path-dependent analysis. Within the framework of a realistic macroeconomic model there would seldom, if ever, be a coincidence between what the individual expected and the macroeconomic outcome, mainly due to uncertainty about the actual situation (present) and about what the future will bring (and, for that matter, also with regard to the consequences of the past).

It is therefore no accident that Keynes has come to stand as the exponent for the realistic, macroeconomic analysis. Keynes's contribution to macrotheory had, methodologically speaking, the opposite point of departure compared to modern neoclassical theory, because our knowledge is ontologically limited and uncertainty cannot be disregarded. Therefore, macroeconomic reality cannot be understood, let alone explained, by a simple aggregation of identical, individual, economic actions based on secure knowledge (and perfect market clearing).

Realistic macroeconomic analysis had, on the contrary, to start 'from above' based on what could be observed of 'the economy as a whole'. To Keynes, persistent, involuntary unemployment was the current problem to be understood, and it could not be explained within the framework of the neoclassical macro-theory that existed at this time. Keynes's colleague Pigou had clearly demonstrated the gap between theory and reality in his book *The Theory of Unemployment* (1933).

Post-Keynesians had the same experience of a wide gap between the macroeconomics of 'the neoclassical synthesis' and of reality. Involuntary unemployment was explained by a rigid real wage within the framework of a general equilibrium model, in accordance with, for example, Modigliani (1944), Hicks (1950) and Patinkin (1956 [1966]). The theoretical paradox was that the neoclassical synthesis was presented as an interpretation of Keynes's macro-theory, despite the fact that within *The General Theory* it was demonstrated that persistent unemployment could be generated independently of whether money wage was assumed to be inflexible or fully flexible.

Post-Keynesian macroeconomic theory is therefore in methodological opposition to both the neoclassical synthesis (old-Keynesians) that dominated the 1950s and 1960s and the general equilibrium model of the new-Keynesians that is dominant today. The overriding difference is how uncertainty is handled analytically. If uncertainty is only identified by stochastic risk, then 'the law of large numbers' applies, and randomly determined mistakes cease to be important at the macro-level and can be treated as calculable risk. If, on the other hand, genuine uncertainty prevails, as described in Chapters 4 and 5, then individual activities are not necessarily random or stochastically independent. In these cases the presence of uncertainty might make the macroeconomic behaviour different from the average of 'rational' individual behaviour. This is so especially if the future is notoriously unknown both at the micro- and the macro-level. Keynes's and the post-Keynesians' important methodological result is therefore that even at the analytical level, the 'whole' can seldom (if ever) be described by a simple summation of the individual economic agents' (so-called) rational behaviour. Or, phrased differently, the total result is different from the sum of the individual agents' intended economic actions.

THE FALLACY OF COMPOSITION AS A CONSEQUENCE OF METHODOLOGICAL INDIVIDUALISM AND GENERAL EQUILIBRIUM

The absence of a model-based consistency between the postulated microeconomic behaviour and an empirically anchored analysis of the macroeconomic landscape is one reason why an analytical fallacy of composition may occur. Sheila Dow phrased it this way: '[I]ndividual actions, if common to a large number of individuals, will generate an outcome different from what was intended by each' (Dow, 1996: 85).

There are two major possibilities of committing the fallacy of composition following Dow's definition. Firstly, we have the micro–macro behaviour problem, when one representative agent is substituted for a group of not entirely similar individuals. Once again the labour market could be a case in point: some workers increase their supply of labour when real wages are expected to rise, whereas others will reduce their supply. This discrepancy between one representative agent and the differentiated reality is further enforced if expectations about the future wage level deviate among the workers.

Secondly, a fallacy of composition might also occur at the market level if a macroeconomic conclusion is drawn on the basis of a single market analysis assuming that all other markets are clearing. Below, it will be demonstrated that in a number of neoclassical textbooks the labour market is analysed using this method.

Hence, both categories of the fallacy of composition might be present when analytical models, which do not reflect World 1, are used to establish policy conclusions pretending to be relevant for the real world (see Figure 7.1).

THE REPRESENTATIVE AGENT: THE MICRO–MACRO DIVIDE

Can relevant supply and demand macroeconomic relations in the labour market be based on the neoclassical, microeconomic theory for one representative agent (Hartley, 1997)? In other words, if at the micro-level the individual actions have a mutually influencing effect, then the behaviour of a representative agent cannot be directly deduced from the behaviour of a single individual (see Chapter 1). In such cases there is a risk that the macroeconomic analysis based on the behaviour of an 'average' rational individual agent will imply a fallacy of composition. Let me give a couple of examples from the labour market.

Labour Supply

When one employee gets a wage increase in a particular industry or company, then the individual experiences this increase as both an absolute and a relative wage increase (compared to other employees). Layard (2005) mentions from empirical experiments that there is a considerable difference in the perceived utility by the individuals, depending on whether the wage increase is absolute or relative. The greatest effect is experienced when there are both types of wage increases but, all things being equal, the relative wage increase gives more satisfaction than an absolute wage increase. In addition Layard's results show that the negative effect of a relative wage decrease is considerably larger than the effect of a corresponding increase. Here is an asymmetry that one representative agent cannot represent, as already discussed in Chapter 4.

One may ask to what extent a rational representative agent will experience 'utility' from a generally higher money wage level. If the agent has rational expectations, then he or she 'knows' that a higher wage only means higher prices, and thereby an unchanged real wage is expected. (We leave productivity increases aside.) In an uncertain environment any individually experienced money wage increase might have a different effect, depending on what is expected to happen to the average wage rate, to the spillover effects on the price level and, finally, to the substitution between income and leisure. Furthermore, individual behaviour is also influenced by the expectation of other individuals' reactions.

An analysis of the impact on the macroeconomic supply of labour of a changed income tax rate comes very much to the same conclusions: that it depends on a number of behavioural characteristics. If agents were identical and had rational expectations then the representative agent should know that lower taxes means either cuts in public expenditure or increased charges for the users of public services, which in the end leave real income unchanged. In that case, a changed taxation of wage income will have no effect on the labour supply.

A similar case can be established with regard to income-related social benefits. According to traditional microeconomic theory, lower social benefits will increase the labour supply. But a rational representative agent would know that reduced public social benefits means higher individual contributions to private social insurance to keep the same risk-free income. This higher contribution is paid out of the reduced income tax. Assuming that the risk of being unemployed is randomly distributed, there will be no impact on the representative agent's labour supply if the private contribution to social security is similar to collective contributions (which are known to be used for a specific purpose). In the real, uncertain world social benefit is not only a benefit for those workers without a job, it is a benefit to all workers who experience the uncertainty of losing their job in the future. That is a part of the so-called flexicurity model, where job flexibility is traded for a relatively generous social benefit, which makes it more acceptable to run the risk of losing one's job, especially within an uncertain environment (Jespersen and Lang, 2006).

The question of the role of trade unions is also a part of the analysis of labour market adjustment. The existence of labour market organizations entails that individual behaviour is no longer representative of the labour market. Through trade unions, wage-earners can establish a degree of market power that may possibly rival that of the employers. These organizations change the market structure away from the assumed atomic behaviour lying behind the demand and supply curves in Figure 7.1. For that reason alone it would be impossible to draw conclusions about overall market behaviour based on a single wage-earner's or firm's atomistic behaviour.

Labour Demand

Individual profit-maximizing firms will aim at marginal revenue being equal to marginal costs. Under the assumptions of a well-behaved production function with diminishing marginal product of labour, and of perfect competition in both the output and labour markets, one can deduce the well-known demand curve for labour. It falls from left to right with real wages measured along the vertical axis and demand for labour on the horizontal axis. If such a microeconomic firm is similar to the representative firm, there should be no interdependence between firms when they act in the goods and labour market. They are assumed to expect an unlimited supply of labour at the ruling (real) wage level. If they collaborate, competition is reduced and the marginal productivity curve no longer represents the demand for labour.

In the real world each firm knows that its market share is not without limit. Furthermore each firm knows equally well that lower wage costs might also imply lower costs for other firms, which in a competitive market means lower prices and unchanged real wages cost. Hence, firms know in an uncertain environment that the microeconomically derived downward-sloping D_L curve is not the effective demand curve for labour.

If the equilibrium is disturbed, the representative microeconomic firm is in the dilemma that, given the atomistic market conditions, it can change neither the price nor the wage. If internal agreements are made within the industry then the real wage can be changed by price and/or wage adjustments; but in that case the crucial assumption of given money wage and product price of a perfectly competitive market analysis is broken, and no conclusion within the conventional textbook figure of the labour market about the macroeconomic impact can be obtained.

Summary

If the 'representative agent' is not representative, then conclusions cannot readily be drawn from the individual agent's optimal behaviour (with or without the assumption of rational expectations) about the macro-behaviour by simply 'counting' the number of market participants. In that case the macro-demand and macro-supply will deviate from the representative microeconomic agent.

FROM MARKET LEVEL TO THE 'ECONOMY AS A WHOLE'

The fallacy of composition might also be committed when a single macro-market is analysed in isolation from the 'economy as a whole'. That would happen if the *ceteris paribus* method was employed and analytical results presented without any consideration to the consequences of having assumed *ceteris paribus.*[6] In that case the error would be that the achieved result in the isolated macro-market analysis is assumed to be valid for the economy as a whole. The neoclassical textbook treatment of the labour market is also illustrative for this fallacy of composition.

An Isolated Labour Market

I have discussed above a number of difficulties that are connected with giving an empirically relevant representation of supply and demand in the labour market by using the method of representative microeconomic agents. Here I put this discussion to one side and look only at the adjustment in the labour market from the neoclassical point of view, where an analysis based on representative agents is considered to be both consistent and relevant. The question that has now to be answered is whether this labour market model will produce a consistent answer to the question of how the real wage and employment will develop in a situation where involuntary unemployment is to be reduced through a policy of lowering the real wage (see Figure 7.2, which can be found in many representative new-Keynesian textbooks, for instance Begg et al., 2001).

Assuming general equilibrium (*ceteris paribus*) in all other macro-markets, then the analysis is carried out by lowering the real wage and by assuming that the market equilibrium follows the demand curve, since

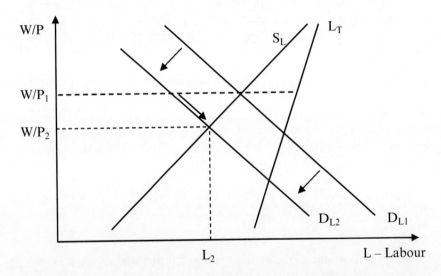

Figure 7.2   The new-Keynesian textbook representation of labour market adjustment

'supply creates its own demand' and the agents have rational expectations. Lower money wages lead to lower real wages and higher employment in the new-Keynesian analysis, on condition that all other things are unchanged. If this model is to be a relevant representation of the adjustment in the macroeconomic landscape, then the analysis would not involve a fallacy of composition. If however there are spillover effects from the labour market adjustment, then 'all other things' will not stay unchanged and the assumption about unchanged equilibrium values cannot be maintained.

As discussed in Chapter 5 there are outside *the* general equilibrium always spillover effects between the macro-markets. Hence *ceteris* cannot stay *paribus* and the assumption of unchanged equilibrium values in all other markets is violated. The often-presented post-Keynesian example of such a macro-market interrelationship is the assumption that the firms' expectations of aggregate demand for private consumption are forward-looking and dependent on the purchasing power of the wage-earners. A reduced real wage might cause the purchasing power of wage-earners to fall, which would more likely than not reduce consumer demand. Wage policy might have a rather complicated spillover effect on the effective demand for goods and services and thereby also on the demand for labour. This analysis will be extended in the next chapter, and has, in a condensed form, been illustrated above in Figure 5.3 with the accompanying text. The point should be emphasized that when there is a mutual interdependency between macro-markets (here the goods market and the labour market) the macroeconomic effect cannot be determined by an isolated macro-market analysis without running the risk of committing a fallacy of composition.

An Increased Propensity to Save

Another, almost as 'classic', example of a fallacy of composition is the question of whether an increase in individuals' propensity to save will increase society's total saving. People who increase their propensity to save will – all other things being equal – naturally increase their savings from a given income. But are all things equal? In an isolated loanable funds equilibrium model (with full employment and the rate of interest clearing the market for real investment and savings) the answer is a straightforward 'yes'. When the propensity to save is increased the rate of interest will fall (see Figure 7.3). A lower rate of interest ensures that intended saving is transformed into an equivalent amount of real investments, whereby the total output and total employment remain unchanged.

A changed saving behaviour thus has no spillover effect on the markets for output as a whole, employment and money. The assumption of *ceteris*

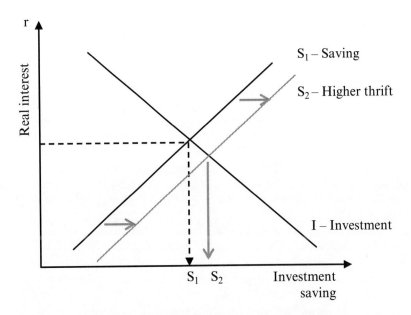

Figure 7.3   A neoclassical isolated saving–investment analysis

paribus isolates the 'market' for saving and real investment and the (real) interest rate ensures that the market clears. An increased individual propensity to save leads automatically to an increased sum of savings at the macro-level due to the assumption of analytical closure.

If however it is argued that this assumed closure is analytically illegitimate because of significant spillover effects between the markets for saving and investment and other markets within the macroeconomy, then we might conclude that the isolated equilibrium model is not a satisfactory analytical device. When *ceteris* is not *paribus*, Figure 7.3 cannot give a full answer to what will happen to saving at the macro-level.

For instance, post-Keynesian economists would emphasize that an increased propensity to save would, firstly, mean reduced consumption and therefore reduced sales. That would influence the firms' expectations and thereby the effective demand for goods and services. If this effect is strong, an increased propensity to save might even result in a reduction of total savings. This integrated analysis will not be pursued further here. The most important thing is to clarify the point that when *ceteris* is not *paribus*, the interplay between the different markets is absolutely decisive for the resulting macroeconomic effect.

One methodological reason why a fallacy of composition is committed at the macroeconomic level is the assumption of *ceteris paribus* when this assumption does not have enough empirical and therefore analytical validity.

SUMMARY

An isolated macro-market analysis entails the risk of committing a fallacy of composition. According to the post-Keynesian methodology hardly any macro-market should be analysed in isolation since the *ceteris paribus* assumption is seldom, if ever, satisfied in the macroeconomic landscape. Therefore it was also underlined several times in the previous chapter that when the so-called open-system *ceteris paribus* method is practised in a macroeconomic analysis, it could only represent a temporary semi-closure. The full analysis could not be completed without the consequences for and repercussions from other markets being evaluated and included. This iterative process could help to avoid committing the fallacy of composition.

In any case there is a risk of falling into the trap of committing a fallacy of composition whenever an ontologically important matter is disregarded. The outstanding example is, of course, when uncertainty is erased as an empirically relevant factor for describing microeconomic behaviour and undertaking macroeconomic analysis. Hence, representative agents and general equilibrium, which may work so well when applied to a closed model, could easily violate some important features of the social ontology of the macroeconomic landscape, because it has an open structure.

The key assumptions which might cause the fallacy of composition to be committed within neoclassical macroeconomics, are the following:

1. Rational microeconomic behaviour → representative agent:
   (macro = n × (stereotype) micro-behaviour)

2. Market clearing → general equilibrium
(*ceteris paribus* and general market clearing)

If these chains of reasoning leading from rational individual behaviour, *via* representative agents and market clearing, to general equilibrium are not a realistic form of analysis within the macroeconomic landscape, then the risk of committing the fallacy of composition is substantial. It could happen each time there is a significant difference between the analytical model and method and the perceived reality. In such cases macroeconomic conclusions cannot be directly based on a generalization of microeconomics; *pace* the quotation from Lucas in Chapter 1, where macroeconomics is made identical to generalized microeconomics.

To avoid committing the fallacy of composition while using a conventional general equilibrium model, it has to be argued convincingly that the social ontology behind the macroeconomic landscape can adequately be analysed in accordance with the following five requirements:

- agents act independently, which makes methodological individualism appropriate;
- rational expectations-formation is empirically relevant;
- representative agents are 'representative' for macroeconomic behaviour;
- agents can change the market price, but still perceive it as externally given;
- market clearing is instantaneous and obtainable in all markets.

If one or more of these requirements is 'unrealistic', that is, violated in practice, then there will be an imminent risk of committing a fallacy of composition when using the general equilibrium method. To the extent that the general equilibrium model, based on the assumptions of representative agents with rational expectations-formation and market clearing, is not empirically anchored, then a fallacy of composition will occur when macro-conclusions are based on a generalization of individual behaviour. To guard against committing such fallacies of composition, it is necessary to support any macroeconomic analysis with an evaluation of the realism of the model. For this reason alone, a descriptively based macro-model is indispensable.

In fact, when the axioms of the analytical model and method do not correspond to the social ontology under consideration, it is not only the risk of the fallacy of composition that is at stake: the analysis is, from a realistic point of view, methodologically in troubled waters and might give misleading results.

NOTES

1. This chapter is an edited version of my contribution to Fenger-Grøn and Kristensen (2001). A more popular version can be found in Jespersen (1996), Chapter 2, 'Neoclassical theory cannot explain reality'.
2. Also quoted in Chapter 1.
3. As explained in the introductory chapter, during the 1990s neoclassical economists split between new-classical and new-Keynesian traditions. They both share the ambition of having a firm microeconomic foundation, but deviate on the question of whether the

economic development can be analysed as a continuous market-clearing process (new-classical school) or there might be short-run deviations due to sluggish price and wage adjustments (new-Keynesian school).

4. Newer economic behavioural research, however, has demonstrated that it is possible, by way of empirical experiments, partly to discover how individuals do react to altered external conditions. This research has actually revealed that individuals' preference structures are not invariant with regard to changes in economic conditions and past experiences; see for example Kahneman (2003), Layard (2005).

5. This is probably also, as mentioned before, the reason why Andersen and Pedersen (2005) reject the question of committing the fallacy of composition as irrelevant with regard to the use of a general equilibrium model like the DREAM model, for, as they argue, all relevant interrelations are built into the general equilibrium model. They seem to interpret the fallacy of composition as an accusation of internal inconsistency of the DREAM model or other applied general equilibrium models, which is not the case. The risk of committing a fallacy of composition is related to macroeconomic conclusions which are derived from a pre-designed ideal market economic system, where macro is equal to $\sum$ micro by means of representative agents and market clearing. This happens when there is an obvious discrepancy between the model and reality. One could, in that situation, perhaps talk about external inconsistency.

6. A procedure which could be compared to a closed-system analysis.

8. Effective demand: a macroeconomic causal relationship

> As I now think, the volume of employment is fixed by the entrepreneur under the motive of seeking to maximise his present and prospective profits; whilst the volume of employment which will maximise his profit depends on the aggregate demand function given by his expectations of the sum of the proceeds. (Keynes, 1936: 77)

PROLOGUE

'Effective demand' is one of the distinctive analytical concepts that Keynes developed in *The General Theory*. Demand and demand management have thereby come to represent one of the distinct trademarks of Keynesian macroeconomic theory and policy. It is not without reason that the central position of this concept has left the impression that Keynes's macroeconomic model predominantly consists of theories for determining demand, while the supply side is neglected. From here it is a short step within a superficial interpretation to conclude that Keynes (and post-Keynesians) have ended up at a theoretical dead end, where macroeconomic development is exclusively determined by demand factors.

To avoid this dead end, this prologue is intended as an encouragement to the reader to abandon this mistaken understanding. In this chapter it will be demonstrated that behind the somewhat ill-chosen expression 'effective demand', there lies a rather refined analysis of how supply factors, market conditions and demand expectations in the business sector as a whole interact and together form the arguments behind the macroeconomic causal relationship that is known as 'effective demand'. It is this mix of supply, demand and institutional considerations that determines how much the business sector as a whole plans to produce and, thereby, how much labour it wants to employ. On what terms labour would be employed was not thoroughly discussed in *The General Theory*. Although Keynes on several occasions emphasized that it is the money wage which is negotiated, he was willing, as an assumption, to accept the so-called first classical labour market postulate: 'In a given state of organisation, equipment and technique, the real wage earned by a unit of labour has a unique (inverse) correlation with the volume of employment' (Keynes, 1936: 17).

INTRODUCTION

This chapter will draw together a number of points from the previous chapters. Effective demand, as I will interpret the concept below, can best be understood by drawing on several methodological elements.

Effective demand is an analytical concept that is used in World 2 in order to understand the dynamics in the macroeconomic landscape. It draws on the theory of microeconomic behaviour under conditions of uncertainty with the aim of developing a macroeconomic behavioural relationship (causal relationship). The theory of effective demand is then presented in the form of a series of semi-closures containing the markets for both goods and labour and based on the open-system *ceteris paribus* method. This produces a geometric presentation of the 'principle of effective demand' originally presented by Davidson and Smolensky (1964). Subsequently, the *ceteris paribus* assumptions will be relaxed, which makes the theory more complex but also more realistic. The principle of effective demand is an example of how supply and demand factors, as well as institutional conditions, can be summed up in one single macroeconomic causal relationship (see Figure 8.1).[1]

MACROECONOMIC 'BEHAVIOUR' WITH A MICROECONOMIC CONSIDERATION

As mentioned, the intention of this chapter is to give an example of how a macroeconomic causal relationship can be modelled on the basis of both

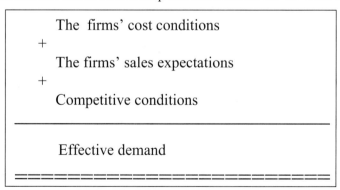

Figure 8.1   Outline for the principle of effective demand

supply and demand factors with the inclusion of specific institutional conditions such as different forms of competition. The choice of the analytical method plays a determining role for the macroeconomic 'behaviour' that can be deduced on the basis of an aggregate model structure supported by rational microeconomic reasoning and empirical observations. The methodological procedure is contrary to methodological individualism and representative agent theory that are more often than not employed within neoclassical macroeconomics, as discussed in Chapter 4.

Unfortunately, it is technically much more difficult to give a simple (aggregate) presentation of the behaviour of heterogeneous actors acting under conditions of uncertainty. The more heterogeneous the underlying microeconomic structure is assumed to be, the more difficult it is to deduce a simple macroeconomic causal relationship that is relevant for understanding the macroeconomic landscape.

However, I will use Chapter 3 in Keynes's *General Theory*, 'The principle of effective demand', as an example of how important analytical results can be achieved by using the OSCP method. When maintaining an open model, there is no *a priori* requirement that the microeconomic behaviour and the institutional anchoring should be predesigned. On the contrary, it will be an epistemological strength if the analytical model by its design contains alternative behavioural hypotheses and institutional organization. A theory is said to be more general if, for example, it can contain markets with both perfect and monopolistic competition.

THE PRINCIPLE OF EFFECTIVE DEMAND

My interpretation of effective demand can explain how Keynes, through this central macroeconomic concept, not only included the economy's supply side (production decisions), but could also make the standard assumption of firms' rational behaviour at the micro-level the basis for understanding the important causal relationship for determining production and employment in the macroeconomic landscape.

It should immediately be conceded that Keynes, as already mentioned, did not make it any easier for the reader when he gave this chapter, which explains how production decisions are made, the title 'The Principle of Effective Demand'. However, it should be noted here that Keynes used the expression 'principle'. I do not think it is a coincidence that Keynes used this expression. It is not merely one of a number of possible theories for understanding the macroeconomic dynamic based on the individual firms' rational behaviour under conditions of uncertainty. A 'principle' is more fundamental than just a theory.[2] A principle is close to an axiom, which in any case should be substantiated empirically in order *a priori* not to close the model. 'Effective demand' hereby appears as a necessary, but not always totally sufficient, theory for understanding the changes in output and employment.

Thus, Keynes takes his point of departure in the firms' behaviour when he explains the basic 'principle' for how total output and employment are determined as a result of firms' optimizing behaviour:

> For entrepreneurs will endeavour to fix the amount of employment at the level which they expect to maximise the excess of the proceeds over the factor cost. ... [F]or it is at this point that the entrepreneurs' expectation of profits will be maximised. ... [T]he point of the aggregate demand function, where it is intersected by the aggregate supply function, will be called *the effective demand* (Keynes, 1936: 24–5).

As I will explain in more detail below, 'effective demand' is a concept that is associated with profit-maximizing firms: it is based on entrepreneurs' expectations with regard to future sales and current costs. It is the behaviour of profit-maximizing firms that is central in *The General Theory*. It is these entrepreneurs' expectations that determine output and employment. The fact that Keynes called this analytical concept 'effective demand' has, as already mentioned, unfortunately contributed to misleading generations of macroeconomists into concluding that it was exclusively the demand for consumer and investment goods that determines the macroeconomic development. On the contrary, it is the interaction between the sum of the individual firms' sales expectations (aggregate demand) and their production costs (aggregate supply) that together determine the development in output and employment 'as a whole'.[3] Thus, I hope to contribute to eradicating the often-presented point of view that Keynes's macroeconomic theory does not have a microeconomic foundation or supply-side considerations.

Firms' Aggregate Behaviour Describes the Supply Side

The supply side in the goods market is determined by the individual firms' cost functions. Keynes's aggregate supply function appears almost to be copied from Marshall's *Principles of Economics*. It shows a relation between what Keynes calls 'supply price', the sales proceeds that, given the production function and cost structures, is needed to 'just make it worth the while of the entrepreneurs to give that employment' (Keynes, 1936: 24). This means that behind the supply curve there is a combination of fixed and variable costs plus a certain expected profit. At each level of demand, firms will be maximizing their profits, so there is no further

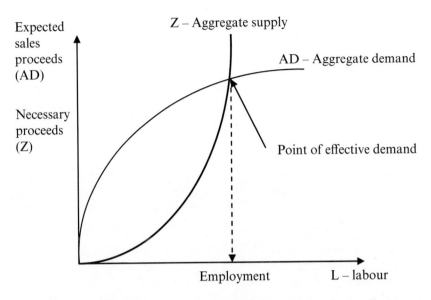

Figure 8.2   Aggregate supply and aggregate demand determine effective demand for labour

incentive for firms to change output or employment. The function of the aggregate demand curve is to show what level of demand firms expect.

Hence, in this chapter Keynes assumed firms to be profit-maximizing, the aggregate production function to represent decreasing marginal productivity with regard to labour, and the market structure to be perfect competition. These assumptions entail that the aggregate supply function (what Keynes called the Z-curve) is upward sloping and represents the proceeds that will be needed by the industry as a whole to make a certain employment 'worth undertaking'; see the Z-curve in Figure 8.2. In fact, this aggregate supply function looks as though it was taken directly from a standard, neoclassical textbook, where decreasing marginal productivity of a representative firm is assumed; but Keynes is dealing with the aggregate supply of heterogeneous firms which do not necessarily take output prices as given. Therefore the interpretation of the upward-sloping aggregate Z-curve is quite different from the neoclassical AS-curve.

Aggregate Demand is Determined by the Firms' Expectations

It should be a simple matter to ascertain that, in relation to the standard macroeconomic literature in the 1930s, Keynes's introduction of aggregate demand for goods and services as a whole was a theoretical innovation.

But Keynes found it puzzling; how the incorporation of demand into macr-oeconomic theory would be considered as a novelty. Why should Marshall, who if anyone, was the father of the supply and demand theory of adjust-ments in a single market, have left out demand at the macro-level?[4]

> You will not find it [effective demand] mentioned even once in the whole works of Marshall, Edgeworth and Professor Pigou, from whose hands the classical theory has received its most mature embodiment. (Keynes, 1936: 32)

To get a full understanding of the principle of effective demand, it is necessary to make a detour *via* aggregate demand. That is defined as 'the proceeds which entrepreneurs expect to receive from the employment of N men' (Keynes, 1936: 25). This concept of aggregate demand can possibly be best understood empirically with reference to the far newer statistical concept of a 'business sentiment index'. The business sentiment index is based on a survey among a representative cross-section of firms of their expectations for sales in the nearer future. This published index helps to form expectations of sales proceeds for the industry as a whole or even for the entire macroeconomy. It is assumed that on this basis, firms form expectations with regard to the most likely development in overall sales (considered as a whole) in the nearer future.[5] This overall expectation of aggregate demand is a useful point of departure for the individual firms when they form their specific expectations of future sales. These sales expectation[6] will therefore centre especially on the future macroeconomic demand level (and today we would also add international competition). Keynes's macro-theory has a microeconomic foundation but differs from neoclassical theory by an explicit introduction of aggregate demand expected by business as a whole, that is, the total expected sales on the macro-level.

In order for firms to act they have to form expectations about future sales which should be both empirically based and forward-looking at the same time:

> let *D* be the proceeds which entrepreneurs expect to receive from the employ-ment of *N* men, the relationship between *D* and *N* being written $D = f(N)$, which can be called the *Aggregate Demand Function*. (Keynes, 1936: 25)

It is undeniably a definition of few words that opens the possibility for a number of hypotheses with regard to how the entrepreneurs' total expecta-tions of earnings are formed. Firstly, it is important for Keynes to make clear that aggregate supply and aggregate demand are two clearly sepa-rated entities. Keynes's main objection against 'classical' theory is exactly as described above, that in his interpretation it equates the macro-supply and macro-demand functions.

But in his critique, Keynes does not explain how the entrepreneurs' expected aggregate demand function can be analytically established on the basis of individual expectations.[7] Here the *D*-curve's shape is explained by 'the psychological characteristic of the community, which we shall call the propensity to consume' (Keynes, 1936: 28) which suggests that during an economic upswing, where employment is increasing, firms considered as a whole will expect an increase in sales. Then he concludes in the following paragraph: '*D* is what we have called above *effective demand*' (Keynes, 1936: 29). Here, I think, there is reason to make an objection, because on page 25 in *The General Theory* (see above) Keynes called *D* the aggregate demand function. He is making an unnoticed slippage in the interpretation of the *D* function, making an unhappy convergence between the sales that the firms expect and the society's psychology, which is quite another thing. Not only are expected sales made equal to the planned demand from households and investors on the macro-level, but the important intersection between aggregate demand and aggregate supply is left out in his page-29 definition of effective demand, which I consider quite confusing.

By making effective demand similar to aggregate demand and equalizing it with actual demand, Keynes did make a number of short-cuts, which removed a number of potential slips between consumers' and investors' planned demand for goods and services and firms' expectations of aggregate demand and effective demand. Unnoticed, Keynes thus made the semi-closure that lies in assuming an analytical convergence between the 'planned demand' at community level, and the sum of the sales proceeds which the firms as a whole expect to be able to get at different levels of employment (aggregate demand). Furthermore, Keynes did not discuss how the individual firms figure out their share of the aggregate demand within their industry. One possible interpretation of the behaviour of the individual firms is that they do not consider their firm-specific demand as infinite at a given market price. In the short period they probably have to behave under the constraint of a rather fixed market share. In that case individual firms do not operate on a horizontal demand curve and do not expect the market price to be solely given 'from outside'. This means that the neoclassical assumption of firms exclusively adjusting their output on the basis of a given price and cost structure, leaving demand neglected, can be discharged. Firms know that the aggregate demand at the macro-level is limited and this has to be included in the individual firm's production planning. This analytical semi-closure of firms operating under the constraint of a limited market share makes it relevant to assume that firms have to react to a change in aggregate demand. In addition, individual firms still try to maximize their profits given the uncertain knowledge about price, aggregate demand, market share and competitive condition (domestic and foreign).

In this case it has been explained why post-Keynesian economics has dismissed the neoclassical abstraction that the macro-supply curve can be presented by the behavioural relationship of one representative micro-firm. In post-Keynesian theory firms are assumed to behave with respect to their uncertain knowledge about aggregate demand, and that they can only achieve a(n) (un)certain share of this aggregate demand. Hence, demand is not unlimited for the individual firm; that is, the individual demand curve is not horizontal within Keynes's principle of effective demand.

The Importance of the Organization of the Market

The degree of competition on the output market determines the size of profit that can be achieved by the entrepreneurs at a given level of demand. Post-Keynesian literature also distinguishes between two distinct market forms: 'perfect competition' and 'monopolistic competition'. This distinction leads to different results with regard to the size of profit and to how much employment a certain level of aggregate demand can be expected to generate. One of Keynes's main points was precisely to demonstrate that his theory was 'general', that it was valid no matter what form of competition prevailed on the goods and labour markets.[8] In fact, effective demand is a relevant analytical concept even in cases where firms are not profit-maximizing. Probably, he chose to assume profit-maximizing behaviour and perfect competition even on the demand side of the labour market for the sake of analytical convenience rather than realism.

As mentioned above, Keynes did undertake his macro-analysis under the assumption of 'perfect' competition in the sense of real wages being determined by marginal productivity – goods prices are given from outside the individual firm while the aggregate demand had to be shared between firms in the market for final goods. In that case effective demand is determined as the intersection point between aggregate supply and aggregate demand, which also determines 'profit equilibrium' (*CWK*, VII: xxxiii; Fanning and Mahony, 2000). At the point of effective demand there will be no inherent tendency in the business sector to change production or employment, because firms are maximizing expected profit.

An assumption of monopolistic competition on the goods market, which however is not directly included in *The General Theory*, will imply that the 'optimal' output level, and thereby also the derived employment level, would lie to the left of the intersection point between Z and AD under perfect competition. This is so because as explained above the level of profit which 'just make[s] it worth the while of the entrepreneurs to give that employment' (Keynes, 1936: 24) is higher. Compared to a market form with perfect competition the Z-curve will be higher up in Figure 8.2 and the point of effective demand to the left, causing a smaller number of people being employed.

Conversely, it can be illustrated that increased competition may – *ceteris paribus* – create an incentive to increase production and employment by lowering the required profit, and the point of effective demand will move to the right. Hence, globalization could cause employment to increase if the generally required profit level was reduced due to increased competition. Furthermore, globalization might also lead to increased real wages, which could boost aggregate demand.

Effective Demand Implies 'Profit-Equilibrium'

Effective demand determines the level of employment (as a whole) given the required level of expected profit (as a whole) and given the market structures. The causal relationship goes from effective demand to employment. When the firms' sales expectations are met and if the firms' competitive position (domestically and internationally) is unchanged, then a realization of the point of effective demand will entail that there will be no behavioural incentive in the business sector to change output and employment (as a whole), because profit is expected to be at the required level.

Keynes did assume that profit was maximized; but one could equally well work with the Kaleckian assumption of mark-up pricing. In any case this is an example of profit-equilibrium, where: 'the equilibrium level of employment, i.e. the level at which there is *no inducement to employers as a whole* either to expand or to contract employment' (Keynes, 1936: 27; emphasis added).

This explains why a situation with a considerable number of involuntarily unemployed workers can remain stagnant as long as there are no private, economic incentives to change employment. The firms are assumed to maximize expected profit, and if expectations are unchanged and by and large fulfilled, there is a situation of 'no change'. This analytical semi-closure will stay as long as the given factors are unchanged, which of course will seldom happen in practice (see Chapter 6).

On the other hand Keynes wanted to emphasize that workers (and firms) within an analytical environment of perfect competition would not expect the wage level to change unless employment changes. According to the logic of the model, a change in costs would immediately be reflected in a similar change in the price level, whereby the real wage will remain unchanged. Even in a situation with monopolistic competition among employers, uncertainty with regard to how a reduction in money wage level would influence aggregate demand and thereby ultimately effective demand could block changes in the general wage level regardless of the level of unemployment. Without a reasonably certain expected change in the aggregate demand and/or the aggregate supply, there is no economic incentive for firms (as a whole) to change the level of employment, if they (as a whole) are operating at maximum profit (or close to it) in their initial situation.

Any change of output that is not caused by a change in effective demand cannot within this model be explained by rational arguments based on private-economy incentives. The fact that unemployment exists at the macro-level does not by itself carry information that the effective demand might change in the future. In other words, idle production factors do not by themselves create economic incentives that would increase effective demand.

However, let us take a closer look at this argument, since it must contain an evaluation of both the development in the firms' expected sales (aggregate demand) and their cost relations (aggregate supply). Involuntary unemployment does not in itself send a signal that a larger amount of goods could be expected to be sold in the future. A lower real wage would rather reduce the employed wage-earners' purchasing power. The theoretical conclusion with regard to the behaviour of employers even in the event of substantial unemployment is that they will go on employing an unchanged number of workers as long as they expect to maximize profit.

In his labour market analysis we know that Keynes at an early stage denied the validity of the second labour market postulate, because it was not considered relevant for a realistic employment analysis. Workers do not have the power to change firms' expectation of aggregate demand or aggregate supply, that is, the effective demand for labour. Even in the case of some trade union power workers can only negotiate for a certain money wage, while entrepreneurs determine the real wage through price-setting. Furthermore, when individual workers are willing to accept a lower money wage they would possibly increase their *individual* likelihood of being considered for a job; but this does not increase the overall macro-employment as long as the effective demand and, it follows, the number of jobs, is unchanged. Of course, changed search behaviour by individual workers might reduce the frictional unemployment, but that is not what Keynes's theory of effective demand is about.

Summary

Effective demand is thus an analytical concept, a causal relationship that makes a significant contribution to the understanding of how output and employment are determined at the macro-level by the interaction between aggregate supply and aggregate demand. It is determined by the firms' expected sales paired with the cost structure, which together determine how much it is optimal to produce and thereby also determine the effective demand for labour as a whole.

However, this conclusion is not dependent on whether there is an assumption of perfect competition or monopolistic competition on the goods market, let alone the labour market. The market form is subordinated to the results of the general analysis. Keynes actually accepted in *The General Theory* both flexible prices and wages, and thereby also a flexible real wage on the labour market, not as a cause, but rather as a consequence of a changed level of employment. He assumed that the first neoclassical postulate – that the real wage is uniquely correlated with the marginal productivity – was satisfied, though the causality was not as neoclassical economists argued.

DIFFERENCES BETWEEN KEYNES'S AND NEOCLASSICAL THEORY OF 'OUTPUT AS A WHOLE'

Keynes's genuinely new macroeconomic theory is thus that at the macro-level, output is determined by effective demand, which includes both the firms' cost conditions and expected aggregate demand.

This theoretically new causal macroeconomic relationship was intended as a direct contradiction to the existing (neoclassical) theory of output, where there is no difference between supply and demand of goods and services at the macro-level. Here it is assumed that the analytical law applies that 'supply creates its own demand'. The microeconomic foundation of neoclassical macro-theory contained the assumption that as long as there was unemployment, firms could expand employment along the D_L line (cf. Figure 7.1), only limited by the supply curve of labour. The individual firm was assumed to maximize profit by equating marginal cost to the given market price, and as long as the money wage did fall – *deus ex machina* – causing the real wage to fall, output could be expanded. The total macroeconomic demand curve for goods and services thus becomes coincident with the firms' aggregate supply function. If the macroeconomic theory is solely deduced on the basis of this neoclassical microeconomic theory, that is, as the sum of the individual atomistic firms' behaviour (presented in the model as one single representative firm), then demand is only limited by the form of the production function and the available quantity of factors of production.

It is at this point that neoclassical macro-theory, presented as aggregated micro-theory, gets into internal difficulties because atomistic firms cannot change the money wage or the market price, and hence the real wage gets stuck.[9] There is a 'missing link' in the neoclassical presentation; see the previous chapter: how can the representative firm be assumed, on a consistent microeconomic foundation, to be able to change either the price level or the wage level?

Hence, there is no neoclassical microeconomic foundation of macro-economic price and wage theory when perfect competition is the case: the representative agent is assumed to act on the basis of an externally given price (and wage). The model lacks a consistent theoretical foundation for a mechanism that can generate the correct price change for full employment.

On the premise of neoclassical theory, that supply creates its own demand, there is one equation missing to make a determination of the production at the macro-level. This is so because, if supply creates its own demand, output is undetermined. Keynes concluded that: 'the amount of employment is indeterminate except in so far as the marginal disutility of labour [i.e. the supply of labour] sets an upper limit' (Keynes, 1936: 26), that is, full employment is the only constraint to expansion. This is why output in neoclassical macro-theory is assumed to adjust itself to the amount of labour that is available in the labour market on the assumption of a prefixed equilibrium:

> Thus Say's law, that the aggregate demand price of output as a whole is equal to its aggregate supply price for all volumes of output, is equivalent to the proposition that there is no obstacle to full employment. (Keynes, 1936: 26)

Keynes's final verdict was that the neoclassical macroeconomic theory is, in the mathematical sense, underdetermined.[10] Outside general equilibrium an equation to determine 'employment as a whole'[11] is missing:

> in other words, that the aggregate demand price (or proceeds) always accommodates itself to the aggregate supply price; so that, whatever the value of N may be, the proceeds D assume a value equal to the aggregate supply price Z which corresponds to N. (Keynes, 1936: 26)

According to Keynes's critique the question of how an increased supply of goods due to lower nominal costs is converted to an equivalent increase in demand for goods remains theoretically unresolved, since neoclassical theory '[i]n its crudest form, [this is tantamount to assuming that] the reduction in money-wages will leave demand unaffected' (Keynes, 1936: 258).[12] After which Keynes continues:

If this is the groundwork of the argument ... , surely it is fallacious. For the demand schedules for particular industries can only be constructed on some fixed assumption as to the nature of demand and supply schedules of other industries and as to the amount of the aggregate effective demand. It is invalid, therefore, to transfer the argument to industry as a whole ... (Keynes, 1936: 259)

Wages and Employment: Output is Measured in 'Wage-Units'

In Keynes's day labour was to an overwhelming degree represented by unskilled labour in the manufacturing, mining and construction sectors. Employment could be calculated in hours and/or persons without making a serious aggregation error of lumping together heterogeneous items. It is more difficult when it comes to output, which by its nature consists of heterogeneous goods and services. To overcome the technical aggregation problem one could calculate all transactions in value terms at market prices, which can be added together to form one single number. But that would leave us without information about the development of output in real terms. This was a practical problem which had to be solved in a practical manner. A unit of labour is much more homogeneous than a unit of gross domestic product (GDP); furthermore, employment and the real wage are at least as analytically interesting as the quantity of goods and services. Therefore, Keynes argued that this index problem of converting output at market prices into quantities could be solved by using the wage of unskilled labour as the overall deflator, which Keynes called the wage-unit.

In this way, the index problem was solved, which would otherwise inevitably have arisen in connection with a macroeconomic presentation of the development in the quantity of heterogeneous output. How could one calculate the total volume of pork, electronics and tourist trips produced, so that it is possible to make a consistent comparison over time? This is impossible when relative prices change: electronics become cheaper, tourist trips become more expensive, and so on. Keynes cut through this problem and suggested that output, calculated at market prices, could be compared year by year, as long as it is deflated with a relevant wage-unit.

The Assumption of a Constant Wage-Unit is a Semi-Closure

Since it is the quantitative change in output (and thereby in employment) that is the object of Keynes's macroeconomic focus of *The General Theory*, until Chapter 19 he assumed for analytical convenience that the wage-unit was constant. Keynes was aware that this simplification could in a superficial reading be misinterpreted, so that his critics would claim that the 'general' theory had a constant wage level as a crucial analytical assumption. In an attempt to pre-empt this misconception that the theory of effective demand assumes a constant wage-unit, he wrote immediately after he had argued for the analytical advantages of this semi-closure:

> But this simplification, with which we shall dispense later, is introduced solely to facilitate the exposition. The essential character of the argument is precisely the same whether or not money-wages, etc., are liable to change. (Keynes, 1936: 27)

The use of the wage-unit as a measure for output as a whole also has the advantage that the unambiguous correspondence between output and employment can be maintained, even in a growth scenario. If the wage-unit as a normal assumption is assumed to grow in step with the trend in labour productivity, then there will continue to be a considerable degree of proportionality between development in output and employment. Keynes did not explicitly touch on this aspect in *The General Theory*, but he dealt with it indirectly in *Economic Possibilities for our Grandchildren* (Keynes, 1930b, reprinted in *CWK*, IX)

Flexible Real Wage was the Basic Assumption

Keynes acknowledged his neoclassical, Marshallian upbringing in several connections. He thus had no problem maintaining the assumptions of profit-maximization and labour-market determination of the money wage, because they did not challenge his main conclusion: that macroeconomic development is caused by changes in effective demand and cannot be understood within the framework of a general equilibrium, market-clearing model.

Although the concept of marginal productivity is assumed to be analytically relevant in *The General Theory*, it does not determine employment, but is used to deduce an indication of how the real wage might change. Keynes was thus willing to assume 'perfect' competition between the employers in the labour market, which has the theoretical implication of the real wage being equal to labour's marginal productivity:

> Thus I am not disputing this vital fact which the classical economists have (rightly) asserted as indefeasible. In a given state of organisation, equipment and technique, the real wage earned by a unit of labour has a unique (inverse) correlation with the volume of employment. Thus *if* employment increases, then, in the short period, the reward per unit of labour in terms of wage-goods must, in general, decline and profits increase. (Keynes, 1936: 17)

Keynes is unambiguous: his theory holds even when perfect competition between firms in goods and labour markets is assumed. This means that competition among firms drives down prices until the calculated level of real wage equalizes the marginal productivity of labour; see the point of effective demand in Figure 8.2. But it is important here to hold on to Keynes's causal ordering, which is in direct opposition to the neoclassical economists. Output and employment are determined by effective demand; then the real wage adjusts through changes in the market price of goods. The causality goes from employment to the real wage – not the other way around:

> But when we have thrown over the second postulate, ... a willingness on the part of labour to accept lower money-wages is not necessarily a remedy for unemployment. (Keynes, 1936: 18)

The quotation above shows that Keynes did not reject the analytical idea of having a flexible money wage as an assumption. To Keynes the important matter was to get the causality right between money wage and employment, and hereby prevent macroeconomists from giving incorrect advice to politicians about the employment effect that could be achieved through increased wage flexibility. This was one of his main points of criticism against Pigou, his colleague at Cambridge (see Appendix 8.1.)

Profitability

Effective demand is determined by expected demand, production costs and attempts to maximize profit. From the analysis above it appears straight-forward that a reduced expected demand will tend to reduce employment (see Figure 8.3). Similarly, an isolated upward movement of the aggregate supply curve will lead to the result that the profit level for unchanged employment will tend to fall below its required level, when Z exceeds AD. In such event, firms have an incentive to reduce employment. An adjustment process will take place. Given the model's premises, an adjustment of the cost level can take on two different forms: (1) a reduction of the cost level either through a fall in money wages; or (2) increased marginal productivity. But a reduction in money wage would at the same instant have an impact on the AD-curve. Firms know, of course, that lower wages also means lower demand for consumer goods.

This indeterminate consequence of lower wage costs brings the second cost-adjusting mechanism into play, consisting of an increased marginal productivity. If Keynes (and the neoclassical economists) are right in their assertion that in the short period there are decreasing marginal returns to

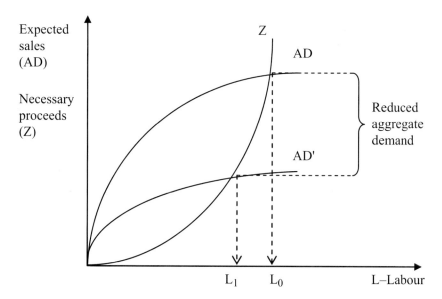

Figure 8.3   A fall in AD leads to reduced employment

labour, then a profit maximum can – though at a lower absolute level of profits – be re-established by a fall in output, determined by the new inter-section point between *Z* and *AD'* in Figure 8.3. In other words, profits are still maximized with regard to the level of demand.

AGGREGATE DEMAND IN THE LONG RUN

> It is my contention that Keynesians of all shades make a fatal strategic error by failing to examine the long-period equilibrium arguments of *The General Theory* because it leaves them unable to offer an effective alternative to the classical vision. (Rogers, 1997: 325) [13]

I have mentioned above the issue that Keynes made it rather easy for himself by assuming that firms, in regard to future sales expectations, have assumed 'correct' expectations in the short period. In *The General Theory* Chapter 5, 'Expectation as determining Output and Employment', Keynes explained how the firms' 'daily' production decisions are determined by the cost of output (that is, the *Z*-function) and expectations as to the sale-proceeds of its output (that is, the *AD*-function). These short-term expectations of proceeds will largely depend on long-term (or medium-term) expectations of other parties, that is, the degree of competition on the goods and labour markets respectively and the consumers' (medium-term) and investors' (long-term) expectations.

Similarly, he did not distinguish sharply between the households' and the firms' demand plans and their actual purchases. Thus, the short-term and long-term expectations of consumers and investors respectively determine aggregate demand, which is an important part of effective demand. Consumption (C) – as a part of aggregate demand – is thus determined by the marginal propensity to consume and changes in (disposable) income for the wage-earners. Higher income and/or more employment increases consumption, but less than proportionally, especially in the short term. The level of investment (I) is determined by the marginal efficiency of capital, the interest rate and 'the state of confidence'.

A critical point in the theoretical construction of effective demand is that aggregate demand is determined as the firms' expectations of households' and firms' demand, $C + I$, which for many purposes is assumed by Keynes to correspond to the realized demand, as in Figure 8.3. Just as the sales expected by the firms can deviate from realized sales, so the demand desired or planned by households and firms can deviate from the realized demand.[14] Keynes focused on equilibrium (understood as 'standstill'), where there is convergence between expected sales (AD) and actual sales. Only when these items coincide will there be a theoretical 'standstill' on the demand side. In practice, there will of course always be deviations; but if they are small they might not necessarily change the overall business mood.

The dynamic effects are in a monetary production economy caused by persistant changes in aggregate demand *and* aggregate supply. One should not exclusively focus on and discuss the distinction between expected, planned and realized demand, since they only represent one part of effective demand. The other part consists, as discussed above, of the supply side: production and cost conditions. Both parts will undergo considerable and partly unforeseeable changes in a more long-term perspective. In the long period the AD- and the Z-curve will be under constant change due to changed technology, increased wealth and a new product mix – things Keynes did not consider.

As mentioned in the introduction to this chapter, it is a barrier of understanding that the theory of effective demand is too often equated only with the households' planned consumption demand and firms' planned investment demand. In that part of the macroeconomic literature, the firms' production behaviour will therefore seem to be following the effective demand exclusively determined by the behaviour of consumers and investors. The two central 'books' in *The General Theory*, Book III 'The Propensity to Consume' and Book IV 'The Inducement to Invest', describe in detail the psychology behind consumers' and investors' behaviour. These form part of the basis for the firms' sales expectations, which should then be matched by the firms' production and cost structures.

SUMMARY

The principle of effective demand is an example of a macroeconomic causal relation based on microeconomic arguments that include both supply and demand factors. It was demonstrated how the methodological approach determines the analytical conclusions that can be drawn from the interpretation of the effective demand. Keynes's point of departure is a specific interest in what had happened to the demand side in the neoclassical macro-theory at his time. Demand at the macro-level is not mentioned at all by either Marshall or Pigou. Demand had vanished as a consequence of Say's Law and reinforced by the assumption of general equilibrium. In that framework, demand had become redundant: 'Supply creates its own demand': output and employment are determined exclusively by the supply side.

In his theory of effective demand, Keynes connects supply and demand factors from microeconomic theory under the assumption of rational business behaviour with uncertain expectations about future aggregate sales. It is shown that the effective demand for output and employment also depends on which market form is assumed to make the analysis applicable to more realistic cases than perfect competition.

It is concluded that effective demand is determined by expected sales together with the cost structure of industry, on the assumption that firms are able to hire enough labour to achieve the level of output which maximizes expected profits.

APPENDIX 8.1:   KEYNES'S CRITIQUE OF PIGOU'S EXPLANATION OF UNEMPLOYMENT

The Connection between the Production Function and the Demand for Labour in Neoclassical Theory

It is well known from traditional, neoclassical macro-theory that the demand for labour is derived from the private sector's production function under the assumptions of profit maximization and perfect competition. The production function $F(x)$ in the short period is assumed to have decreasing returns to labour based on existing technical production conditions and a given capital stock. The real wage that is consistent with profit-maximizing behaviour is determined by the marginal productivity of labour that geometrically can be determined by the slope of the tangent to $F(x)$. In other words, the demand for labour is dependent on the real wage, which is set equal to marginal physical productivity due to profit maximization and perfectly competitive conditions within the industry. This is illustrated in Figure 8A.1.

Keynes's critique of Pigou's 'unemployment theory' in *The General Theory* goes as follows:

> The 'real demand for labour' is regarded as a factor which is susceptible of wide short-period fluctuations ... , and the suggestion seems to be that swings in 'the

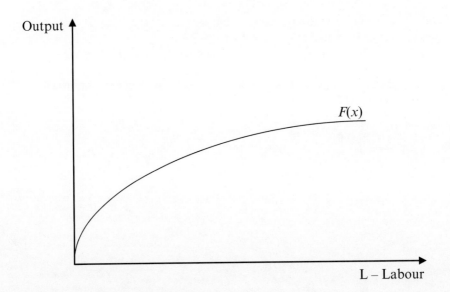

Figure 8A.1   The production function

real demand for labour' are, in combination with the failure of wage policy to respond sensitively to such changes, largely responsible for the trade cycle. ... But if we go back to the definition of the 'real demand for labour', all this loses its plausibility. For we shall find that there is nothing in the world less likely to be subject to sharp short-period swings than this factor.

Professor Pigou's 'real demand for labour' depends by definition on nothing but $F(x)$, which represents the physical conditions of production in the wage-goods industries, and $\emptyset(x)$, which represents the functional relationship between employment in the wage-good industries and total employment .... . Certainly there seems no reason to suppose that they are likely to fluctuate during a trade cycle. For $F(x)$ can only change slowly, and, in a technically progressive community, only in the forward direction; whilst $\emptyset(x)$ will remain stable, unless we suppose a sudden outbreak of thrift in the working classes, or, more generally, a sudden shift in the propensity to consume .... . I repeat that Professor Pigou has altogether omitted from his analysis the unstable factor, namely fluctuations in the scale of investment, which is most often at the bottom of the phenomenon of fluctuations in employment. (Keynes, 1936: 278–9)

Keynes's point is that Pigou, in his verbal description of the causes of the short-term swings in employment and unemployment, seems to argue as if the demand curve for labour can move downwards in Figure 8A.2 when demand for goods falls off. But, says Keynes, that is nothing less than a failure of logical reasoning, if the model's mathematical structure should be respected. The demand curve (MP_L) for labour (as derived from the stable production function) can only change location in the neoclassical

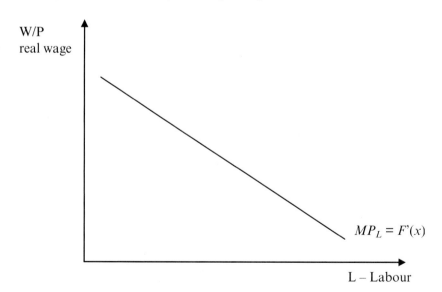

Figure 8A.2   Demand for labour determined by the production function

model when the production function changes position, which, as Keynes argues, will only happen slowly and upwards 'in a technically progressive community'. It is simply not plausible to assume that the MP_L-curve should move inwards.[15]

Increased unemployment can, on Pigou's neoclassical terms, only be explained by an excessively large real wage increase, which is subsequently difficult to adjust downwards. This leads Keynes to point out that the considerable variations in the real wage of more than 20 per cent, which had actually taken place in the years 1924–34, are almost totally caused by fluctuations in the price level, since the monetary wage in that period had only moved within an interval of 6 per cent. The conclusion that Pigou should therefore have reached if he had reasoned correctly within the framework of his mathematical model and had used the available numbers must be, according to Keynes, that prices during the period in question had been too flexible (especially downwards). According to Pigou's model, this price flexibility had made a number of firms unprofitable and thereby forced up unemployment. But Pigou argues to the contrary, that it was the money wage that was too inflexible. This made Keynes remark a bit harshly:

> [P]oliticians are entitled to complain that money-wages *ought* to be highly flexible; but a theorist must be prepared to deal indifferently with either state of affairs. A scientific theory cannot require the facts to conform to its own assumptions. (Keynes, 1936: 276, emphasis as original)

A Paradox in the History of Theory

The above quotation was written over 70 years ago. The macroeconomic debate has not changed considerably since then. As mentioned earlier, the figures used above for the labour market remain a fixed part of the curriculum in modern, neoclassical textbooks, not for reasons related to the history of theory, but because they are still considered to provide an important contribution to the understanding of the causes of unemployment in modern society. The proposed cure for involuntary unemployment is today, just as it was 70 years ago, increased wage and price flexibility. The only noteworthy difference now is that unemployment caused by wage and price inflexibility is, ironically, consistently referred to as Keynesian unemployment. (See for example Romer, 1996; Begg *et al.*, 2001.)

NOTES

1. Keynes's monetary theory, summed up under the name of 'liquidity preference', is another example of such a macroeconomic causal relationship that builds upon a basis of supply and demand factors within the financial sector under considerations of uncertainty and specific institutional conditions.

2. Longman's dictionary gives three partly overlapping definitions of the word 'principle' which could be summarized the following way: 1. a moral rule for behaviour – how one should behave, 2. rule of a physical or intellectual process – carrying argument and 3. belief – the basic view (the example which is given is 'the principle of free markets'), Longman (1995).

3. One can always discuss what the most effective strategy is when new theories are to be presented. For Keynes it was critical to include demand on an equal footing with the supply conditions in the macroeconomic analysis as a counterweight to the existing dominance of Say's Law. This is probably part of the explanation for the choice of his terminology. This choice was so effective that few subsequently doubted that Keynes placed special emphasis on demand – unfortunately, so effective that ever since, Keynes's and Keynesian economics, on a more superficial reading, are often presented as exclusively demand-oriented theories. This is an exaggeration of at least the same dimension as the classical emphasis on supply. As mentioned above, Keynes was wondering why the 'inheritance from Marshall' did not include a macroeconomic theory comprising demand and supply for output as a whole?

4. One exception should be mentioned, because in classical macro-theory all the way back to Smith, there is one macro-demand function for money, which together with the given money supply, determines the aggregated price level *via* the quantity theory. It was the methodological dichotomy in the analysis of, on the one hand, relative prices, and, on the other hand, the absolute price level, that was a constant challenge for Keynes. When finally during the 1930s he solved the methodological problem, he used the expression 'a monetary theory of production' for his integrated macro-theory.

5. 'Nearer future' means an analytical period that corresponds to the time of implementation of decisions related to hiring and firing in the labour market.

6. How the total sales would be distributed among the individual firms within the industry would be of lesser importance in a macroeconomic perspective. Keynes assumed that expansion or contraction of overall activity would fall on firms proportionally.

7. 'Those who complain that there is no theory of the formation of expectation of demand are entirely correct' (Chick, 1983: 102).

8. The post-Keynesian literature distinguishes between 'fundamental-Keynesian' and 'Kaleckian' economics. (The latter is named after the Polish-born economist Michal Kalecki, 1899–1970). An often rather subtle distinction (King, 2002) that with regard to pricing on the goods market two different principles are used, marginal-cost pricing and mark-up pricing respectively. These can be attributed to two different competition assumptions. The distinction is not important for the macroeconomic theory, since Keynes can be interpreted as covering both market forms for the macroeconomic theory.

9. There is a certain irony that neoclassical economists today accuse Keynes of assuming rigid prices and wages and state that this assumption is the cause of involuntary unemployment.

10. This discussion is anticipated in Chapter 1.

11. Seen in the light of the modern theory-of-science discussion about 'open' and 'closed' systems respectively, it is particularly ironic that Keynes characterizes the closed classical model as mathematically underdetermined.

12. The history of macroeconomic theory, as described in Chapter 1, provides a number of examples of how the neoclassical interpretation of *The General Theory* has provided several attempts to add the missing demand equation to the neoclassical macro-model, see for example: Modigliani (1944) and Patinkin (1956 [1966]).

13. Rogers (1997) explicitly discusses the importance of whether general equilibrium has analytical validity for the long period. On the other hand, he sidesteps the core issue: whether it is theory or methodology that divides macroeconomists on the use of the general equilibrium method. For Rogers, the dividing line is between models that can generate persistent unemployment and models that automatically move towards general equilibrium. For Keynes (and many post-Keynesians), the decisive difference from (neo)classical macro-theory is not only the possibility of constructing a consistent model that can generate permanent underemployment, but the understanding of the fact that in a world characterized by genuine uncertainty, general equilibrium is analytically irrelevant. Only when this acknowledgement has been reached is it clear why the analysis of sticky prices, wages, interest rates and so on become rather unimportant, because then it becomes obvious that they are no longer theoretical necessities for persistent unemployment. On the contrary, in an open model it is failing effective demand, as described above, not inflexibilities which is the cause both in the short and the long run.

     When Rogers (1997: 336–8) gives Harrod (1947) credit for having explained underemployment as caused by a 'wrong' interest rate, it is an example of a too-high rate of interest held up by liquidity preference and, hence, causing unemployment. This argument might give the impression that 'if only the interest rate (and all other prices and money wages) had been correct', then there would have been no unemployment. In the same way, it is a neoclassical-inspired statement to blame 'wrong' expectations for causing macroeconomic imbalances. Wrong in relation to what? It can of course, *ex post* be ascertained that the expectations were incorrect, but that is a completely different story: we may learn from previous mistakes (learning by doing), but we can never know in advance what are correct expectations.

14. If we look at an economy with foreign trade, there will also be the modification that the desired demand can be realized though imports, which breaks with the narrow, causal connection from realized demand to realized output and further to employment.

15. It should be noted that the failure in reasoning discussed here also seems to be embodied in the argument of Begg et al. (2001) which is discussed in Chapter 5 and also in the following paragraph.

9. Methodological perspectives for realistic macroeconomic research: a summary

DIVIDING LINES

Macroeconomic theory is not unambiguous. Snowdon and Vane (2005) counted no less than ten different macroeconomic schools, which to various degrees are different from each other. It would be wrong to pretend that these macroeconomic theories are all genuine alternatives. They are not. As was evident from the 'family tree' in the introductory chapter, a number of theories develop from one another. This evolution is due partly to changes in society which changes the institutions and attitudes within the macroeconomic landscape and partly to the attainment of new analytical techniques in step with, among other things, the expansion of computer capacity. They vary quite considerably from strict theoretical models to models of a more descriptive nature.

In this book I have chosen primarily to let the methodology which the different theories use determine the overall division of the macroeconomic schools. In the introductory chapter it was demonstrated that the assumption of the existence and analytical relevance of the term 'general equilibrium' was a very important division criterion for the evaluation of the macroeconomic models' realism. That led to distinguishing between the 'ideal' models and the 'realistic' models, which simply have a different aim. The ideal models are useful to examine the conditions for proving existence and stability in a perfect market economy where general equilibrium is assumed. The realistic models have, to the contrary, the aim of uncovering causal relations which are relevant for understanding the actual macroeconomic development. Between those two distinct macroeconomic approaches we find the new-Keynesian models, which on one hand are built on the method of general equilibrium with the assumption of rational expectations-formation, but at the same time often have an ambition of giving the macroeconomic model some adjustment mechanisms, which would add some realistic characteristics (for example transaction costs, asymmetric information, efficiency wage) to the analytical model.

This leads to three major and separate theoretical schools: new-classical, new-Keynesian and post-Keynesian theory. Their relevance for understanding a number of different macroeconomic aspects of reality will be summed up below.

New-Classical Economic Theory

New-classical and post-Keynesian theories are, from a macroeconomic perspective – as regards to subject fields, economic theory and analytical method – opposites.

New-classical theory has, according to Lucas, cancelled the border-lines between micro- and macroeconomics. In his theoretical universe there only exists 'economics' in the meaning of conclusions derived from rational individual behaviour within a simple construction of well-behaved (clearing) markets. The answers to macroeconomic questions can, in this methodological framework, be analysed by using generalized microeconomic theory. The theoretical model they have chosen to use is strictly axiomatic and based on individual (economic) behaviour, rational expectations coordinated through a general equilibrium assumption. This makes Lucas conclude that: 'involuntary unemployment is not a fact or a phenomenon which it is the task of theorists to explain' (Lucas, 1978: 243). In fact, *An Equilibrium Model of the Business Cycle* is the title of one of Lucas's papers (Lucas, 1975). The methodology is clear and has been summarized in Figure 9.1 which is subdivided into 9.1a: vision and 9.1b: method. New classical economics is a theory which is only relevant on the analytical level (World 2), and where theoretical deductions are purely hypothetical.

The hypothetical deductive method secures the internal logic of the transition from axioms to formulation of hypotheses which together shape the analytical model. This is the 'laboratory' where conclusions about the ideal economic market-system can be established. Hence, the new-classical

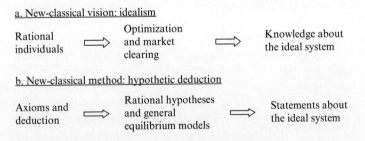

a. New-classical vision: idealism

Rational individuals ⟹ Optimization and market clearing ⟹ Knowledge about the ideal system

b. New-classical method: hypothetic deduction

Axioms and deduction ⟹ Rational hypotheses and general equilibrium models ⟹ Statements about the ideal system

Figure 9.1   The new-classical methodological sequence

practice is to prioritize theoretical deduction over empirical anchoring, of which Hartley (1997) among others gives a number of illustrative examples.

The new-classical school has an ideal market economy as its subject field, which quite clearly differs ontologically from the realistic macroeconomic schools; but the methodology supports Lucas's earlier stated intention of removing any distinction between micro- and macroeconomics.

Post-Keynesian Macro-Theory

Post-Keynesian macro-theory is intentionally a contrast to new-classical theory. King (2002: xv) characterizes post-Keynesian economies as follows: 'The focus is predominantly macroeconomic, though Post Keynesians have made important contributions to microeconomic theory and policy and on questions of economic philosophy, methodology and research methods.'

The subject field is the macroeconomic reality. The ambition is to formulate relevant economic political advice on the basis of an analytical model which has a solid empirical foundation. With theory-of-science inspiration from critical realism the post-Keynesian school has developed a (retroductive) method, described in Chapter 2, where all three methodological levels – the real, the analytical and the operational – are included in the scientific procedure.

The point of departure is the scattered knowledge of the macroeconomic reality (World 1), which is assumed to have an open and socially structured ontology, which initially can be given an analytical presentation by drawing up a macroeconomic landscape, as shown in Chapter 3. All methodological dispositions have to respect the common feature that the ontology is open, which is caused partly by behavioural uncertainty, and partly by the lack of knowledge about the macroeconomic system.

The following are characteristics of post-Keynesian models:

- That on the real level there is an inherent uncertainty regarding what the future will bring and regarding the consequences of actors' dispositions. Both considerations are important for the analytical hypotheses of how expectations are formed at the macroeconomic level and hence the relevant form of macro-behavioural relations (causal mechanism).
- That the macro-model should include the economy as a whole, which might be different from the sum of the individual parts due to uncertainty and related non-market-clearing structures, partly hidden organizations and power institutions.

- That analytical results should mirror the historical context and inter-disciplinary interdependence, according to Figure 3.1. Therefore, in many cases it might be useful to undertake a path-dependency analysis by employing the open-system *ceteris paribus* method.

'[T]he essence of *uncertainty* in Post Keynesian economic theory is grounded in a nonergodic, nondeterministic world [view] understood as an open-system' (Arestis, 1996: 117, quoted from Dunn, 2004: 42).

In practice there might be quite some differences in the analytical methods employed by post-Keynesian macroeconomists. Some are mostly inclined to emphasize deduction, others retroduction; but they share the emphasis that empirical anchoring in a macroeconomic landscape is indispensable and analytical results have to be interpreted within the actual context.

Employing the retroductive method should contribute to making the research at the analytical level (World 2) more realistic through an empirical anchoring, which is schematically presented in Figure 9.2a and 9.2b.

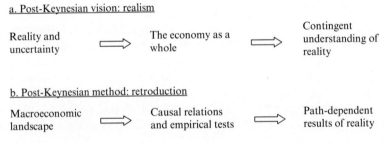

a. Post-Keynesian vision: realism

Reality and uncertainty ⟹ The economy as a whole ⟹ Contingent understanding of reality

b. Post-Keynesian method: retroduction

Macroeconomic landscape ⟹ Causal relations and empirical tests ⟹ Path-dependent results of reality

Figure 9.2   The post-Keynesian methodological sequence

I have in Chapters 3–6 above given a methodologically reasoned presentation of post-Keynesian macroeconomic analysis. Here the term 'uncertainty' was the pivotal point in the discussion of how to include the inescapable aspect of reality in the analysis of 'the economy as a whole'. It was difficult to make this analysis operational due to lack of knowledge about the kind of missing information. A suggested short-cut was the use of the open-system *ceteris paribus* method when applicable, but with the implication that the analytical results had to be interpreted with respect to the assumptions made and the quality of the empirical tests.

New-Keynesian Macro-Theory

The new-Keynesian macroeconomics has a foot in both the ideal and the practical camps by using an axiomatic, deduced model and at the same time aiming at giving the analytical results with relevance to macroeconomic policy. The new-Keynesian models therefore have many of the same methodological features as new-classical theory: general equilibrium, market clearing and rational expectations are included in their benchmark model. On the other hand the ambition to reach an analytical result that is relevant to the macroeconomic reality has meant that the new-Keynesian models contain a number of market-adjustment mechanisms, which are inspired by real phenomena in the form of, for instance, fluctuations in the output gap and involuntary unemployment. An important conclusion is that a well-designed economic policy can lessen and shorten the adjustment process towards the general equilibrium solution within the analytical model. Unfortunately, an evaluation of whether the analytical results are relevant for the macroeconomic reality is seldom carried out in detail and there is hardly any consideration of the importance of disregarding uncertainty.

The ambition of new-Keynesian macroeconomists – within the Danish context represented by Andersen (2000) – to make their policy recommendations relevant at the operational level (World 3) is difficult always to fulfil, when they insist that empirical realism should be subordinated to deductive rigour. Hence, securing empirical anchoring of analytical results is given a rather low priority. There is thus a tension between the axiomatic reasoning within their closed analytical model and their policy recommendations, which are claimed to have relevance to the real world. The new-Keynesians' analytical results are solidly anchored in World 2 by the use of the general equilibrium method, giving clear-cut hypothetical-deductive results, which are rather uncritically used to give advice about what to do in World 3. It is this suppressed duality which causes the ambiguity of new-Keynesian macroeconomics: the difficulties of formulating policy recommendations which are consistent with, and therefore relevant for, the social ontology of the real world.

On the other hand it is indisputable that the new-Keynesian economists have ambitions to reach results which are used for policy advice. This is one reason why they have chosen to call themselves new-Keynesians (Mankiw and Romer, 1991); through this choice of name they wished to signal a clear dissociation with the new-classical theory and not least its conclusion of policy ineffectiveness. Their ambition to contribute policy recommendations runs counter to their choice of analytical model and method, which is kept within the axiomatic use of the closed-system, laboratory approach. Therefore the new-Keynesian analytical results can only demonstrate a restricted room for manoeuvre for short-run demand management policies, which in any case should be corrected when general equilibrium is achieved (Sørensen and Whitta-Jakobsen, 2005). The *raison d'être* for economic policy is established through the insertion of a number of market-adjustment mechanisms into the standard general equilibrium model. These mechanisms introduce inertia into the working of the market system, which causes a certain delay in the traverse to the general equilibrium solution. It is argued that these mechanisms are derived from rational individual behaviour in the form of 'menu costs', 'efficiency wages', 'asymmetric information', and so on, which are quite similar to what Keynes in 1934 (*CWK*, XIII: 486) called 'creaks and groans and jerks and interrupted by time lags, outside interference and mistakes'. These inertias make it possible within the analytical model to show that a well-designed short-run policy can lessen the deviations from the initial general equilibrium and reduce the adjustment time of the traverse, because the new-Keynesian model takes it as an axiomatic fact that a 'well-behaved' macroeconomy should adjust to general equilibrium (Andersen, 2000).

Within new-Keynesian economics there is a split between their vision of reality and their employed method based on logical positivism as illustrated in Figure 9.3.

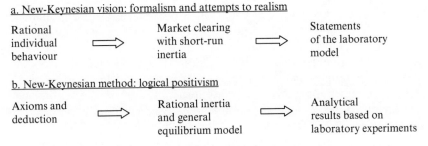

a. New-Keynesian vision: formalism and attempts to realism

Rational   Market clearing   Statements
individual   ⇒   with short-run   ⇒   of the laboratory
behaviour   inertia   model

b. New-Keynesian method: logical positivism

Axioms and   Rational inertia   Analytical
deduction   ⇒   and general   ⇒   results based on
                      equilibrium model   laboratory experiments

Figure 9.3   The new-Keynesian methodological sequence

The crucial dividing line between new-Keynesian and post-Keynesian macro-theory is methodologically determined. New-Keynesian macroeconomics has firmly placed itself on the side of the gulf opposite to Keynes, which contributes to the special irony attached to use of the term 'Keynesian' by the new-Keynesian school. As explained in Chapter 1, Keynes was very conscious of this methodological gulf between his macroeconomic methodology on one side and Pigou as a representative of the dominant neoclassical school on the other. For Keynes there was little doubt that general equilibrium and a self-regulating macroeconomy had its historical roots in an analytical tradition, which he for years struggled to escape from. His ambition was to draw a picture of the real world which we happen to live in. The harsh experiences of the interwar period had taught him the empirical lesson that it did not make sense with regard to policy recommendations to make an *a priori* assumption of the macroeconomic system always adjusting towards general equilibrium. The inappropriate methodology of the new-Keynesian approach has an affinity with a number of Pigou's contributions which led Keynes (1936: 276) to conclude: 'A scientific theory cannot require the facts to conform to its own assumptions.'

It is in many ways easier to understand that the old-Keynesian economists, in their early presentations of Keynes's new 'principle of effective demand', were willing to build a bridge over the gulf by establishing the 'neoclassical synthesis' shortly after the publication of *The General Theory*. Of course, they should have known better, because Keynes had given a clear warning (among others to Tinbergen and Harrod; see *CWK*, XIV) not to overstretch the use of the methodology of natural sciences within economics. Social sciences do not have the required homogeneity and behavioural stability to make use of closed-model reasoning for realistic analyses. It was not yet understood that inescapable uncertainty had to be incorporated. At that time the methodology of uncertainty was not yet distilled. That came much later when, as a part of the post-Keynesian (II) reasoning, it became clearer that effective demand cannot be understood without taking uncertainty seriously into the analysis. Uncertainty became even better understood through the 'philosophical' debates exposed by the rediscovering of Keynes's early writings (especially *A Treatise on Probability*) and undertaken by among many others: Lawson and Pesaran (1987), Carabelli (1988), Fitzgibbons (1988), O'Donnell (1989) and Skidelsky (1983 and 1992). Against this background it is a paradox that the new-Keynesian school could establish itself partly on the ashes of the neoclassical synthesis in the beginning of the 1990s. That it did so signals that the importance of the Methodological Gulf is still with us.[1] One may wonder why.

MAKING MACROECONOMIC REALITY OPERATIONAL: FROM WORLD 1 TO WORLD 3

We have stressed above the crucial difference made by the choice of methodology and subject field in the new-classical, new-Keynesian and post-Keynesian macroeconomic schools. The new-classical school has as its main focus the analysis of the ideal market system, which can be meaningfully analysed within a general equilibrium model. Macroeconomic theory within this tradition primarily contributes to a better and more general understanding of the assumptions needed in order to establish a formal proof of the existence of market-clearing equilibrium. This is an important research field in its own. The new-classical theory has made an important contribution to the understanding within this research field.

Opposed to the 'economics of the ideal' approach, we find the Keynesian tradition, which has macroeconomic reality as its subject field. Keynesian macroeconomists share the aspiration of getting analytical results that are relevant for the understanding of reality. As has been shown, Keynes-inspired macroeconomists are separated into two camps determined by their methodology. This conclusion leads, as we have seen, to very distinct analytical models (closed and open), and thereby also to policy recommendations which differ quite considerably.

In Chapter 2 it was shown that, when undertaking realistic macroeconomic research, the methodological field could with advantage be split into three levels: the real level (World 1), the analytical level (World 2) and the operative level (World 3). But quite quickly the two Keynes-inspired schools split on methodological grounds. New-Keynesians choose to make their analysis on the basis of certain knowledge put into a rigorous framework, where the construction is built upon a number of logical deductions, ensuring that rationality is respected. If reality deviates from this analytical model it must be because the assumption of individual rationality is violated one way or another. To put it into a single phrase: what the new-Keynesians know, they know with certainty.

By contrast, post-Keynesian economists consider uncertainty as an important fact of life. Therefore, one might phrase the post-Keynesian methodological research programme this way: we simply do not yet know how much uncertainty matters for the understanding of macroeconomic reality. But they have the aspiration of giving a scientific answer. The post-Keynesians' vision is to understand and analyse the macroeconomic landscape as realistically as possible. Hence, the challenge is to produce a realistic macroeconomic theory through a retroductive analytical process in World 2, whereby there can be established a scientific foundation which can generate results containing expanded knowledge with relevance for the operational level (World 3).

Seven Theses with Relevance for a Realistic Macro-Analysis

Below you will find seven tentative conclusions about macroeconomic methodology in a post-Keynesian perspective where uncertainty matters. This is an attempt to emphasize that the inclusion of uncertainty is a necessity in most cases in order to make the analysis relevant for policy recommendations. My intention is to increase the awareness of uncertainty at the analytical level and thereby to contribute to making the research of macroeconomic issues and the analytical results more relevant for macroeconomic policy.

1. The 'macroeconomic landscape' is embedded in a historical context and can best be understood in an interdisciplinary perspective.

Forming a macroeconomic landscape as an initial analytical step should make the macroeconomic theory more coherent and prepared for the open-system *ceteris paribus* method. From this starting point hypotheses regarding causal mechanisms, institutional settings and organized macroeconomic behaviour can be formulated and tested. Then an open macroeconomic system describing dynamic processes anchored in historical time can be developed. These processes are constantly changing, because they are not reversible and not necessarily continuous in time. Actions carried out today can have lasting consequences for the macroeconomic development in the future and should be presented within the frame of a path-dependent analysis.

2. The social ontology is open, which means the economic actors have uncertain knowledge of both micro- and macro-issues. This has a special importance for the formation of expectations of future events and of the consequences of individual activities.

Aggregate macroeconomic behaviour, which is the outcome of millions of microeconomic decisions, is partly based on expectations about future economic developments. Furthermore, the macroeconomic future is partly determined by the present transactions, which are made today. Here we are dealing with a path-dependent process, which makes expectations endogenously determined. Volatile microeconomic expectations lie behind the aggregate macroeconomic behaviour, which at the very same time become both cause and effect. This micro-macro interdependency rules out by its nature that the future can be known with certainty.[2]

3. Only the surface of the macroeconomic landscape is directly observable. Structures in the 'deeper' strata are assumed to make an impact on how the 'economy as a whole' changes through historical time. Therefore, one cannot make a one-way deduction from observed microeconomic behaviour to macroeconomic tendencies.

The analytical road leading from micro to macro is not just a matter of simple aggregation. Actors with shared interests might benefit from organizing themselves into larger units to reduce the individual uncertainty and to achieve some market power which gives macroeconomic weight. This kind of organization is well known, not least as regards the labour market institutions. Individual uncertainty can also be reduced through public welfare

institutions. Norms and conventions further safeguard some predictability in aggregate behaviour. Financial markets can diversify individual
uncertainty and make it less risky, and these markets can be supported by
legislation. Insurance companies and financial institutions can also trans-
form individual risk by the systematic use of the law of large numbers. A
yet unsolved question is how to devise an 'anchor' which can safeguard the
expected value of money. The independence of the courts also contributes
to lessen the uncertainty surrounding to the fulfilment of contracts. Laws
contribute to the predictability of the future by setting up a framework
for human behaviour, especially in areas where the uncertainty can have
serious consequences. It is not enough that rationality tells us that all of us
should drive on the same side of the road; convention and legal force are
also needed to secure that it actually happens. Social control is not always
strong enough, when the consequences of uncertainty are severe.

The understanding of organizations, institutions and social structures in
the deep stratum makes the macroeconomic landscape analytically more
transparent – both horizontally and in depth.

> *4. The importance of the distribution of income, wealth, ownership and
> power on macro-behaviour and thereby the macro-dynamic processes are
> also important elements within the deep stratum.*

Macro-behavioural relations are not necessarily stable; they change over
time, among other things as a consequence of the changes in economic
distribution and institutions. Here, the distribution of income, wealth and
access to credit obviously play an important part. The causes and effects
of inequality are only vaguely described empirically and their impact
on macroeconomics has a weak theoretical foundation. For instance, a
change in relative wages may have a larger incentive effect than a change
in the absolute wage level. The function of macro-markets is partly
determined by organizational and institutional frameworks, for example
fix-price or flex-price markets, and partly by the power structures (the
market-makers). These conditions influence how an impulse is transmitted
through the macroeconomic landscape and thereby becomes a part of the
macroeconomic *quaesitum*.

> *5. Investing in real capital, in contrast to financial capital, is an irrevers-
> ible process.*

Real investments are physically irreversible. When a real investment has
been carried out it is, in macroeconomic terms, a free good except for
running costs. We need a macroeconomic and institutional framework

to understand why 'free' real capital and 'free' labour (for that matter) might stay idle and people stay unemployed. In real life, when a bridge has been built, it is difficult to argue for not using it. Railways will not be dismantled until the expenditure to operate them exceeds their current and expected future income. It is often cheaper to keep a power plant running than to build a new one and pay to decommission the old one. The expenditure on real investment consists of the real resources which were used while producing the goods. The calculus for making private microeconomic investment decisions, dependent on expected profits discounted by a market rate of interest, might be misleading looked upon from the angle of 'the economy as a whole'. In macroeconomics the past is given. Unemployed labour is lost forever, whereas accumulated real capital becomes a part of the present structural framework. This makes some future paths through the landscape more likely than others. A new power plant does facilitate the future supply of electricity, but the impact on the climate depends on the type of power plant: based on conventional, nuclear or renewable resources. Uncertainty concerning the environmental impact of future energy supply has increased; any conclusion depends so much on the likely alternatives.

6. Demography and technology are under constant change, causing uncertainty on micro- and macro-levels.

Here we are talking of irreversible processes. A changed demographic structure requires changes in the society's institutions. More nursing homes will be needed to care for a greater number of elderly. This development is actually quite certain. But even if the number of people stays constant on macro-level, a changing population may cause renewed microeconomic activity. Each year approximately 60 000 people leave the Danish labour market and approximately the same number, but with a rather different educational profile, enter the labour market. This requires both a dynamic and a flexible labour market to fill vacancies with new people without creating frictions. This happens through upgrading the qualifications of people already in the workplace, dismantling some redundant jobs and establishing new jobs and functional relationships. An adjustment process that is challenged by continual technological innovation makes certain job functions superfluous and creates new ones. This whole job rotation and exchange process takes place within the framework of the macroeconomic space which effective demand establishes.

7. Natural resources are not unlimited: as regards sustainable development, 'we simply do not know'.

The macroeconomic landscape is, as described in Chapter 3, limited by the 'framework of nature', which in an analytical sense can be interpreted as a semi-closure. But here it should not be overlooked that the supply of energy from the sun makes this semi-closure of given energy resources less binding, just as the individual country's access to fossil fuel is determined not only by its own resources but also by the size of its international currency reserves. At present, the high dependency on oil contributes to its increased price and in general to the uncertainties related to future political and economic development.

Uncertainty with regard to the consequences of the disposal of waste in the ground, in the oceans and not least in the atmosphere also has to be integrated into the macroeconomic analysis. Although we know very little, increased uncertainty should not in a realistic analysis be neglected. Pollution does not disappear if it is disregarded, and uncertainty will not go away.

SUMMING UP

The above seven theses are each a contribution to the understanding of the importance of not neglecting uncertainty when the economy as a whole is under investigation. Unfortunately, uncertainty makes a realistic macroeconomic analysis quite complex and the outcome is path-dependent. Analytical results are context-specific and have to be interpreted with respect to that, before they are converted into policy recommendations at the operational level of World 3.

This leads to the conclusion that also at the operational level we are dealing with an open system, which can be used to produce politically inspired and macroeconomically realistic scenarios where the elements of uncertainty are made explicit before the policy conclusions are drawn.

The suggested open-system *ceteris paribus* method has inspiration from the method Keynes used in *The General Theory* where he, with a number of reservations, sketched several semi-closed models. This model-building procedure helped to uncover some of the causal mechanisms with roots in the deeper strata. These causal mechanisms would otherwise have remained hidden. Through increased knowledge about the underlying forces within the macroeconomic landscape, reasons can be given for the observed tendencies, such as for instance the multiplier effect, liquidity preference and effective demand. In this methodological perspective the term 'equilibrium' has reduced importance as a temporary standstill in the otherwise permanently changing environment. Hence, it has become more relevant within macroeconomic analyses to search for explanations of the statistically robust tendencies, which are more relevant for a realistic macroeconomic understanding. The inclusion of the above-mentioned seven macroeconomic theses, which all have connotations with uncertainty and are rooted in the 'deep' stratum, could make the post-Keynesian analysis even more relevant for a richer understanding of the real economy as a whole. The analytical method should therefore be characterized by macro-dynamics (Cornwall, 1979), which can better be used to describe the historical growth processes which have characterized the macroeconomic development since the end of the Second World War. The macroeconomic dynamics have been caused by the interaction of demand and supply factors in a historical context determined by existing institutions and structures. Within such macroeconomic processes there is not just one dominating factor, but a complex interaction between many factors, undergoing constant change. Therefore:

> [It] should be clear that in Post Keynesian macrodynamics growth is both endogenous and path dependent, since there is no growth trajectory acting as a 'center of gravity' towards which the economy is inexorably and inevitably drawn. (Setterfield, 2001: 95)

Macroeconomic Disagreement is Based on Methodological Differences

In an attempt to avoid too many repetitions I have summarized the three described macroeconomic schools in Table 9.1, where the most important differences are emphasized. The full use of the content of the table can only be obtained through reading the previous chapters, where a number of reservations are made and illustrative examples given. The table serves as a summary of a number of methodological points which it is important to be aware of when a macroeconomic analysis is planned.

Methodological difference is the foundation for the understanding of the disagreement among macroeconomists which has been the prevailing characteristic at least since Keynes wrote *The General Theory* and which, paradoxically, has been even more dominant in the post-war period. The crucial dividing line today, as it was 70 years ago, is however the question of defining on which side of the methodological gulf the macroeconomic analysis is anchored. The relevance of the analysis has to be evaluated in the light of the social ontology of the object field, what analytical axioms are considered indisputable, what analytical method is preferred and in what way policy recommendations are shaped. The overarching guiding principle for this investigation is to detect the methodological choices, which determine the character of the subsequent analysis and its relevance to macroeconomic policy.

Table 9.1   Schematic overview of macroeconomic positions[1]

	New-Classical	New-Keynesian[2]	Post-Keynesian
Theory of science	Idealism[3]	(Logical) positivism	(Critical) realism
Model picture	Clockwork	'Pebbles in the clockwork'	Organicism
Model frame	Closed	Closed	Open
Analytical method	General equilibrium	General equilibrium with inertia	Path-dependent causal analysis
Behaviour	Rational economic man; Market clearing	Representative micro-agents	Macroeconomic causal relations
Expectation model	Rational expectation-formation	Rational expectation-formation process[4]	All available information
Knowledge level	Full information	Sluggish adjustment to full information	Limited information, uncertainty
Analytical subject field	Perfect market system	Laboratory model	Macroeconomic landscape
Empirical anchoring	Accidental	Calibration	Verification/counter examples
Supply policy	More markets, flexible prices	Improving the dissemination of information	Institutions, reduced uncertainty
Demand policy	Inefficient	Temporary effect	Lasting effect

Notes
1. This schematic overview must by its nature be concise and does not pretend to be exhaustive. It can only serve to give some central features, which mark important similarities and especially differences between the three schools of thought.
2. If rational expectations and the requirement of an explicit microeconomic foundation are removed, old-Keynesian (the neoclassical synthesis) also falls into this category.
3. The term is used to mean subjective idealism. The reality exists but is solely viewed through an idea-based model where the agents are fully rational and the market system always clears.
4. The Monetarists most often use an adaptive expectations-formation hypothesis.

The central purpose of this book has been to promote theories which relate to macroeconomic reality and to recognize the analytical ambiguities caused by the presence of uncertainty in social sciences.

NOTES

1. Andersen (2000), in his review paper on macro-theory, does not make one single reference to post-Keynesian literature even though he is rather conscious about the importance of methodology and has published in the *Journal of Post Keynesian Economics*.
2. Keynes's presentation in Chapter 12 of *The General Theory* of the expectations-formation process on the financial markets is here especially illustrative.

Bibliography

Note: for Danish letter 'Ø' entries please see under 'O'.

Akerlof, G.A. (2002), 'Behavioral macroeconomics and the macroeconomic behavior (a Nobel Lecture)', *American Economic Review*, June, pp. 411–33.

Andersen, E. (1975a), *En model for Danmark – 1949–1965,* København: Akademisk Forlag.

Andersen, E. (1975b), *Træk af makroøkonometriske modellers historie og udvikling*, København: Akademisk Forlag.

Andersen, T.M. (2000), 'Makroteori', in Chr. Hjorth-Andersen (ed.), *Udviklingslinjer i økonomisk teori*, København: DJØFs Forlag.

Andersen, T.M. (2004), *Velfærdssamfund – økonomiske aspekter*, København: Velfærdskommissionen.

Andersen, T.M. and L.H. Pedersen (2005), 'Debat om fremtidens velfærd – opsamling og replik', *Nationaløkonomisk Tidsskrift,* **143** (2), pp. 275–98.

Arestis, P. (1992), *The Post-Keynesian Approach to Economics: Alternative Analysis of Economic Theory and Policy*, Aldershot, UK and Brookfield, US: Edward Elgar.

Arestis, P. (1996), 'Post-Keynesian Economics: Towards Coherence, Critical Survey', *Cambridge Journal of Economics*, **20**, pp. 111–35.

Arestis, P., A. Brown and M.C. Sawyer (2001), *The Euro: Evolution and Prospect,* Cheltenham, UK and Northampton, MA, USA: Edward Elgar.

Arestis, P. and S.C. Dow (eds) (1992), *On Money, Method and Keynes, Selected Essays by Victoria Chick*, London: Macmillan and New York: St Martin's Press.

Arestis, P., S.C. Dow and M. Desai (eds) (2002), *Methodology, Microeconomics and Keynes: Essays in Honour of Victoria Chick*, London: Routledge.

Arestis, P., G. Palma and M.C. Sawyer (eds) (1997), *Essays in Honour of Geoff Harcourt*, Vols 1–3, London: Routledge.

Arestis, P. and M. Sawyer (eds) (1994), *The Elgar Companion to Radical Political Economy,* Aldershot, UK and Brookfield, US: Edward Elgar.

Arrow, K. and G. Debreu (1954), 'Existence of an equilibrium for a competitive economy', *Econometrica,* **26**, pp. 522–52.

Arrow, K. and F. Hahn (1971), *General Competitive Analysis,* San Francisco, CA: Holden-Day.

Barr, N. (2004), *Economics of the Welfare State,* 4th edn, Oxford: Oxford University Press.

Bateman, B. (2003), 'The end of Keynes and philosophy', in Runde, J. and S. Mizuhara (eds).

Baumol, W. (1952) 'The transactions demand for cash', *Quarterly Journal of Economics,* **66**, pp. 545–56.

Begg, D., S. Fischer and R. Dornbusch (2001), *Foundations of Economics,* 2nd edn, New York: McGraw-Hill Education.

Bhaskar, R. (1975), *A Realist Theory of Science,* London: Verso.

Bhaskar, R. (1978), *The Possibility of Naturalism,* Hemel Hempstead: Harvester Press.

Bhaskar, R. (1989), *Reclaiming Reality: A Critical Introduction to Contemporary Philosophy,* London: Verso.

Birk, L.V. (1925), *Europas svøbe, staternes gæld. Beskrevet, forklaret og historisk belyst,* Copenhagen.

Blaug, M. (1980), *The Methodology of Economics: Or How Economists Explain,* 2nd edn 1992, Cambridge: Cambridge University Press.

Blaug, M. (ed.) (1995), *The Quantity Theory of Money: From Locke to Keynes and Friedman,* Aldershot, UK and Brookfield, US: Edward Elgar.

Blaug, M. (2002), 'Developments in modern economics', in Mäki, U. (ed.).

Boland, L.A. (2003), *The Foundation of Economic Method: A Popperian Perspective,* 2nd edn, London: Routledge.

Bresser-Pereira, Luiz Carlos (2005), 'The two methods of economics', unpublished paper, available at www.bresserpereira.org.br.

Caldwell, B.J. (ed.) (1982), *Appraisal and Criticism in Economics: A Book of Readings,* Boston, MA: Allen & Unwin.

Capra, F. (1986), *Vendepunktet: videnskaben, samfundet og det nye verdensbillede,* København: Borgens Forlag.

Carabelli, A. (1988), *On Keynes's Method,* Basingstoke: Macmillan.

Carabelli, A. (2003), 'Keynes: economics as a branch of probable logic', in Runde, J. and S. Mizuhara (eds).

Chick, V. (1978), 'The nature of the Keynesian revolution', *Australian Economic Papers,* **24** (1), pp. 3–16; reprinted in Arestis, P. and S.C. Dow (eds) (1992).

Chick, V. (1983), *Macroeconomics after Keynes: A Reconsideration of the General Theory,* Oxford: Philip Allan and Cambridge, MA: MIT Press.

Chick, V. (1998), 'On knowing one's place: formalism in economics', *Economic Journal*, **108**, pp. 1850–69.

Chick, V. (2003), 'On open systems', *Brazilian Journal of Political Economy*, **24** (1), pp. 3–16.

Chick, V. and M. Caserta (1997), 'Provisional equilibrium', in Arestis, P. et al. (eds).

Chick, V. and S.C. Dow (2001), 'Formalism, logic and reality: a Keynesian analysis', *Cambridge Journal of Economics*, **25**, pp. 705–22.

Clower, R.W. (1998), 'Keynes in retrospect', in P. Arestis (ed.), *Method, Theory and Policy in Keynes: Essays in Honour of Paul Davidson*, Vol. 3, Cheltenham, UK and Lyme, US: Edward Elgar.

Colander, D. (ed.) (1997), *Beyond Microfoundations: Post Walrasian Macroeconomics*, Cambridge: Cambridge University Press.

Cornwall, J. (1979), 'Macrodynamics', in Eichner, A. (ed.).

Cornwall, J. and W. Cornwall (2001), *Capitalist Development in the Twentieth Century: An Evolutionary-Keynesian Analysis*, Cambridge: Cambridge University Press.

Daly, H. (1997), *Efter væksten: den bæredygtige udviklingsøkonomi*, Århus: Hovedland.

Dasgupta, P. (2002), 'Modern economics and its critics', in Mäki, U. (ed.).

Davidsen, Bjørn-Ivar (2000), *Bidrag til den økonomisk-metodologiske tenkningen*, Ekonomiska Studier (unpublished PhD dissertation), Nationalekonomiska Institutionen, Handelshögskolan vid Göteborgs Universitet.

Davidson, P. (1972), *Money and the Real World*, London: Macmillan.

Davidson, P. (1994), *Post Keynesian Macroeconomic Theory: A Foundation for Successful Economic Policies for the Twenty-first Century*, Aldershot, UK and Brookfield, US: Edward Elgar.

Davidson, P. (2003), 'Keynes's *General Theory*', in King, J. (ed.).

Davidson, P. and E. Smolensky (1964), *Aggregate Supply and Demand Analysis*, New York: Harper & Row.

Davis, J.B. (1998), 'Davidson, non-ergodicity and individuals', in P. Arestis (ed.), *Method, Theory and Policy in Keynes: Essays in Honour of Paul Davidson*, Vol. 3, Cheltenham, UK and Lyme, USA: Edward Elgar.

Debreu, G. (1959), *Theory of Value: An Axiomatic Analysis of Economic Equilibrium*, Cowles Foundation Monograph no. 17, New Haven, CT: Yale University Press.

DeCanio, S.J. (2003), *Economic Models of Climate Change: A Critique*, Basingstoke: Palgrave Macmillan.

De Long, J.B. (2000), 'The triumph of monetarism', *Journal of Economic Perspectives*, **14** (Winter), pp. 83–94.

Desai, M. (2002), 'On Chick and equilibrium: the nature of equilibrium in Keynes's *General Theory*', in Arestis, P. et al. (eds), Vol. 2.

Dow, S. (1990), 'Beyond dualism', *Cambridge Journal of Economics*, **14**, pp. 143–57.

Dow, S. (1996), *The Methodology of Macroeconomic Thought: A Conceptual Analysis of Schools of Thought in Economics*, Cheltenham, UK and Brookfield, US: Edward Elgar.

Dow, S. (1999), 'Post Keynesianism and critical realism: what is the connection?' *Journal of Post Keynesian Economics*, **22** (1), pp. 15–33.

Dow, S. (2001), 'Post Keynesian methodology', in Holt, R.P.F. and S. Pressman (eds).

Dow, S. (2002), *Economic Methodology: An Inquiry,* Oxford: Oxford University Press.

Dow, S. (2003), 'Probability, uncertainty and convention: economists' knowledge and the knowledge of economic actors', in Runde, J. and S. Mizuhara (eds).

Dow, S. and J. Hillard (eds) (1995), *Keynes, Knowledge and Uncertainty*, Aldershot, UK and Brookfield, US: Edward Elgar.

Downward, P. (ed.) (2003), *Applied Economics and the Critical Realist Critique*, London: Routledge.

Downward, P. and A. Mearman (2002), 'Critical realism and econometrics: a constructive dialogue with post Keynesian economics', *Metroeconomica*, **53** (4), pp. 391–415.

Dunn, S. (2004), 'Transforming Post Keynesian economics: critical realism and the Post Keynesian project', in P. Lewis (ed.).

Eatwell, J., M. Milgate and P. Newman (eds) (1987), *The New Palgrave: A Dictionary of Economics*, London: Macmillan.

Eichner, A.S. (ed.) (1979), *A Guide to Post Keynesian Economics*, New York: M.E. Sharpe.

Estrup, H., J. Jespersen and P. Nielsen (2004), *Introduktion til den økonomiske teoris historie,* København: DJØFs Forlag.

Fanning, C. and D.O. Mahony (2000), *The General Theory of Profit Equilibrium: Keynes and the Entrepreneur Economy*, Basingstoke: Macmillan Press.

Favrholdt, D. (1998), 'Logisk positivisme', in Birgitte Rahbek (ed.), *Da mennesket begyndte at undre sig*, Århus: Spektrum.

Fenger-Grøn, C. and J.E. Kristensen (eds) (2001), *Kritik af den økonomiske fornuft*, København: Hans Reitzels Forlag.

Fitzgibbons, A. (1988), *Keynes's Vision: A New Political Economy*, Oxford: Clarendon Press.

Fleetwood, S. (ed.) (1999), *Critical Realism in Economics: Development and Debate*, London: Routledge.

Flyvbjerg, B. (1991), *Rationalitet og Magt*, Vol. 1, København: Akademisk Forlag.

Foss, N.J. (1994), 'Realism and evolutionary economics', *Journal of Social and Evolutionary Systems*, **17** (1), pp. 21–40.

Franses, P.H. (2002) *A Concise Introduction to Econometrics: An Intuitive Guide*, Cambridge: Cambridge University Press.

Friedman, M. (1953), 'The Methodology of positive economics', reprinted in M. Friedman (1966), *Essays in Positive Economics*, Chicago, IL: Chicago University Press.

Friedman, M. (1968), 'The Role of Monetary Policy', *American Economic Review*, **58**, pp. 1–17.

Fuglsang, L. and P. Bitsch Olsen (eds) (2004), *Videnskabsteori for Samfundsvidenskaberne*, Frederiksberg: Samfundslitteratur.

Fullbrook, E. (ed.) (2004), *A Guide to What's Wrong with Economics*, London: Anthem Press.

Gerrard, B. (1997), 'Method and methodology in Keynes's *General Theory*', in Harcourt, G.C. and P.A. Riach (eds).

Gerrard, B. (2003), 'Keynesian uncertainty: what do we know?' in Runde, J. and S. Mizuhara (eds).

Giddens, A. (1998), *The Third Way: The Renewal of Social Democracy*, Cambridge: Polity Press.

Godley, W. and M. Lavoie (2007), *Monetary Economics: An Integrated Approach to Credit, Money, Income, Production and Wealth*, Basingstoke: Palgrave, Macmillan

Graziani, A. (2003), *A Monetary Theory of Production*, Cambridge: Cambridge University Press.

Hahn, F.H. (1973), 'On the notion of equilibrium in economics', Inaugural Lecture, reprinted in Hahn, F.H. (1984).

Hahn, F.H. (1984), *Equilibrium and Macroeconomics,* Oxford: Blackwell.

Hahn, F.H. (2001), 'The macroeconomic foundation of microeconomics', Lecture given in Cambridge to the Marshall Society (mimeo)

Hahn, F.H. and R. Solow (1996), *A Critical Essay on Modern Macroeconomic Theory,* Cambridge, MA: MIT Press.

Hands, D.W. (ed.) (1993), *Testing, Rationality, and Progress: Essays on the Popperian Tradition in Economic Methodology*, Lanham, MD: Rowman & Littlefield.

Hands, D.W. (2001), *Reflection without Rules: Economic Methodology and Temporary Science Theory*, Cambridge: Cambridge University Press.

Hansen, B. (1970), *A Survey of General Equilibrium Systems*, New York: McGraw Hill.

Harcourt, G.C. (1972), *Some Cambridge Controversies in the Theory of Capital,* Cambridge: Cambridge University Press.

Harcourt, G.C. (ed.) (1977), *The Microeconomic Foundations of Macroeconomics*, London: Macmillan.

Harcourt, G.C. (2001), *50 Years a Keynesian and Other Essays*, Basingstoke: Palgrave Macmillan.

Harcourt, G.C. and P.A. Riach (eds) (1997), *A 'Second Edition' of the General Theory*, 2 vols, London: Routledge.

Harris, S.E. (ed.) (1947), *The New Economics; Keynes's Influence on Theory and Policy*, New York: Alfred A. Knopf.

Harrod, R.F. (1939), 'An essay in dynamic theory', *Economic Journal*, **49**, pp. 14–33.

Harrod, R.F. (1947), 'Keynes, the economist', Chapter VIII in S. E. Harris (ed.).

Hartley, J. (1997), *The Representative Agent in Macroeconomics*, London: Routledge.

Hausman, D. (1992), *The Inexact and Separate Science of Economics*, Cambridge: Cambridge University Press.

Hawking, S.W. (1988), *A Brief History of Time*, London: Bantam Books.

Heilbroner, R. and W. Milberg (1995), *The Crisis of Vision in Modern Economic Thought*, Cambridge: Cambridge University Press.

Hicks, J. (1937), 'Mr Keynes and the "classics": a suggested interpretation', *Econometrica*, 5 April, pp. 147–59.

Hicks, J. (1939), *Value and Capital*, 2nd edn (1946), Oxford: Oxford University Press.

Hicks, J. (1950), *A Contribution to the Theory of Trade Cycle*, Oxford: Oxford University Press.

Hicks, J. (1989), *A Monetary Theory of Markets*, Oxford: Clarendon Press.

Hodgson, G. (2004), '*Can* economics start from individuals alone?' in Fullbrook, E. (ed.).

Holt, R.P.F. and S. Pressman (eds) (2001), *A New Guide to Post Keynesian Economics*, London: Routledge.

Hoover, K.D. (2001), *The Methodology of Empirical Macroeconomics*, Cambridge: Cambridge University Press.

Ingrao, B. and G. Israel (1990), *The Invisible Hand: Economic Equilibrium in the History of Science*, Cambridge, MA: MIT Press.

Jespersen, J. (1996), *Økonomi og Virkelighed*, København: Fremad.

Jespersen, J. (ed.) (1998), 'Hvorfor så megen makroøkonomisk uenighed?', *Samfundsøkonomen*, **6**, p. 3.

Jespersen, J. (2001), 'Den atomistiske fejlslutning', in C. Fenger-Grøn and J.E. Kristensen (eds).

Jespersen, J. (2002a), *John Maynard Keynes – den makroøkonomiske teoris oprindelse og udvikling*, København: DJØFs Forlag.

Jespersen, J. (2002b), 'Why do economists disagree on the EMU?' in Arestis, P. *et al.* (eds).

Jespersen, J. (2003), 'Makroøkonomisk metode: Keynes og lærebøgerne – to adskilte verdener', *Økonomi og Politik*, **76**, December, pp. 33–46.

Jespersen, J. (2004), 'Kritisk Realisme – med makroøkonomiske eksempler', in Fuglsang, L. and P. Bitsch Olsen (eds).

Jespersen, J. (2005), *Introduction to Macroeconomic Theory: A Post Keynesian Perspective*, København: DJØFs Forlag.

Jespersen, J. (2009), 'Bridging the gap between monetary circuit theory and post-Keynesian monetary theory', in J.F. Ponsot and S. Rossi (eds).

Jespersen, J. and D. Lang (2006), 'The Danish (un)employment "miracle": aggregate demand, profitability and labour market policies', *European Studies Review*, **7**, pp. 71–92.

Journal of Post Keynesian Economics (1999), 'Post Keynesianism and critical realism', Special Issue, Spring/Fall, **22**(1).

Kahneman, D. (2003), 'Maps of bounded rationality: psychology for behavioural economics', *American Economic Review*, **93** (5), pp. 1449–75.

Kahneman, D. and A. Tversky (1979), 'Prospect theory: an analysis of decisions under risk', *Econometrica*, **47**, 313–27.

Kaldor, N. (1973), 'Equilibrium theory and growth theory', reprinted in M. Boskin (ed.) (1979), *Economics and Human Welfare: Essays in Honor of Tibor Scitovsky*, New York: Academic Press.

Kaldor, N. (1985), *Economics without Equilibrium,* Armonk: Sharp.

Katzner, D. (2003), 'Equilibrium and non-equilibrium', in King, J. (ed.).

Keen, S. (2003), 'Growth Theory', in J. King, (ed.).

Keynes, J.M. (1972–89), *The Collected Writings of John Maynard Keynes*, 30 vols, D.E. Moggridge (ed.), London: Macmillan and Cambridge: Cambridge University Press for The Royal Economic Society. Literature sources are given as '*CWK*' followed by the volume number in roman and original date of publication is given where relevant.

Keynes, J.M. (1921), *A Treatise on Probability*, *CWK*, VIII.

Keynes, J.M. (1923), *A Tract on Monetary Reform*, *CWK*, IV.

Keynes, J.M. (1930a), *A Treatise on Money*, Vols 1 and 2, *CWK*, V and VI.

Keynes, J.M. (1930b), 'Economic possibilities for our grandchildren', reprinted in *CWK*, IX, pp. 321–32

Keynes, J.M. (1931), *Essays in Persuasion*, *CWK*, IX.

Keynes, J.M. (1933), *Essays in Biography*, *CWK*, X.

Keynes, J.M. (1934), 'Poverty in plenty: is the economic system self-adjusting?', *The Listener*, 21 November; reprinted in *CWK* XIII, pp. 485–92.

Keynes, J.M. (1936), *The General Theory of Employment, Interest and Money*, *CWK*, VII.

Keynes, J.M. (1937), 'The General Theory of Employment', *Quarterly Journal of Economics,* 51, pp. 209–23; reprinted in *CWK*, XIV.

Keynes, J.M. (1938), *Preface to the German edition*, reprinted in *CWK*, VII.

Keynes, J.M. (1939), 'Relative movements of real wages and output', *Economic Journal*, **49**, pp. 34–51, reprinted in *CWK*, VII, pp. 394–412.

Keynes, J.M. (1973a), *The General Theory and After: Part I, Preparation*, *CWK*, XIII.

Keynes, J.M. (1973b), *The General Theory and After: Part II, Defence and Development*, *CWK*, XIV.

Keynes, J.M. (1980), *The General Theory and After: a Supplement* (to Vols 13 and 14), *CWK*, XXIX.

Keynes, J.M. (1989), *Bibliography and Index*, *CWK*, XXX.

Kincaid, H. (1998), 'Methodological individualism and atomism', in J.B. Davis, D. Wade Hands and U. Mäki. (1998), *The Handbook of Economic Methodology*, Cheltenham, UK and Lyme, US: Edward Elgar.

King, J. (1995), *Conversations with Post Keynesians*, New York: St Martin's Press.

King, J. (2002), *A History of Post Keynesian Economics since 1936*, Cheltenham, UK and Northampton, MA, US: Edward Elgar.

King, J. (ed.) (2003), *The Elgar Companion to Post Keynesian Economics*, Cheltenham, UK and Northampton, MA, US: Edward Elgar.

Kirman, A. (1992), 'Whom or what does the representative individual represent?' *Journal of Economic Perspectives,* **6**, Spring, pp. 117–36.

Kregel, J.A. (1976), 'Economic methodology in the face of uncertainty: the modelling methods of Keynes and post Keynesians', *Economic Journal*, **86** (June), pp. 209–25.

Kriesler, P. (2003), 'Traverse', in King, J. (ed.).

Kurrild-Klitgaard, P. (2004), *Adam Smith: Økonom, filosof, samfundstænker*, København: DJØFs Forlag.

Lakatos, I. (1974), 'Falsification and the methodology of scientific research programmes', in I. Latakos, and A. Musgrave (eds), *Criticism of the Growth of Knowledge*, Cambridge: Cambridge University Press.

Latsis, S.J. (1976), 'A research programme in economics', in S.J. Latsis (ed.), *Method and Appraisal in Economics*, Cambridge: Cambridge University Press.

Lawson, T. (1997), *Economics and Reality*, London: Routledge.

Lawson, T. (2001), 'Background notes, Lectures 1–4', Michaelmas Term, Cambridge University (not published).

Lawson, T. (2002), 'Social explanation and Popper', paper presented at University of Galway, September.

Lawson, T. (2003), *Reorienting Economics*, London: Routledge.

Lawson, T. (2005), 'The (confused) state of equilibrium analysis in modern economics: an explanation', *Journal of Post Keynesian Economics*, **27** (3), pp. 423–44.

Lawson, T. and H. Pesaran (eds) (1987), *Keynes's Economics: Methodological Issues*, London: Croom Helm.

Layard, R. (2005), *Happiness: Lessons from a New Science*, London: Allan Lane.

Leijonhufvud, A. (1981), *Information and Coordination: Essays in Macroeconomic Theory*, New York: Oxford University Press.

Lewis, P. (ed.) (2005), *Transforming Economics: Perspectives on the Critical Realist Project*, London: Routledge.

Lindbeck, A. (1998), 'New Keynesianism and aggregate economic activity', *Economic Journal*, January, pp. 167–80.

Lodewijks, J. (2003), 'Bastard Keynesianism', in King, J. (ed.).

Longman (1995), *Dictionary of Contemporary English*, 3rd edn, Harlow, Essex: Longman Group.

Lucas, R.E. Jr (1975), 'An Equilibrium Model of the Business Cycle', *Journal of Political Economy*, **83**, pp. 1113–44.

Lucas, R.E. Jr (1978), 'Unemployment policy', *American Economic Review*, **68**, May, pp. 353–57.

Lucas, R.E. Jr (1981), *Studies in Business Cycle Theory*, Cambridge, MA: MIT Press.

Lucas, R.E. Jr (1987), *Models of Business Cycles*, Oxford: Basil Blackwell.

Lucas, R.E. Jr and T.J. Sargent (1978), 'After Keynesian macroeconomics', in *After the Phillips Curve: Persistence of High Inflation and High Unemployment*, Federal Reserve Bank of Boston, Conference series No. 19, pp. 49–72, reprinted in the Federal Reserve Bank of Minneapolis *Quarterly Review*.

Mäki, U. (ed.) (2002), *Fact and Fiction in Economics: Models, Realism and Social Construction*, Cambridge: Cambridge University Press.

Mankiw, G. and D. Romer (eds) (1991), *New Keynesian Economics,* Cambridge, MA: MIT Press.

Marshall, A. (1890), *Principles of Economics*, 8th edn, 1920, London: Macmillan.

Matzner, E. (2003), 'Third Way', in J. King (ed.).

Mayer, T. (1992), *Truth versus Precision in Economics*, Aldershot, UK and Brookfield, US: Edward Elgar.

McCloskey, D.N. (1986), *The Rhetoric of Economics*, Brighton: Wheatsheaf.

McCloskey, D.N. (1996), *The Vices of Economists – the Virtues of the Bourgeoisie,* Amsterdam: Amsterdam University Press.

Meyer, G. (2004), *Ekspert og samfund – en interviewbog om offentlig diskussion og videnskab*, Frederiksberg: Forlaget Samfundslitteratur.

Milgate, M. (1987), 'Equilibrium: development of the concept', in Eatwell, J. et al. (eds).

Minsky, H. (1975), *John Maynard Keynes*, London: Macmillan Press.

Modigliani, F. (1944), 'Liquidity preference and the theory of interest and money', *Econometrica*, **12**, January, pp. 45–88.

Modigliani, F. (1999), 'Interview', in Snowdon, B. and H.R. Vane (eds).

Moore, B. (1988), *Horizontalists and Verticalists: The Macroeconomics of Credit Money*, Cambridge: Cambridge University Press.

Muth, J.F. (1961), 'Rational expectations and the theory of price movements', *Econometrica*, **29**, July, pp. 315–35.

Nielsen, P. and H. Buch-Hansen (2004), *Kritisk Realisme*, Frederiksberg: Samfundsfagslitteratur.

O'Donnell, R. (1989), *Keynes: Philosophy, Economics, and Politics: The Philosophical Influences of Keynes's Thought and their Influence on his Economics*, London: Macmillan.

Ormerod, P. (1998), *Butterfly Economics: A New General Theory of Social and Economic Behaviour*, London: Faber & Faber.

Oswego (2006), 'Microeconomic notes', available at www.oswego.edu/~economic/eco101/cap1/cap1.htm.

Østrup, F. (2000), *Money and the Natural Rate of Unemployment*, Cambridge: Cambridge University Press.

Oxford English Dictionary (on line): http://dictionary.oed.com/cgi/entry.

Patinkin, D. (1956), *Money, Interest, and Prices: An Integration of Monetary and Value Theory*, 2nd edn 1966, New York: Harbor & Row.

Pålsson Syll, L. (2001a), *Den dystra vetenskapen – Om nationalekonomins och nyliberalismens kris*, Stockholm: Atlas Akademi.

Pålsson Syll, L. (2001b), *Ekonomisk teori och metod*, Lund: Studentlitteratur.

Pålsson Syll, L. (2006), *John Maynard Keynes*, no. 28, Pocket bibliioteket, Stockholm: SNS Förlag.

Petersen, T.W. (1997), 'Introduktion til CGE-modeller', *Nationaløkonomisk Tidsskrift*, **135** (2), pp. 113–34.

Phelps, E.S. (1987), 'Equilibrium: an expectational concept', in Eatwell, J. et al. (eds).

Pigou, A.C. (1920), *The Theory of Value*, London: Macmillan.

Pigou, A.C. (1933), *The Theory of Unemployment*, London: Macmillan.

Ponsot, J.-F. and S. Rossi (eds) (2009), *The Political Economy of Monetary Circuits – Tradition and Change in Post-Keynesian Economics*, Basingstoke: Palgrave Macmillan.

Popper, K.R. (1996), *Historicismens elendighed*, København: Samlerens Bogklub.

Popper, K.R. (1999), *All Life is Problem Solving*, London: Routledge.

Raffaelli, T. (2003), *Marshall's Evolution*, London: Routledge.

Robbins, L. (1932), *An Essay on the Nature and Significance of Economic Science*, London: Macmillan.

Robinson, J. (1956), *The Accumulation of Capital*, London: Macmillan.

Robinson, J. (1962), *Essays in the Theory of Economic Growth*, London: Macmillan.

Robinson, J. (1972), 'The second crisis of economic theory', *American Economic Review*, **62** (2), Papers and Proceedings, pp. 1–10.

Robinson, J. (1974), *History versus equilibrium*, Thames Papers in Political Economy, London: Thames Polytechnic.

Robinson, J. (1977), 'What are the questions?', *Journal of Economic Literature*, **15** (4), pp. 1318–39.

Robinson, J. (1978), *Contributions to Modern Economics*, Oxford: Basil Blackwell.

Robinson, J. (1985), 'The theory of normal prices and reconstruction of economic theory', ("spring cleaning") in G.R. Feiwel (ed.), *Issues in Contemporary Macroeconomics and Distribution*, London: Macmillan.

Rogers, C. (1997), '*The General Theory*: existence of a monetary long-period unemployment equilibrium', in G.C. Harcourt and P.A. Riach (eds).

Romer, D. (1996), *Advanced Macroeconomics*, New York: McGraw-Hill.

Rotheim, R. (ed.) (1998), *New Keynesian Economics/Post Keynesian Alternatives*, London: Routledge.

Rotheim, R. (1999), 'Post Keynesian economics and realist philosophy', *Journal of Post Keynesian Economics*, **22** (1), pp. 71–103.

Runde, J. (1998), 'Assessing causal economic explanations', *Oxford Economic Papers*, **50** (2), pp. 151–72.

Runde, J. and S. Mizuhara (eds) (2003), *The Philosophy of Keynes's Economics – Probability, Uncertainty and Convention*, London: Routledge.

Sayer, A. (2000), *Realism and Social Science*, London: Sage Publications.

Schultzer, B. (1957), *Relativitet – i filosofisk belysning*, København: G.E.C. Gads Forlag.

Setterfield, M. (1997), 'Should economists dispense with the notion of equilibrium?' *Journal of Post Keynesian Economics*, Fall, pp. 47–65.

Setterfield, M. (2001), 'Macrodynamics', in Holt, R.P.F. and S. Pressman (eds).

Setterfield, M. (2003a), 'Critical realism and formal modelling: incompatible bedfellows?' in Downward, P. (ed.).

Setterfield, M. (2003b), 'Effective demand', in King, J. (ed.).

Skidelsky, R. (1995), 'J.M. Keynes and the quantity theory of money', in Blaug, M. (ed.).

Skidelsky, R. (1983), *John Maynard Keynes: Hopes Betrayed, 1883–1920*, London: Macmillan Press.

Skidelsky, R. (1992), *The Economist as Saviour, 1920–37*, London: Macmillan Press.

Skidelsky, R. (1996), *Keynes*, Oxford: Oxford University Press.

Smith, Adam (1759), *The Theory of Moral Sentiments*, edited by D.D. Raphael and A.L. Macfie (1976), Oxford: Clarendon.

Smith, Adam (1776), *Inquiry into the Nature and Causes of the Wealth of Nations,* Vols 1 and 2, R.H. Campbell and A.S. Skinner (eds) (1976), Oxford: Clarendon.

Snowdon, B. and H.R. Vane (1999), *Conversations with Leading Economists: Interpreting Modern Macroeconomics*, Cheltenham, UK and Northampton, MA, US: Edward Elgar.

Snowdon, B., H. Vane and P. Wynarczyk (1994), *A Modern Guide to Macroeconomics*, Aldershot, UK and Brookfield, US: Edward Elgar.

Snowdon, Brian and H.R. Vane (2005), *Modern Macroeconomics: Its Origin, Development, and Current State*, Cheltenham, UK and Northampton, MA, US: Edward Elgar.

Solow, R.M. (1956), 'A contribution to the theory of economic growth', *Quarterly Journal of Economics,* **70**, pp. 65–94.

Solow, R.M. (1986), 'What is a nice girl like you doing in a place like this? Macroeconomics after fifty years', *Eastern Economic Journal*, July–September, pp. 191–8.

Sonnenschein, H. (1972), 'Market excess demand functions', *Econometrica*, **40**, pp. 549–63.

Sørensen, P.B. and H.J. Whitta-Jakobsen (2005), *Introducing Advanced Macroeconomics: Growth and Business Cycles*, Maidenhead: McGraw-Hill Education.

Summers, Lawrence H. (1991), 'The scientific illusion in empirical macroeconomics', *Scandinavian Economic Journal*, **93**, pp. 129–48.

Sutton, J. (2002), *Marshall's Tendencies: What can Economists Know?,* Cambridge, MA: MIT Press.

Togati, T.D. (1998), *Keynes and the Neoclassical Synthesis: Einsteinian versus Newtonian Macroeconomics*, London: Routledge.

Toporowski, J. (2003), 'Kaleckian economics', in J. King (ed.).

Varian, H.R. (1999), *Intermediate Microeconomics: A Modern Approach*, 5th edn, New York: W.W. Norton.

Vercelli, Alessandro (1991), *Methodological Foundations of Macro-economics: Keynes and Lucas*, Cambridge: Cambridge University Press.

Walras, L. (1874), *Elements of Pure Economics,* translated by W. Jaffe (1954), London: Allen & Unwin.

Weintraub, E.R. (1985), *General Equilibrium Analysis: Studies in Appraisal*, London: Macmillan.

Young, W. (1987), *Interpreting Mr Keynes: The IS–LM Enigma*, Cambridge: Polity Press.

Index